Discovering Images of God

Narratives of Care among Lesbians and Gays

Larry Kent Graham

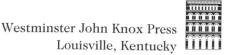
Westminster John Knox Press
Louisville, Kentucky

For information, address Westminster John Knox Press,
100 Witherspoon Street, Louisville, Kentucky 40202-1396.

Book design by Jennifer K. Cox
Cover design by Kevin Darst

First edition
Published by Westminster John Knox Press
Louisville, Kentucky

This book is printed on acid-free paper that meets the
American National Standards Institute Z39.48 standard. ∞

PRINTED IN THE UNITED STATES OF AMERICA
98 99 00 01 02 03 04 05 06 — 10 9 8 7 6 5 4 3 2

Library of Congress Cataloging-in-Publication Data

Graham, Larry Kent.
    Discovering images of God : narratives of care among
lesbians and gays / Larry Kent Graham.
       p.   cm.
    Includes bibliographical references and index.
    ISBN 0-664-25626-0 (alk. paper)
    1. Church work with gays—United States. 2. Gays—
Religious life—United States. I. Title.
BV4437.5.G73   1997
261.8′35766—dc20   96-44111

Discovering Images of God

TO ALL WHO
HAD THE COURAGE AND GENEROSITY
TO SHARE THEIR NARRATIVES
OF CARE

Contents

Preface

This book is about the lives of lesbian and gay persons, and those whom they love and who love them. Some of the stories are sad and incredibly painful to read. Others are inspiring and convey a sense of pride and hope. Most are mixtures of pain and beauty, loss and fulfillment. In all cases, one discerns a mystery of otherness, a sense of familiar strangeness, that both connects the reader to these persons and punctuates their intractable uniqueness.

These stories are a testament to an often denied, but firmly shared, common humanity. One cannot read them without somehow feeling them as "familiar," even though they convey the uniqueness of individuals and groups of people who are "strangers" and "outcasts" in our society. The struggle to love, to see a cherished face smiling back at the beginning and end of the day, to be rewarded for achievements, to walk the streets in safety, and to have one's gifts and graces welcomed and utilized are common values familiar to us all. To be perplexed about our bodily state and sexual feelings, to have mixtures of attraction and repulsion toward other bodies, and to struggle with guilt as well as delight in the sexual arena are feelings not uncommon to most humans whose instincts and moral sensibilities contend for a viable partnership. To grieve the ending of relationships, to confront untimely death and unwarranted suffering, and to incorporate the abyss of God's abandonment as well as the baffling emergence of God's sustaining grace are familiar to most who are attuned to our place in the world we are given. As we read these stories, we will learn to know ourselves better, because they touch in a fresh manner on the familiar, the common, and much of what is compelling for all of us.

At the same time, this book will be an introduction to strangers whose orientation to life may seem queer, or quaint, or qualitatively disgusting to some. It will be difficult, if not impossible, for some readers to support the argument that lesbians and gay men can help straight people discover that same-sex love is a positive expression of the traditional religious and family values of love, justice, community, and hospitality toward the outsider that is required of all of us. Rather than providing a vehicle to understanding and further identifying with and welcoming the stranger in all of us, these stories will reinforce for some that lesbians and gay men are outsiders with whom familiarity would be detrimental.

Of course, it is my intention that this book, through narratives of care, will be a bridge to the common and familiar, and that destructive abysses will no longer divide.

Yet this book also wants to protect our strangeness, to hold out for irreducible mystery and diversity at the heart of things. Bridges connect differences; they do not eradicate them. Differences, as thematicized in religious concepts of transcendence, holiness, and parable, are essential for life to be rich and love to be possible. Differences are the foundation for mystery. They give rise to the great dramas and narratives in which are forged the small and large meanings giving form and direction to human living. Indeed, the Jewish and Christian traditions out of which my commitments grow, and that comprise the framework for interpreting the narratives of this book, see in the stranger and outsider both a point of identification for all human beings and a basis for the sacramental encounter with the distinct "otherness" characterizing the mystery of God's being. It is my profoundest hope that the reader of these narratives will encounter the grace that weaves strangers into a familiar common destiny, while reverencing the mystery of an uncontained otherness at the heart of our existence.

One of the outcomes of discovering and interviewing lesbians and gay men was the emergence of a great indebtedness to scores of people and institutions. There is no way that I can name them all, but I must name many. Iliff School of Theology provided a sabbatical year to conduct the research, and generous relief from other duties to complete the manuscript once the leave was finished. Dean Jane I. Smith particularly provided wise counsel in helping me to select this topic, among other possibilities for that sabbatical year, and ensured institutional support for the approach taken in this project. The Association of Theological Schools in the United States and Canada provided a generous faculty grant for travel, consulting, and other costs of the research.

The field trips to New York, San Francisco, and Atlanta were assisted by many people in those communities. Margaret Kornfeld, Ronald Harris, and Robert Parkin were particularly helpful in providing lodging, contacts, and interview settings in New York City. Archie Smith and Randall Mixon helped me with these necessities in the San Francisco Bay Area. Ulrike Guthrie, E. Claiborne Jones, and Brian Childs were the contact points for my work in Atlanta. In Denver, the Revs. Toni Cook, Constance Del Zell, and Lucia Guzman made possible several timely interviews. Had these persons not validated me and my research with lesbian and gay persons whom they knew, there would have been no way that this research could have been completed. They were the critical bridge between people who before this study were complete strangers to one another. Through them I entered a network. As a result of the interactions in the interview process over a year's time, I now feel embedded within a "living communion." Not only has my understanding of pastoral theology taken a new and deeper turn through this project, but also I have found myself spiritually connected to gifted and inspiring persons in a way I would never have imagined before the study.

Many persons read the manuscript in part or total as the project unfolded. Andrew J. Lester of Brite Divinity School shepherded the process by which my research data could be formulated into a viable working arrangement with Westminster John Knox Press. My friend and colleague Joretta Marshall provided invaluable ongoing consultation and critical assessment. Randall Mixon was a wise guide at several points along the way. Doctoral students Jeanne Hoeft and Darryl Fairchild took an ongoing interest in ensuring that the text was both "pastoral-theological" and applicable beyond the lesbian and gay experience. Dennis MacDonald and Delwin Brown expanded the biblical and theological linkages to the concept of the image of God and made useful suggestions about how to formulate my constructive ideas. Sharyl Bender Peterson hammered several textual infelicities into coherence and spent considerable effort ensuring that the references and the analyses went together. My secretary, Gene Crytzer, brought his word-processing expertise and quirky good humor to the many drafts that I placed on his desk. Jon Berquist, my editor at Westminster John Knox Press, provided wise and patient guidance in the final stages of preparation. My spouse and most cherished colleague at Iliff, Sheila Greeve Davaney, added her uncanny capacity for incisive reading of texts to a generous tolerance for the weeks I was away from our family in order to conduct this research.

In all of these instances the book is considerably stronger than it would have been without their contributions. I am deeply in their debt and regret that my own limitations rendered it impossible to use all of the suggestions pressed upon me by these accomplished allies. Finally, words cannot express my gratitude for the gracious manner in which I was received and assisted by all those whose stories are told here, as well as those whose interviews are not included in this book. For their openness, wisdom, and persistent hopefulness, I dedicate what follows to them.

INTRODUCTION

Pastoral Theology and Lesbian and Gay Experience

What unique contribution might a pastoral theologian make to the raging debate in the church concerning lesbian and gay persons? Where is a pastoral theological voice among the cacophony? Do pastoral theologians await firmer outcomes concerning biblical interpretation before we speak? Are we silent until ethicists and theologians resolve their differences? Or do we simply lie low, biding our time until a more general cultural consensus has emerged, and then speak up?

Certainly, we will continue to do all of these things, and wisely so, since much of pastoral-theological activity requires sustained listening and restraint in the face of ambiguity and conflict. We draw our very lifeblood and make our most effective contribution, to the extent that we can "be present to" symptomatic persons and communities, especially when these are in conflict or crisis about matters requiring spiritual guidance, theological reconstruction, and ethical analysis. When relationships become fractured through conflicts about ultimate meanings and loyalty to cherished traditions, the pastoral theologian should be among the first to show up and among the last to "give answers," as any good introductory course in pastoral care attests.

Yet at a certain point, pastoral theology requires more than empathic and receptive presence. It is also a theological discipline that presses what it hears into constructive religious interpretation. Pastoral theology provides guidance for responding with authenticity and theological power to struggling persons and communities. Its voice becomes public, adding its unique standpoint and experience to the discourse.

As I wondered how to go about adding a uniquely pastoral-theological interpretation to the discussions on lesbian and gay persons, I found myself thinking of the scores of pastoral situations I have encountered over the years involving issues related to lesbian and gay concerns. I have often been asked as a professor of pastoral theology and care how to help pastors work with their congregations on gay and lesbian issues. Lesbian and gay individuals have sought my counsel or the counsel of pastors or students who then in turn sought my consultation or supervision. Clinical case conferences have frequently focused on what might be the best mode of response to individuals, couples, and families wrestling with their sexual orientation and its impact on their lives and the lives of those around them.

These concrete human lives in the situations of care and counseling became the starting point for considering the question of what unique contribution pastoral theology might make to the current debates about the Christian church's response to lesbians and gays. For pastoral theology contends that unaddressed theological issues often arise from the particularity of human experience, including the actual practice of ministry, and that further interpretation of what actually takes place in concrete experience has the potential for constructing new theological understandings or clarifying unresolved matters in the tradition.[1]

The initial questions that emerged as I reflected on these cases were the following: Why would these persons want to be Christian when the source of so much of their pain is from their denigration and rejection by such a large part of the Christian church and its teachings? If the church of Jesus Christ could not discover the deeper truth about lesbian and gay persons and provide the love and acceptance promised by the gospel, would not the best pastoral counsel be to help them find God's love and human fellowship outside of the church? Could I do less, as one who is committed to the belief that God's love is not confined to the church, but potentially emerges in surprising ways outside of the religious setting?

On further reflection, however, it was clear that to counsel people away from their desires to be a part of the life of the church was neither pastorally nor theologically appropriate. On the one hand, I believed that Christian lesbian and gay persons *belong* in the church and that pastoral care ought to help make possible Christian worship, fellowship, and mission. On the other hand, most Christian lesbian and gay people whom I encountered in the context of pastoral care and counseling wanted to be in the church because they felt called by God to be Christian and to serve God and the world as part of the church. It therefore became important for me to continue thinking about how pastoral theology might build bridges between the faith and calling of lesbian and gay people and the ongoing life of the churches to which they felt called and to which they offered their gifts of love and service.

Thinking more fully about the experiences of care with some lesbian and gay persons whom I had known over the years, I realized something even more profound. I realized that sometimes pastoral care was a format in which the life of the church and the aspirations of lesbian and gay persons came together in mutually positive ways. Through the acceptance

2

and support mediated in pastoral care, the message and life of the church sustained, affirmed, and guided lesbian and gay persons in the concrete decisions of their lives. In turn, the pastoral-care relationship was sometimes the bridge on which the "gifts and graces" of lesbian and gay persons were welcomed into the church.

By participating in and supervising pastoral care with lesbian and gay persons, I discovered the depth of Christian commitment and maturity at the foundation of many of their lives. The quality of their resiliency and hope, their capacity to heal and serve others, and their passion for justice and the love of the earth embodied some of the most authentic Christian vitality I had ever seen. If lesbian and gay persons, claiming to be Christian, found grace in their relationships and lived thankfully before God and in service to neighbor, ought not the status of their lifestyles be reevaluated by the church? And might not the lifestyles that were in part made possible through the ministry of care of the church be a source of theological knowledge for the church? It seemed so to me.

This "discovery" of vital Christian "gifts and graces" in the lives of lesbian and gay persons challenged many negative cultural and religious stereotypes and brought new experiential data to the theological table. I realized that ancient biblical texts, selective historic practices of the church, abstract ethical and theological positions, and modern behavioral and social sciences could not alone set the agenda and define the norms for Christian reflection on the lives of lesbian and gay persons. Concrete experience with "living human documents" in the practice of the ministry of the church also generates data that must be taken seriously in the larger discourse.

If an examination of the concrete experience of care received by lesbian and gay persons, and their families of origin and choice, has the potential to uncover significant dramas of Christian living and human wholeness, ought not we learn more about this? If lesbian and gay persons experienced a deep sense of God's companionship and affirmation, should not we ask what this means pastorally and theologically? Would not a fuller knowledge of the nature and consequences of pastoral care and counseling with lesbians and gays provide an enrichment for all concerned? Might not more precise knowledge disclose a fuller dimension of the gifts that lesbian and gay persons bring to the church and provide a basis for rethinking the theological, ethical, and spiritual dimensions of the lesbian and gay experience and its positive relationship to God and the church? In short, might not the discoveries of the transformative journeys disclosed in the context of caregiving provide the foundation for answering the key question of what compelling and salvific contribution pastoral theology might offer to the church and to lesbians and gay men?[2]

Examining Positive Care

To answer the question of pastoral theology's possible contribution to a Christian understanding of gay and lesbian experience, I realized that I needed to have more details about effective caregiving with lesbian and gay persons and their larger networks. The scores of pastoral-care situations that I had been involved with were largely addressed from the point of view of the pastoral helper, rather than from the lesbian or gay person receiving care. Usually I did not have a record of the outcome of the caregiving, and I had no way to relate what was happening in pastoral caregiving to a wide array of caregiving experiences that lesbian and gay persons sought outside the religious context.

Another problem was whether there were sufficient examples of positive care available in the first place. In spite of the positive examples I described above, it was more often reported by lesbian women and gay men that the church failed to be an environment that demonstrated nurture and care for its same-sex members. Over the years, lesbian and gay persons reported horrible accounts of rejection, vilification, and condemnation on the part of the church. Indeed, preliminary responses to my study were commonly cautious, even discouraging. I was told that I would find very few examples of positive help and that to emphasize the good examples could mask the larger reality of injury inflicted by the church on lesbian and gay people. These responses housed a great deal of anger, pain, and mistrust, even among those who remained somehow connected with Christianity.

Therefore, in order to gain the fullest picture of positive care, I realized that I needed to look beyond what happened in the context of the church. I needed to explore any experience of positive and effective care, both inside and outside the church. It also became clear that I needed to be realistic about the pervasive negative influence that the church has had on the well-being of those oriented in a lesbian and gay manner. I needed to learn about the kinds of things for which care was sought, how it was communicated, where it was impeded, and some of its enduring outcomes.

Although it would have been more in keeping with pastoral-theological methodology directly to observe or examine the case material of pastoral and other clinicians—as well as the practices of less formal caregivers— there was no practical or ethical way to gain access to an adequate amount of this material. Instead, I would have to find a way to get access to their experience of care retrospectively, by asking the recipients of care about what happened in the caregiving setting that was positive, and to explore their assessment of its ongoing contribution to their lives.

In order to discover the varieties of positive care experienced by lesbian and gay persons, I received a year's sabbatical leave from Iliff School of Theology and a grant from the Association of Theological Schools in the United States and Canada to interview lesbian and gay persons in Denver, New York, San Francisco, and Atlanta. During 1993–1994 I conducted over sixty tape-recorded semiclinical interviews, each averaging one hour and forty-five minutes. I also observed various settings of ministry in which lesbian and gay persons found positive care. The population I interviewed is by no means representative of the wide spectrum of lesbian and gay experience. Most of the persons whom I interviewed were committed or nominal Christians; several had advanced theological training. I interviewed about an equal number of men and women, but most were white. I interviewed several African Americans and Latinos/Latinas. The ages of the persons I interviewed ranged from middle adolescence to septuagenarians. Most, however, were in their thirties and forties.

The interview was structured around several questions. I began with an introduction to the study. We contracted about confidentiality, anonymity, and ongoing review of the write-ups. I asked four basic questions:

1. When you understand care in the broadest terms as any assistance that you have received in your life related to your needs, with special emphasis on your sexuality, where have you found care? Who provided it, what did they do, and what impact did it have on you?

2. Were there particular religious dimensions to the care you received? For example, was the care in a religious context, carried out by representatives of religious communities? Were religious concepts, images, and methods used? Were there religious consequences—positively or negatively or mixed—connected with the care you received?

3. In what way have your relationships with other lesbian and gay persons been a source of care for you? How is this conveyed, and what has been its impact on you?

4. How does the geographical setting in which you now live affect the care that you need and that is available to you? Are there differences between this environment and others in which you have lived?

In each of the cities, I was hosted by at least one person who had a high level of credibility among the lesbian and gay community, and who was willing to make contacts for me. In some cases, they actually scheduled the interviews and provided a safe environment for the interview. Nearly without exception, I was received positively by those of whom I requested an interview. The questions were engaged seriously. Once trust was established, persons were quite candid and even vulnerable. Only two or three persons were unable to accept my invitation for an interview. Schedule conflicts were reported as the basis for declining. All expressed regret. Because of time constraints, I was not able to interview all those who volunteered.

In addition to the interviews, I visited several settings in which ministry to lesbian and gay persons was central. I interviewed clergy in several Metropolitan Community Church (MCC) congregations. On two occasions, I visited an AIDS support group in New York City. I visited several congregations in all the cities and attended some AIDS healing services. I visited a lesbian and gay counseling center in San Francisco, interviewing some of its staff. I worshiped at City of Refuge, a gay-affirming African-American United Church of Christ congregation in San Francisco, and at Congregation Beth Simchat Torah, a lesbian and gay Reform congregation in New York City. In all of these settings, I gathered information about their ministries and draw on them in describing positive caregiving.

One of the most significant outcomes of all these encounters was the sense of acceptance and welcome I experienced. At first I defined my activity as identifying and entering the lesbian and gay network. As I was welcomed and affirmed, and as a variety of persons gave themselves to the success of this project, I felt that the network had become transformed into a "communion of partners" working together on a project of mutual importance.

My Motivation and Accountability

The two most frequently asked questions about this project by the persons I interviewed, or by those whose assistance I otherwise requested, were, "Why are you doing this?" and "What will you do with the information you get?" The answer to each of these questions grew in clarity as the study progressed, and became an important part of the project itself. The way they were asked, answered, and incorporated into the interview process was a major part of how this project contributed to developing a strong working relationship with the gay and lesbian network that I entered.

Why am I doing this? At the most basic level I can identify, I am doing this out of my sense that the gospel of Jesus Christ, to which I have committed my life, requires it. For me and for the community of faith in which

I am an ordained minister, the gospel requires that all Christians minister with suffering persons and work with one another to undo the structures of injustice that account for our suffering. When this call is linked to the concrete lives of lesbian and gay persons and their families, I realize that I would not only be disloyal to the gospel and to my ordination, but I would betray many lesbian and gay friends, former students, counselees, academic colleagues, and fellow pastoral counselors and ministers if I did not do my part to expand resources appropriate to their healing and fulfillment. It simply became impossible to be silent to a church and society that so unheedingly persists in undervaluing or destroying those who are a very important part of my life and ministry.

Another motivation is drawn from the discipline of pastoral theology and the fields of pastoral care and counseling themselves. I became increasingly aware over the years that there was virtually no literature from either the field of pastoral care and counseling or that of pastoral theology which addressed the care of lesbian and gay persons. At the same time, both groups were consciously trying to reach out to "other voices," such as women, persons of color, and persons with a variety of "other than" mainline liberal Protestant perspectives. Little was said about lesbian and gay persons. As a pastoral counselor and pastoral theologian, I began to feel dissatisfied with this negligent silence and heard a deeper call within me to address it. It seemed that I was in a position to contribute to the development of a literature on caregiving that might be a partial touchstone for a wider, more public discussion of these issues.[3]

In spite of these motivations, there were particular problems connected with this project. As a straight white male, I ran at least two dangers. On the one hand, I could co-opt or misrepresent altogether the voices of lesbian and gay persons themselves, leading to further marginalization and distortion. On the other hand, I could remain silent and contribute to what I believe is the abuse and neglect of the gifts of lesbian and gay persons. Thus the question, What are you going to do with the information you get? became a critical part of the question of accountability and the basis for decisions about how to write this book.

I have three foci of accountability. The primary accountability is to the narratives of the persons I interviewed. The second is to the Christian faith of which I am a minister. The third is to the fields of pastoral care and counseling, and pastoral theology. These accountabilities, of course, interconnect.

In terms of my accountability to the lesbian and gay community, I am aware that it may be presumptuous and condescending to attempt to report and interpret the experience of another group of persons, especially persons who have been so injured by the culture that has benefited me so greatly. I have therefore taken steps to ensure that I am faithful to the experience of those whom I have interviewed, as well as to those beyond the study. I have developed a small, trusted, and forthright advisory group of lesbian and gay persons who have read everything I have written and have consulted with me on every aspect of the study. I have also asked all those whose experience I have used in this book to read the portions that recount and interpret their experience. I have modified my reports in accordance with their guidance. I have also made it clear in our discussions, and in the written release forms signed by the interviewees, that they could withdraw their participation at any time. I also emphasized that whatever level of public identification the interviewees desired would be honored. Some wanted total anonymity; some wanted full disclosure of identities and institutional location. I have kept faith with those agreements and certify that everything included in this book has been favorably reviewed by the individuals whose narratives are presented by name.[4]

Perhaps the most significant manner in which I have sought to be accountable to the experience of lesbian and gay persons is the decision to organize this book around the narratives of care coming out of the interviews. That is, the narratives themselves ground the organization of the book and shape much of the theological interpretation and the suggested guidelines for practice. Further, the guidelines themselves are consistent with reputable and substantial "cognate secular" literature pertaining to psychotherapy and care of lesbian and gay persons. In all of these conversations, I have sought to be a learner; in my write-ups I have endeavored to be a "faithful witness" to what I have heard.

In writing the text, I have tried to present real lives in a real way. Some of the stories have very unpleasant and painful aspects to them. Some of the behaviors described may jar against the moral sensibilities of some readers. Some may find themselves in fierce disagreement with people in this book, including the author's relative inattention or outright neglect of something held dear by the reader. I have not tried to say everything that could or should be said. But in keeping with my fundamental conviction that for care to be real and for God to be real in our experience of living, we too must be real. Christianity is not about plastic saints and idealized piosities, but about real people, in real situations, with real glories, real sins, and real loves. An overriding accountability, therefore, has been to present "real people" seeking "real care" and encountering a "real God." In reporting and interpreting these stories, I have taken pains to be accountable to the criteria set by Dorothy Allison, a lesbian writer:

> Every time I pick up a book that purports to be about poor people or lesbians and gay men or Southern women, I do so with anxiety, an awareness that the books about us have often been

cruel, small and false. I have wanted our lives taken seriously and represented fully—with power and honesty and sympathy—to be hated or loved, or to terrify and obsess, but to be real.[5]

Allison goes on in the article to say that the reason she writes is to "remake the world into a place where the truth would be hallowed, not held in contempt, where silence would be impossible."[6] It is my profoundest hope that this book is not "cruel, small and false," but that it truthfully breaks the silence and leads to the increase of love toward those whose lives I have tried to take seriously and represent fully with "power and honesty and sympathy."

I am aware that lesbian and gay experience is diverse, and that the need for and experience of care reported to me by the sixty interviewees is not necessarily reflective of the full range of care experienced in the lesbian and gay community. Yet, based on my reading of a great deal of literature generated by lesbian and gay caregivers, the credibility of those whose narratives I include in this volume, and critical feedback from those who do have access to a wider range of caregiving in the lesbian and gay community, I believe that this book provides a viable beginning framework for understanding the major dimensions of positive caregiving in a Christian context with same-sex oriented persons. The majority sentiment of those who read this text prior to publication was summarized by a lesbian who said, "Thank you for the opportunity to read these chapters. You have captured much of the breadth and depth of lesbian and gay life. It is beyond me how anyone might read these narratives and not be moved toward love, acceptance, and justice."

At the same time that I have tried to present faithfully the voices of lesbian women and gay men, I have also added my own voice. I believe that responsibility for the church and its ministry is a shared responsibility, and that I have special training and resources to bring some elements of that ministry to light and into focus. I look at this work as my part in a larger partnership between lesbian, gay, and heterosexual persons who love God and the church and who want to create the kind of church that reflects our spiritual experiences and our faith commitments. Thus there is a third option between silence and co-option—a partnership of learners and teachers who are seeking a better way together. For me, this partnership became real in the course of my research and was a source of spiritual nurture. It was not uncommon for those involved in the study to report a similar outcome. Robert Parkin, a gay psychiatrist, wrote in a personal letter: "I was enormously interested and informed by your understanding of the ideas about which you wrote. . . . Of course, the richness you found as you studied lesbians and gay men was 'a window into understanding' that means much to me. The hair on my neck, always a reliable emotional barometer, stood tall as I identified with many of the stories you related."

My second focus of accountability is the ministry of the church of Jesus Christ. I have already spoken of my belief that it is counter to the will of God for lesbian women and gay men to suffer so at the hands of the church and society. For many reasons, I have become sensitive to the great harm done to the oppressed and marginalized people in the name of Christianity dominated by white male power structures. I have also become aware that the white male power structure is fundamentally heterosexist. I believe that any structure of domination and subordination is against the love of God as expressed in the life, death, and resurrection of Jesus Christ. The gospel accepts and validates us as we are; our sinfulness is not in our sexuality but in the directions of our motivations and the quality of our relationships to God, ourselves, our neighbors, and to the ecosystems that contain and produce us all. Christianity, as interpreted through these ecological and liberative theological convictions, is the second focus of accountability to the narratives of care reported by gay and lesbian persons.[7]

Finally, I am accountable to the disciplines of pastoral care and counseling, and pastoral theology. This book is fundamentally addressed to lay and clergy providers of pastoral care and counseling, and offers a serious theological foundation for concrete acts of care with lesbian and gay persons. The "canons" of the disciplines—as diverse, flexible, and developing as they are—are also addressed in the production of this volume. One of these is the need to proceed from experience and practice to theory—hence the emphasis on discovering narratives of care as a basis for theological construction and practical guidelines.

These foci of accountability are not contradictory, but require one another. They come together in a variety of ways in the structure and development of the book.

The Thesis, Plan, and Style of This Book

Most of the chapters will combine narrative with theological interpretation and practical guidelines. The main part of these chapters will recount in narrative form some of the experiences of the persons I interviewed between September 1993 and January 1, 1995. The power of stories to convey emotional meaning and the presence of God is unparalleled. In October of 1993, I visited a seminar at Union Theological Seminary in New York on pastoral care of gays and lesbians, taught by John McNeill, an influential Roman Catholic writer on gay liberation.[8] At this seminar McNeill stated that in the retreats he has led, the most important moment, psychologically and spiritually, is when each person tells his or her story. "The power of God in each of them is so strong that you simply can't deny it. When we tell our stories, we reclaim our lives. We are brought to life and healed by our own stories years later."

Throughout the interview process, I found that telling stories of care in itself had a healing effect on the teller. Therefore, in order to convey the power of stories to connect us to our common humanity and to mediate psychological and spiritual healing, I have organized the chapters around common themes that presented themselves in the narratives and that must be taken account of theologically and practically in developing pastoral care with gay men and lesbian women.[9]

The heaviest weight of chapters 1–5 is on the narratives themselves, with some attention to their practical and theological dimensions. In chapters 6–8, I move to more explicit guidelines and theological construction, without losing touch with the stories that generate and illustrate these ideas.

The thesis of this book is that an examination of the concrete lives of lesbian women and gay men, especially in the context of a variety of caregiving situations, discloses the capacity of lesbian and gay persons for creative, deep, and loving communion with God, self, neighbor, and the natural order. Theologically, when lesbian and gay persons embody "creative, deep, and loving communion," characterized by relational justice, they reveal themselves as full human beings who reflect what it means to be created in the image of God. These creative and diverse modes of love, communion, and justice reflect the image of God, who also loves freely and justly in diverse and creative ways, according to major strands within the Christian witness. Appropriate pastoral caregiving is therefore characterized by full acceptance of the sexual orientation of lesbian women and gay men, and seeks to promote a greater capacity for relationally just, creative, and loving communion in all dimensions of their experience. From the disclosure of the image of God in caregiving with lesbian and gay persons, it is possible to discern more clearly what it may mean for all persons to be in the image of God. On the basis of a reconsideration of an expanded view of the image of God to affirm and include authentic lesbian and gay sexuality, it is possible to devise comprehensive strategies of care applicable for all humans as well.[10]

The concept of relational justice will be central throughout the book, for the concept of love requires more specific moral definition, especially in light of the dominant culture's unjust response to the lesbian and gay experience. Too often persons glibly say that they love lesbian and gay persons while treating them individually and as a group in a variety of unjust ways. Too often, within lesbian and gay loving—like all others—

unjust domination and subordination patterns persist. Therefore the concept of relational justice is understood as the positive norm for realizing the meaning of love in the image of God. Relational justice points to shalom, or rightness of relationship and well-being between creator, creatures, and the people of God, and opposes injustice that takes the forms of coercion, denigration, marginalization, and disvaluation of created life, including human life. Pastoral care, drawing on these theological constructions, therefore assumes and is informed by a liberative ethic and a strategic or prophetic political agenda.[11]

These themes, and others appropriate to the issues under consideration, are all discussed in relation to common issues for which lesbian and gay persons seek care. In chapter 1, I provide a detailed narrative of two persons in order to lay the foundations for the dimensions of positive care to be expanded later in the book. Caregiving in relation to the process of coming out and establishing partnerships is the foci of chapters 2 and 3. Attention to care for families established is considered in chapter 4.

Chapter 5 addresses the various ways in which recovery from loss emerges as the focus of care, with special attention to losses through AIDS and the ending or reconfiguring of relationships. Chapter 6 offers a comprehensive communal framework for organizing care with lesbian, gays, and others.

Chapters 7 and 8 revisit the question, What unique contribution might a pastoral theologian make to the raging debate in the church concerning lesbian and gay persons? To answer this question, chapter 7 examines a variety of ways in which the doctrine of the image of God has been understood in Christianity and why it cannot simply be equated with heterosexual norms, as contended by many in today's church. Chapter 8 provides a constructive reinterpretation of the image of God in relational terms. Viewed thus, rather than through "essentialist" and "biological" lenses, lesbian and gay persons can be understood to reflect the image of God, like all others, when their lives embody creative loving communion and relational justice at all levels of interaction within God's world. Specific guidelines for care are summarized at the end of chapter 8.

1

AFFIRMATION AND SOLIDARITY

Establishing the Framework of Care

What counts for effective care for gay men and lesbian women? To answer this question, two narratives will be explored in detail. A framework, or profile, of the main features of care will be developed to guide future endeavors for lesbian and gay persons, as well as care for all persons. The narratives we explore will also provide a foundation for thinking about the relationship between Christian pastoral care and the realization of the image of God in human beings, including lesbian and gay persons.

William Carroll:
A Formative Narrative

The research for this project is anchored in my friendship and pastoral relationship with William, a former Doctor of Ministry student whose project I had advised.[1] After a presentation I had made on depression, he sought me out to discuss his own situation. He said that during my presentation he thought that I was speaking directly to him. He said that for many years he had wrestled with depression and had begun to realize that his depression was related to his struggle to deal with his sexual orientation. He was a successful minister, well-respected in his community, successfully married, and the father of two daughters. Periodically he had been under psychiatric care for his depression and to help him remove or contain the homosexual fantasies that constantly plagued him. He admitted to a great deal of guilt at having purchased gay magazines and, on occasion, having acted on his sexual impulses.

William poured out his story to me. He described his attempts to cure his homosexual fantasies before his marriage, and the conflict he had about marrying in the first place. He told of the tension he felt over preaching about a God who accepts us as we are, but whose acceptance he himself had never experienced because of his struggles. He wrestled with

13

whether he could ever affirm that he was gay, and what it would mean to tell his wife and children. He suspected that he would have to leave the ministry, and he had no doubt that his marriage would have to end. His wife had for a long time been unhappy with their sexual relationship, and he felt that she deserved better. He was hopeful that his children would be affirming of him because of the nature of their past relationship and because he had taught them to be accepting and open-minded persons. He realized that he would probably have to leave the small city in which he lived if he acted on his feelings. He knew that he could not have any kind of openness about his orientation and have his ministry survive in that community; indeed, a divorce itself—apart from any mention of sexual orientation—would put great strains on his standing in the community, if not the congregation.

William elaborated on the tension he felt as a minister and as a Christian. For years he had been searching for an authentic spirituality and had spent considerable efforts researching contemporary spiritual movements. He came up with three facets of a spirituality that "I badly needed for my own life: (1) recognizing and celebrating life as a good gift from God, (2) responding to the God-given impulse planted within us to grow toward our full potential, and (3) reaching out to others in Christlike, self-giving love." As good as he felt about these ideas and as helpful as they were in his pastoral guidance of others, they "did not translate into my own life. On every point of my spirituality I struck out: (1) I did not see life as a good gift. My life was a burden—sometimes a curse (even though there have been some great joys along the way, which include my wife and children). (2) I tried to grow toward my full potential, but felt trapped, thwarted, and divided. (3) And I certainly could not reach out to others, even my wife, in self-giving love. I couldn't even face myself, let alone reveal myself to my wife, friends, or colleagues."

As a husband, William felt like a phony. While driving home on their twentieth wedding anniversary, he reported that his wife confronted him "in a gentle but direct way, with her suspicion that she was not my preference for a sexual partner, that she had suspected it for years, and that she didn't think she could take another twenty years like the last." Ten years earlier he had spoken to her of his sexual conflict in college, but had assured her that it was all in the past. "So, on our twentieth wedding anniversary, I was in no way prepared to deal with her concern, but there it was. I tried to tell her that, yes, it was a problem, but not an insurmountable one. I told her how badly I felt about it, and in the process became so distraught I had to stop the car by the side of the highway. I told her how sorry I was for causing her pain. She expressed great concern over AIDS and was fearful that I would bring it home to her. I told her that I had been tested and would not risk that for myself or her. I felt terrible.

14

At one point I told her that it would have been better for all concerned if I had never been born. That is exactly how I felt. I did not fit in this world. There was no place for me, and all I seemed to do was cause pain for myself and her."

After William shared all of this in our initial session, I suggested that it might be too early to make any decisions about what to do, but that accepting himself for who he was seemed to be the first step. I affirmed his courage in sharing this with me and told him that although I had had great respect and affection for him before, this only enhanced my estimation of him. He said that this was the first time that he had ever shared his struggles with a friend and Christian pastor, and that he felt enormously relieved that I listened so affirmatively. He knew he had come to the point where some decisions had to be made, but he wasn't sure just how things would go. He admitted to feeling both shaky and hopeful. We left the door open for further conversation at his initiative.

William's story was only beginning when he left my office. He later reported orally and in a letter to a friend that he cried the whole three hours' drive home. He said that a logjam inside him seemed to break. "Larry was the first person I had ever talked to, as a friend, about my homosexual feelings. What was different about seeing Larry, unlike going to a psychiatrist, was that he had known me in the past and had seen me as a competent, well-functioning minister and graduate of Iliff. I had some fear about how he would see me after our visit—and how I would see myself. I told him of my dying faith in God. If God were real, then God had created me as a misfit, and it was a cruel joke. I told him that I felt like an utter phony in the ministry, in my marriage, and in my life!"

William recounted that the drive home was very difficult. "I was in terrible pain as I felt my world unraveling. I didn't know where I would go, what I would do, how people would react, how my wife would cope, how my children would feel. And yet there was a kind of relief too." A day or two after he got home, he looked at himself in the mirror. "Was that a homosexual person I was looking at? I saw a face and form I had hated and despised since teen years. I saw a person who had little or no self-esteem. Then I saw someone else. I saw a person who was deserving of love and not contempt. I had misunderstood myself. I owed myself an apology. I deserved better treatment. . . . For the first time in my life I really cared about that person in the mirror. Was this a gift of God's grace? Was the big 'sin' in my life that I had been so estranged from myself, not willing to be who I really was?"

William began reading books and other literature on homosexuality that he had acquired but had been too terrified to look at. These were both "frightening and healing." He found that his homosexuality was not curable, but neither was it bad or sinful. He realized that it was the way he was created. "It was not anything that I did or didn't do . . . and it wasn't something that my mother did to me." Reading about married homosexual men, he recognized that he was tormented at having to pretend that he was something he was not. And yet he could not simply "negate, deny, or forget the significance of twenty-three years of marriage and the joys and companionship that have gone along with that. My wife has given me the beautiful gift of love that I could never give myself. I have agonized that I haven't been able to give it back to her in the same way. And I wouldn't have wanted to miss out on the awesome experience of being a father and having two daughters whom I love so much and who have brought such love to me."

William decided to tell his wife on New Year's Day that he had come to the conclusion that he was more homosexual than heterosexual. "She was quite tearful, and I felt miserable. The next day was hard. I wished I hadn't told her. How do you take back words like those? But as each day went on, I felt that I had done the right thing. I was trying to be honest, and I remembered the words of Jesus, 'You will know the truth, and the truth will make you free.'" Two weeks later, William attended the Week of Lectures at Iliff, where he went to a workshop led by Beverly Barbo, an author and mother who spoke of her love for her gay son who had died of AIDS.[2] William also attended the worship services. At one service, the hymn "Nobody Knows the Trouble I've Seen" spoke strongly to him. He said that the service as a whole was an emotionally and spiritually lifting experience. "When I received communion, it was something new and positive. I didn't feel unworthy or like a phony going through the motions. I think God was in it, and I think that healing started to take place in me. . . . I'm thankful for Iliff; I think it's a healing place, and I'm thankful for the acceptance and love I sense there."

After this initial coming out to himself, to me, and to his wife, William told his children and several close friends and associates. In each case he was affirmed. He and his wife took steps to divorce, which occurred on friendly terms. His wife subsequently remarried, and on several occasions William has shared Christmas with her and her new husband and their children. He became very involved in AIDS ministry in his local community and became known as a gay-friendly minister. He found his way into the gay and lesbian network in his denomination and was successful in finding new employment in a large metropolitan area. He started attending a gay/lesbian-affirming church, entered therapy, joined a number of gay support groups, and began dating.

During the two years from his coming out to me to the new life he established in a large city, William and I had ongoing contact. He shared how more congruent he was feeling, while still having some anxiety about the unknown future. He was quite encouraged by the support and understanding that he received from his former wife and his children, and from most of the individuals to whom he came out. He shared a profound article that he wrote for *The Christian Century,* reinterpreting the story of the prodigal son.[3] He also shared some of his struggles and victories connected with dating, and in making a transition from a small city to a major metropolitan area. Coincidentally, he renewed his long-term friendship with a person who turned out to be a close pastoral-counseling associate of mine. She introduced him socially to a gay psychiatrist who befriended him. This psychiatrist had been my therapist when I was in graduate school and had subsequently come out of the closet. His connections to them and to me provided a stabilizing network for William, and entry into a larger welcoming community of support and solidarity. Alongside these friendships, William was invited to participate in a support group for persons with AIDS and their friends and lovers, led by the pastoral caregiver. He found a therapist and church-related support groups to assist with his coming-out process. I was subsequently able to draw on these relationships for many of the interviews during the field trip portion for this book.

William was one of my interviewees. He reflected on his life and some of the dimensions of care he had experienced in relation to being gay. He realized that when he was twenty-five years old and was kissed by another young man, such a forbidden kiss could be an "act of care." He has been shaken and excited about how deeply the kiss had touched him, yet he went through two more decades of inward struggle before he could allow himself to feel love for another man. That happened when he became a caretaker for Ivan, a thirty-one-year-old gay man with AIDS, who died nine months later. William said that Ivan was "the first man to whom I could say 'I love you' and feel it at a deep, congruent level." At the funeral service, William gave the homily. The central theme was "God didn't make any mistakes when he made Ivan." Through that experience William discovered in a new way how caring can be a reciprocal process. He both supported and received support from Ivan and his family. As a Christian minister, William gave Ivan's family permission to love and accept Ivan as he was. In return, William, as a newly "out" gay man, was warmly welcomed and affirmed by Ivan's parents. "When you get parents on your side, you have powerful caring."

In addition, it was significant for William that a bishop and his wife in another denomination reached out to him over the miles and affirmed him. These parents had lost a gay son and were well known for their activism and support for gay and lesbian people in the church. William found additional support from Parents and Friends of Lesbian and Gays, a national advocacy and support group with a local chapter accessible to him.

William wondered if his wife and children got adequate support. His coming out was also a coming-out process for them. His ex-wife initially did not want people to know the reason for the divorce because she was afraid other men would not want to date her for fear of AIDS. She also thought that "people would wonder why she put up with it so long." Some gay-friendly people in the congregation supported the family in its transition, but it was "hard to get care when you have to be careful who you tell. But the friends we told did okay with it. And my daughters told me that they were more proud of me than they ever have been." He reported that now he asks his daughters "how to go about dating. They've had much more experience and have given me some great advice."

William said that a big part of his care was that I, as a representative of the church, affirmed his orientation as a positive reality in his life. He said, "I needed permission to be gay from someone representing the church. It was very helpful when you told me that I have been trying long enough to deny or overcome something unalterably true about myself." William said that not only did he need permission to come out, to resolve his conflict, but his wife needed him to resolve it, too. She was unhappy in the marital situation and needed for him to come out so that they could both discover the genuine relational intimacy for which they were created. William was further assisted in coming out by reading some of the literature produced by the gay and lesbian caucus of another denomination: "a homosexual orientation is formed long before puberty; a certain percentage of the population discovers itself to be gay or lesbian. He said, "I didn't know that many reputable scholars believed that! I thought it was abnormal or thwarted development. Later, psychotherapy helped me go to yet a new stage of acceptance and freedom. It is very important that my therapist could affirm that homosexuality is a normal variation in human sexuality, not a sickness. From a spiritual perspective I needed to hear that God had created me the way I was."

Forming intimate relationships has not been easy for William. Recently he has drawn on a reputable dating service as he seeks both friendships and a romantic relationship. This has been a positive experience for him, though the relational arena is still frightening and bewildering. As one of his friends said, "He is in the middle of a terrifying and exhilarating struggle to learn what it means for him to be gay." His church is only nominally a spiritual home for him in this struggle, and he is not sure what God means to him now. He believes that God will have meaning for him in relation to people, so he is conscientiously trying to build a relational network that is genuine and viable. Overall, he believes that his life is going well, and he has hope that it will continue to do so.

Sources and Outcomes of Care

Reviewing William's story, it is clear that he found many sources of positive care. Perhaps first and foremost is his own psychic and spiritual strength to endure so much internalized conflict and tension, including chronic depression and significant family loss. When his internalized conflict surfaced, he had the psychological and spiritual means to seek out a trusted colleague and friend and to risk the disclosure of years of hidden turmoil. This capacity to endure, trust, and seek positive help in crisis is a critical dimension of care, based on a lifetime of personal growth and development.

A second source of care for William was a reliable environment that provided a basis for support and solidarity for his transition. When he came to a crisis of identity and chose to disclose his orientation, he already had a wife and family who loved and respected him, and who faced together the truth about his orientation. He had friends and sources of support and influence in his denominational structure that allowed him to make both internal personal changes and expanded vocational choices. He had established a relationship with Iliff and with me. In their own ways, these prior relationships communicated to him in a prevenient way that he would find respect and acceptance for the truth about his life, and ongoing support through his crisis. In the large city to which he moved, he discovered an open and affirming congregation, numerous educational and support groups, a helpful therapist, and opportunities for voluntary service in the gay community. The city itself was characterized by strong diversity, and William felt relatively safe in identifying with the visible lesbian and gay community. Though his transition was intensely personal and individual, it would have been extremely perilous without the solidarity and care mediated through a reliable environment.

A third source of care for William was his particular friendship and pastoral relationship with me. At a time of acute crisis, he found somone whom he trusted and respected who listened to him without judging; and, of more importance, he found someone representing the church who gave him permission to be himself as a gay person. This act of listening with acceptance and the promise of ongoing presence represent fairly conventional pastoral care in many respects. But when they were experienced by a man who had internalized much of the contempt that the church and society holds for gay men, they had an intensely powerful effect on William. His self-image changed, and he was able to take a huge step in overcoming profound estrangement within himself. He was also able to build a more authentic relationship to God, his wife, and his church. The pastoral relationship was for him an anchoring and pivotal event that opened the possibility for other good things to take place.

A fourth source of care was affectional erotic relationships that William was finally able to explore as a gay man. He said that when he was kissed by a man, he realized that "such a kiss was an act of care." His new relationships, although conflicted, also made him feel more vitally alive, true to himself, and emotionally present for others. As he was able to affirm and experience the goodness of his erotic desires, so also was he able to sense that he was a person whom God loved rather than one whom God hated.

Finally, William's religious heritage and its symbol systems and liturgical practices were sources of care for him. He found comfort in the view that God created him gay, once he could break through to this interpretation. When he could apply Christian teachings about God's love to himself, he was able to challenge internalized self-contempt. The sacrament of communion was an important part of his healing and further conveyed the sense of possibility of God's participation in his life. His concept of sin was revised to challenge his alienation rather than his orientation, providing further relief and empowerment. And although he never articulated a sense of gracious providence attending his transitional process, I was quite taken by the ways opportunities opened rather than closed for him as he stepped out on this terrifying and exhilarating journey. Rather than divine judgment and opposition, there seemed to me to be divine presence and empowerment each step of the way. In spite of the losses, missteps, and terror, the journey for William has been graced and has graced others.

What have been the outcomes of this positively experienced care in William's life? I find six results of the care William received that will prove instructive for our subsequent thinking about care for all persons, and especially lesbians and gays.

1. *The ability to move from self-hatred to self-esteem.* William described how through care he looked in a mirror and saw for the first time the face of a person worthy of respect rather than contempt. The internalized self-hatred arising in a heterosexist context was challenged and forever altered. I regard this as ultimately empowered by the gospel of God's validation of our being, including our sexuality, which liberates us from the "bondage to decay" at the hands of a condemning world.

2. *The ability to move from alienation from God to tentative reconciliation.* William had thought, at least unconsciously, that God hated him for his sexual orientation. As a result of care, he was able to see that he was created this way by God and therefore valued by God. In a subsequent communion service he experienced greater healing and sensed the possibility of God's presence. When he looked in the mirror, he saw for the first time a person whom God loved rather than hated. And although he still struggles with the meaning and place of God in his life, and associates God with a punitive and rejecting church, he also believes that it may be possible to find a meaningful relationship to God through other people.

The core conflict between belief in God who loves us as we are and internalized contempt for oneself as a homosexual person is very common for lesbians and gays. It is nearly pervasive for those who were reared in the Christian faith or who seek to find a place in Christianity as either a lay or clergy person. As we will see, effective care will need to recognize and help resolve this core conflict.

3. *The ability to move from phoniness and dishonesty to truthfulness and genuineness in relationships.* William felt that he was living a lie, and in many ways he was. He did not dare let himself or others know the truth about his sexuality because of real or imagined negative consequences. When he was able to come out and was supported through the intense phase of the coming-out process, he could be authentic with himself, his family, and his church. He did not have to live a lie, but could discern the truth and its power to set himself and others free. His relationship to his family and ministry became more genuine; he did not feel like a phony. There is now honest engagement, and he is in a variety of settings where he can discover and explore the truth about himself and his relationships, rather than live in the oppressive conflict between distortion and honesty. He interpreted this in biblical terms as "knowing the truth" so that the "truth will set you free."

4. *The ability to move from self-absorption to self-giving love.* William's life was largely self-absorbed until he came out of the closet and found larger possibilities for himself. He was consumed by his struggle to contain his conflict, to live a divided life, to puzzle out his confusion about the truth about himself, to handle his depression, and to fulfill the demands of marriage, parenthood, and ministry. When he was able to resolve these conflicts and to live more truthfully and honestly, he was freed from the sin of being "curved in upon himself" and was able to share self-giving love in a variety of relationships. He could minister to persons with AIDS and their families, giving them permission to love him as a gay person. His love for his ex-wife and family became deeper and more genuine. He was able to explore committed rather than fantasized or clandestine relationships with sexual partners.

5. *The ability to move from vocational malaise to vocational vitality.* Related to his capacity to engage in genuine and honest relationships characterized by greater dimensions of self-giving love is William's capacity to move to a renewed and larger sense of vocation. He had earlier been in a vocational malaise, feeling dragged down because what he preached to others was not available to himself. Even when he came out to his family and a few close parishioners, he had to keep his orientation a secret in his rural community and with the congregation at large. For a time he considered that he would have to leave the Christian ministry if he were to continue his journey as an openly gay man. The challenge to be truthful and remain as a minister contributed to a debilitating

vocational malaise. However, through the forces of care outlined earlier, he was able to find a setting of ministry that allowed him to be relatively more open and authentic. Observing him in this ministry has led me to conclude that for now his talents and gifts are well matched for the vocational responsibilities to which he has been called, and that he is making a valuable difference in the lives of those with whom he works. He seems to feel gratified in this setting, and his ministry appears to have a vitality that it did not previously have. Care has expanded his capacity for ministry and mission, as well as enabled him to find a context that is fitting for him at this point in his life.

6. *The ability to move from sexual shame to erotic pleasure.* William's sexual experience before coming to terms with his orientation was characterized by conflict and shame. He was conflicted and ashamed in his inability to be the kind of sexual partner that his wife deserved. His disclosures to her about his struggles were embarrassing and difficult. His clandestine homosexuality further shamed him because of its secrecy and ultimately ungratifying consequences. He also lived with fear of AIDS and exposure.

Through the acceptance and public affirmation of his orientation, William was able to experience the erotic dimensions of his sexuality as a mode of care and love, rather than a source of fear and shame. He did not feel contempt for his sexuality, but discovered the pleasure intended by God for humans to have in their most intimate communion with one another. He recognized the "kiss as an act of care." He was able to find in his sexuality a source of love and affiliation rather than contempt and alienation. This discovery, through the care mediated by erotic pleasure with significant others, is a rich source of healing and vitality for William, as for other lesbian and gay persons. We will return to its theological significance below.

Christina: From Outsider to Activist for Christ

Christina Troxell is an African-American woman in her forties who lives in the San Francisco Bay Area. She is a minister at Safe Harbor Community Church, a multicultural congregation in the heart of the San Francisco Bay Area, as well as a teacher and student of theology. She also has affiliations with The Safe Place, Inc., a nonprofit agency that provides housing and services for people living with AIDS, and with other local community-based service projects. She is fully out of the closet and was extremely generous with her time and perspectives.

She said that she had not reflected much on the question of where she had found care over the years, even though she had had numerous occasions to need care. She detailed how she grew up in an economically marginalized and emotionally dysfunctional family. There had been residues of sexual and racist abuse from past generations. Her mother was struggling with issues of abuse and abandonment, and Christina felt that she was in an early caretaker role with her mother. Christina herself was brutally sexually assaulted by men outside her home. From a very early age she learned that she had to look inside herself to make sense out of what was an "insane world" around her. Self-reliance and self-care were prominent themes in the interview.

Christina laughingly said that the early sexual training in her home was for "girls to keep their panties up and their dresses down." She was told that "boys only want one thing." She said that she had typical little girl crushes on boys in class, but that she also had crushes on little girls. "This did not confuse me, since both felt the same." She said that at age eight she "had a major sexual awakening." She began having sexual dreams. She said that this seemed normal and positive. "I never discussed them with anyone because I didn't think they were unusual."

When Christina was thirteen she endured a "brutal and night-long gang rape." She had a succession of boyfriends after this and became a delinquent juvenile as a reaction to traumas in her home and to her assault. She said that the assault resulted in the separation of pleasure from sex in her early life, but she did not think it had anything to do with her "becoming" lesbian. "My getting into trouble as a teenager didn't have anything to do with being gay. My acting out from rape landed me in juvenile hall. While there, I fell in love with another girl. I was fourteen when I discovered for sure that I liked women. I didn't know what to do with this *emotion* of love, rather than feeling confusion that it was toward a girl. I knew I had to be discreet, but I didn't feel like something was wrong with me. I didn't think of myself as gay, I was just me. It didn't occur to me to 'be gay,' but to engage with women just to add a little spice to my life. I thought I was going to grow up and get married. I didn't know there was a gay culture or lifestyle." She said that she had never internalized the split between straight and gay that people talked about. "In my community lesbians were identified with the word 'bulldaggers,' which was used negatively, but I wondered what was so bad about them."

When Christina was nineteen, she "fell headlong in love" with the father of her son. "I have a great son. He is the best son one could have. He is wonderful. But I felt emotionally battered by my relationship to his father. At age nineteen I decided to be gay. I had had both types of relationships, and the relationships with women were more positive. I had never thought strongly about it, but one day I just sat down and recognized that I liked women better. Women treated me a lot better. For ten years I thought this was a deliberate choice, arrived at rationally, because the relationships I really liked emotionally were with women."

Christina began to live openly as a lesbian and began educating her son about this when he was two. "I asked him what he would do if someone came up and told him that his Mama was different. As he got older, those conversations became more pointed. I built up in him some awareness of how he could respond. If he wasn't prepared it would hurt him. I needed to counter what society was sure to say about this. During twelve years of conversations, at no time did I try to hide the nature of the relationships I was in. At fourteen, he told me, 'Whatever makes you happy, makes me happy.' As he grew older, I did not have a series of lovers through the house. No one should model a series of sexual partners just parading through. I tried to carry myself with respect in relationships. I wanted to model positive sexual relationships. Then when my child reached puberty he would have a model of sexual responsibility."

In retrospect, Christina sees the hand of God. "My parents couldn't help me parent my child. When I was a child myself and the grown-ups around me were not making sense, someone had to make sense. Positive thoughts seemed to just spring up inside me, which helped me in life to trust myself. I have always trusted myself. I can see God's guidance. I think God writes his laws on our hearts, and it is there when we need it most."

For a while Christina was militantly pro-gay. "I wore a button like the Coca-Cola ad: 'Gay love—it's the real thing!' How else could I have lived my life at nineteen and twenty? If I was ashamed of who I was, it could not have been positive for my son. This is my life. From my experience in my own family, I knew that an unhappy woman could not raise a happy child. I knew I had to be at ease in my lifestyle if I was going to be positive with my son. I did have enough strength and internal fortitude to make that decision and stay with it. I wanted to be happy, confident, at ease in my lifestyle, and loving toward him."

For Christina, "self-care" was an important resource, and from age thirty on, strong religious foundations supported her life. These were essential sources of care by which to overcome some huge challenges. She said, "If you look at a lot of definitions, I have a lot against me: I am black, female, in my forties, I'm gay, I'm a single mother, in a lower economic class, raised by a single parent from a dysfunctional household, I had limited education and was sexually abused, all of those things. I learned, if you don't have some sense of worth you might as well shoot yourself. I really believe that a sense of self that is internally generated is very necessary for a successful life. A successful life for me means a life of happiness, not riches or so-called accomplishment. We are supposed to love our neighbor as we love ourselves. Loving our neighbor comes after loving ourselves, and loving ourselves can come after finding out that God loves us. Certainly you are worth something, if you have worth to the Almighty!"

Christina has internalized God's acceptance of her life and understands her life fully from a Christian perspective. There is no conflict within her between her Christian faith and her sexuality. At one time, she oriented her identity around a militant Black Nationalist stance. "I was militant against Euro-American culture; there was no white music in my life, and there were no white friends. I learned to speak Swahili, listened only to African and African-American music, and dressed in African clothing." She said that whenever people center their identity on some aspect of their history or psychology, then there is a lifestyle or a culture connected with that. She thinks some gay and lesbian people do that, but she scoffed at the idea that her lesbian orientation constituted a unique lifestyle. "My mother said she would never understand my lifestyle, but, she said, 'Whatever makes you happy is okay with me.' I wanted to say to her, 'Look, my lifestyle is not any different than yours. I get up in the morning and have breakfast. I go to work, come back, do some volunteer work, clean up, return phone calls, talk to my friends, go to the store, buy food, cook dinner. Maybe on the weekends I go out to dinner or see a movie. I may sit around home on Saturday night and eat popcorn. I go to church on Sunday morning. Now that's my lifestyle.' (Laughs) That's as healthy and bland and typical as can be. That's the American lifestyle. So what is this that she can't understand my lifestyle? One of these days I am going to write about this: 'What Lifestyle Are You Talking About?' If I could get that as well publicized as the 'gay' lifestyle has been, I think that we will have come a long way. I think that people who talk about a gay lifestyle are those who identify their humanity as gay, rather than identifying themselves as human beings who have many experiences."

In reflecting on religious faith as a source of care, Christina said that "the gospel helped me see that I matter. When I look back, I see that the hand of God has always been with me. I did take myself to church when I was seven, eight, nine, but I was offended and left the church when the pastor berated me in front of the congregation. I had asked him a question that I understand now challenged his teaching and doctrine about Jesus. His reaction was to berate and insult me from the pulpit, and demand that I never ever challenge his teaching again. But even at eight or nine years old, I knew that God was my advocate. God was for me. That whole confession of Christ took place when I was eight or nine, but I didn't go back to church for twenty years. Yet spiritual things stay with you. God told Jeremiah that before he was born God knew him. Scriptures help us to talk about things that are already in us. The Spirit is in our hearts. I can look back thirty years and see how God was with me."

Christina said that her identity is no longer oriented around her blackness or her sexuality, but "my primary identification is that I am an activist for Christ. I don't need a public platform. I try to work with people who are suicidal because they can't cope with all this. I try to help people one at a time to come out of a trap that is the limit of their own self-definition. Limits on self-definition in any area extend to other areas. I am against the party line about gays and lesbians. I think that sexual coming together is like the coming together of the Father, Son, and Holy Spirit. It is private and very spiritual. The permanent monogamous marriage that we live out in our lives is like the relationship between God the Father and Christ and the church. We learn about our relation to God through the example of the church. Permanent, monogamous, one-flesh union is a type of how Christ lives in the church. Our one-flesh experience points to God's relation to the church. God's one-flesh union is holy, submissive, celebrative, giving. It is compassionate and respectful, esteeming another as higher than oneself. We see in our holy, celebrative, directed, purposeful, and fulfilling love a type of the relation that we have in God. Paul said not to be joined to harlots, as opposed to becoming joined as flesh of my flesh and bone of my bone. We can talk about this with people who are desperate, because there is no condemnation in Christ."

Christina said that she worked with gay and lesbian couples to understand this possibility of love in permanent relationships. She said that both straight and gay people need to have healthy relationships "and forget the stereotyping. If God is not judging, then neither can we. I don't believe God judges homosexuality any differently than heterosexuality. I don't justify this, it just is. I believe that homosexual relationships can reflect God's will for relationships just like others. I work on the quality and meaning of relationships, not their orientation."

To come to this point in her life was not easy for Christina. After her conversion to Christianity, she took the Bible literally and decided that she had to make major changes in her life, including her sexuality. "I thought I had to give up my lesbian partner, give up alcohol, astrological charts. Everything that was not holy had to go. I lived this way for years, based on literal interpretations of the Bible. I was mostly celibate. I was miserable and felt like dying when I failed to stay in the 'holy life.' I couldn't accomplish being a eunuch for the kingdom of God. I felt like I couldn't give my body for God. I was driving myself crazy living this sinless, spotless life that I thought the Bible literally wanted. In church, I was getting the preaching of grace, but this conflicted with my literal interpretation. I began to get more distant from life. I didn't go out and associate with my old friends, didn't return certain people's calls, etc."

A female pastor befriended Christina and began to challenge this interpretation of Scripture and the Christian life. She asked Christina,

"What would you do if God says it is okay to be gay?" Christina realized that this question reflected both pastoral concern and active sexual interest in her on the part of the woman minister. Christina's reply was, "I would pack my bags and be at your door!" Christina prayed and fasted about this. "I knew that I did not have to fear God. I could talk straight with him. I asked him if it was okay to be gay. He said, 'What do you like?' Two days later, I said, 'I like women. I enjoy them more.' He said, 'Then go do that.' I understood in a flash that there was no condemnation in the way that I felt. I went to her house with my bags. I knew that I was not under any condemnation for having 'lesbian tendencies.' I stopped beating myself. God gave me permission to be who I was."

After this, Christina said she returned to "having the life I had vowed to have when my son was born. I was going to have a life that I was happy with and that could be an instrumentality for others. In the name of Jesus I had fallen back from that, instead of forward into it. I had fallen into law, not grace. Now my pastor's preaching on grace had meaning. Grace accepts me just as I am. Because I had some experience of being accepted as worthy, now I could hear the message. It made sense. Now I could live my life as one approved by God rather than by people. I know what I have is an unacceptable gospel in most circles. I just don't care. I would rather be with one person who is dying and who doesn't have a relationship with God than with fifty people who think they are right. I don't care to enter into debates about homosexuality and the Bible. I avoid those who make an issue out of sexual orientation. I just don't have time to deal with them and those who are rejected too. I can't deal with those who injure others *and* those who are injured by them. I need to work with the injured."

Christina finds her congregation as a place for her ministry, a place where she feels welcome as she is. She says that the preaching is based on "grace and truth. People who are marginalized and disenfranchised come in, including me. My sexuality is not an issue here. God doesn't condemn you or require you to change. Scads of homosexuals are in the church. There are drug addicts, criminals, alcoholics, disabled, HIV-positive people—the church is full of misfits. The doors don't close on anyone. What we have in common is an emotional wounding and a need for healing. There is a range of socioeconomic status, lifestyle, etc. Our church struggles not to have a group mind. You can be yourself, not have to be like anyone else. It is essential to have autonomy in relation to God. That sense of autonomy helps create balance. The drive toward autonomy and relationship is very helpful and healthy."

When reflecting on the larger environment as a source of care, Christina thought that "people flock to a place where they are welcome." The Bay Area of California provides a place where "people are welcomed in social and political ways. There is a search for social justice here. People can find community here, though," she chuckled, "not necessarily love relationships. This sense of community gives people a place to belong. The gay community has closed in to help deal with AIDS. There is fabulous support and fund-raising."

Yet Christina realized that there were limits on this network, as well. "You can get comfortable in a gay network. There is an air of militancy. An African-American man who is gay, however, still suffers from racism, even from white gays. Addressing gay issues can create unity for gay issues only; racism and sexism still go on. Just recently, black and white gays were split over a gay issue that had racist overtones. Women of either ethnicity weren't invited into the debate because of sexism issues; white gay men still wanted to be in charge of the movement, to own both the problem and the solution. Gays of color and women were relegated to a secondary position. Unity existed only when orientation alone was the issue."

Christina shared how her partners have been a source of care for her. She realized that as a black lesbian she had to be selective in expressing her relationships, and partners had to be discreet. Further, because she brought a baby into the relationship and "was adamant about my responsibility as a mother, there were special needs in our relationships. Because of my strong personality, people have been somewhat dependent on me to take care of them, think for them, and protect them from the harshness of the world. It is a role I play. I found myself with a succession of people who would hide behind that. I became very unhappy with it. I am not living with those people today because of it."

Today, Christina is in a relationship with "a woman who is as secure about herself as I am, in fact, more so. We have respectively come to terms with our sexuality, and we have put it where it belongs. We have come to the point where we can serve as a model. This is a relationship that God has ordained. All the other things before were what we call 'practice and rehearsal.' They were the kind of things that could make us into people who could have a successful relationship today. My ex-partners couldn't do this. Society works against successful gay relationships; we are supposed to be unhappy and clandestine. People come into relationships tormented and twisted by social pressures concerning themselves. Societal pressures about being gay warp the mental and emotional growth of the individual and make it hard to have what it takes to make a good relationship. It makes them difficult and fleeting. If you look at it, a lot of what makes those relationships difficult is the societal message that says they cannot be natural, normal healthy couples."

Yet Christina is confident that "one-flesh unions" are gifts from God and great sources of joy. "I believe that permanent, monogamous relationships are the way to go—not in order to mimic heterosexual marriage, but because these are the relationships that work out. I always go back to discovering God in flesh and blood union, in discerning the value in some-one else, and in knowing with security that God has placed a prop up un-der you. I am a fan of a relationship God has chosen rather than one I have chosen. I try to tell people about this—the difference between a God-chosen relationship and randomly running around trying to create something. There is no higher source of joy. Marriage is a greater miracle than childbirth, because two disparate people have found one another. My son is not different than me. I have to love him; he came out of this body. But this woman—I didn't even know she was alive, and yet we have a one-flesh union. Now, that's a miracle. And I guess that is against the party line!"

Sources and Outcomes of Care

For Christina, care is many faceted. It shares many of the features that we found in William's experience. Personal strength and self-reliance are more central for Christina, but shared by each. The importance of a reli-able network is underscored by Christina as well as William, though for Christina the church has been more supportive. For each, a particular pastoral relationship was critical for self-affirmation and reconciling sex-ual orientation to Christian faith. Both found that erotic one-flesh unions with mutually consenting partners were positive sources of care, and each found the liturgical practices and theological symbol systems of Chris-tianity helpful once they were freed from heterosexist and homophobic interpretations.

Along with these general parallels, Christina's experience as an African-American lesbian has some unique features. As a woman, she daily faces the pervasive influence of male privilege in our culture. She is a survivor of sexual abuse at the hands of presumably heterosexual males. She also struggles against racial oppression and economic marginalization. There was extreme dysfunction in her family of origin. She "did time" as a juve-nile delinquent. She was a single parent who did not have the ongoing love and support of a former marital partner, as William did.

The care Christina has needed and received has been comprehen-sive; it is neither limited to nor isolated from her sexual orientation. From her report, three aspects of care seem primary. First, there is a theological message that says in strong terms and in many ways "that in Christ there is no condemnation." She is a person whose life and be-ing are under assault in this culture. Yet the gospel not only helps her fight back, it has enabled her so far to prevail over these destructive in-fluences on her body, her personality, her sexuality, her race, her gen-der, her parenthood, and her economic situation. She is a living witness that "nothing in all creation can separate us from the love of God in Christ Jesus."

Second, there is a spiritual presence that makes the theological message of the gospel real for her. Christina believes that God has called her for special purposes and that God's law is written on our hearts. She seeks God in prayer and Bible study, and senses God's response to her. She believes that God has told her that her sexual orientation and relational commitments are pleasing to God when they reflect love and mutual respect and when they serve as a foundation for ministry to others. Indeed, her one-flesh union with her partner mirrors or images the kind of love God has for the church.

Third, Christina demonstrates a huge capacity for self-care and finely honed survival skills. She knew early as a child that she had to look after herself and provide sanity in an insane world. She knew that if she did not ensure her own happiness, her son would be impaired. She knew that some relationships were bad for her and was able to move out of them. She recognized that she did not have to "take in" everything that was around her, but had to use her resources to act on what was positive. She sets limits on whom she will respond to in ministry, and she has been able to move from imbalanced power arrangements to mutuality in her intimate relationships. All of these capacities for self-care and survival are supported by her theological conviction that in Christ there is no condemnation for her sexual orientation (and all other aspects of her life). They are also supported by her personal spirituality. She recognized that in all the events of her life, God's grace has been available in both apparent and hidden ways. Identifying and living the truth about her own strengths and resources has been a way for her to discover God's underlying presence and ongoing guidance and acceptance of her life.

The outcomes of care for Christina are somewhat different, though they overlap with those we identified in William's case. Christina did not seem to experience as much self-rejection as did William, but she too found that pastoral care helped her resolve the core conflict between her sexual orientation and her religious commitment. Through her friendship and sexual intimacy with a female minister of another congregation, she discovered that her attempts to live a sexually abstinent life were alienating her from herself, others, and God. She found God's support of her sexuality through this relationship.

Like William, care assisted Christina to move from fragmented interpersonal relationships to greater mutuality and wholeness. She reported that as she grew in faith and experience, she was able to develop a relationship with someone as strong and self-confident as she is. This relationship is a role model for others and a basis for understanding God's love more fully. She is seeking a stronger relationship with her mother and appears to have overcome many of the negative consequences of damaging relationships in her past.

Another result of care for Christina is the capacity for mission and ministry growing out of a fuller acceptance of her sexuality. She feels called by God to help, among others, those who are suicidal because of internalized homophobia, and to be a role model for committed relationships. She wants to be a part of a community of faith in which all are accepted for who they are, and where unique individuality is prized over a group mindset. She sees herself as an "activist for Christ," confronting heterosexism, racism, and sexism, and affirms her sexuality as a resource in this ministry. Finally, as in William's case, care has assisted Christina in affirming the erotic dimensions of her sexual orientation and overcoming the separation of sexuality and pleasure. And although it does not appear that shame and fear are as large a part of her experience as for William, she acknowledges that she has struggled to find erotic pleasure in her sexuality as a result of early abuse and her later attempts at religiously motivated abstinence. The extent of her healing is revealed in her affirmation that one-flesh unions convey the quality of God's love for the church and help us to know what God is really like. Indeed, her sexuality constitutes a kind of "hermeneutical," or interpretive, lens through which we know the grace and purpose of God's love. It is the basis for disclosing, at least in part, the being and intentions of God. In this respect, the care Christina has received has disclosed for her the image of God in the human experience of erotic, loving, same-sex partners. We will expand the theological implications of this discovery in the pages ahead.

Conclusion:
A Preliminary Profile of Care

These narratives provide a basis for sketching a preliminary profile of care that is viable for lesbian and gay persons, as well as for others. This profile will be elaborated throughout the remainder of the book.

1. *Care as active welcome and full affirmation.* Care is based in and conveys an active welcome for persons in their total humanity, including a full affirmation of their sexual orientation. Active welcome is grounded in the gospel of Jesus Christ, which affirms that in Christ "there is no condemnation." William and Christina illustrate the central importance of acceptance of their sexuality as a condition and mode of care. The need for care in the first place derives from rejection and condemnation. It only follows that true care must have the power to overcome this negative message through individual, communal, theological, and liturgical efforts.

Pastors, congregations, and other communities convey care when they actively seek lesbian and gay persons, and welcome them as full participants in the community of faith. Ongoing pastoral presence and response to crisis also conveys active welcome.

2. *Care as normalized participation.* A corollary of active welcome is normalizing the involvement of lesbian and gay persons in the community of faith. Christina said that it was important for her to be in a congregational setting where there were lesbian and gay persons, as well as other kinds of persons. She wanted an environment where diversity was normal. People did not have to blend into social sameness, but could be uniquely themselves. William found it very important that he could live in a diverse urban environment where it was normal to be around other gay men and to talk about their experiences naturally. Other persons I interviewed emphasized how important it was for them to be a normal part of the congregation rather than "token" lesbian and gay persons, or "tolerated" just like everyone else.

For some, to feel like a normal part of the congregation meant that they had to seek out the Metropolitan Community Church where lesbian and gay experience was predominant. Others said that felt abnormal to them, because life was fuller than lesbian and gay experience. All said that it was important that they felt actively welcomed as lesbian and gay persons in communities where they would not have to hide or deny what that meant for them in the context of their religious life. In order to feel like they were normalized in the congregational setting, lesbian and gay persons expected pastoral visits, social invitations, stewardship campaigns, church directory registrations, sermons, prayers, and announcements to recognize their same-sex relationships and commitments in a manner similar to the way these would be recognized for heterosexuals.

3. *Care as using life experience in ministry.* One of the clear outcomes of care, as well as a means of extending care, is to draw on the life experience of lesbian and gay persons for the mission and ministry of the church. We have seen how William overcame vocational malaise and discovered new dimensions of ministry through his coming-out process. Rather than losing his ministry as he feared, he found that his ministry took on new depth and significance for him. Because his gifts were used rather than denigrated or rejected by his religious community, William felt cared about, even though he still had to remain largely "closeted" in his work setting. In Christina's case, her congregation demonstrated care by recognizing that her life experience would enable her to enter into the needs of others as a guide and resource. Lesbian and gay persons, as we will discover in the narratives ahead, have much to offer the church and larger society. To care for them, as for any person, care providers must seek to find ways to use their experience as a source of grace and ministry for others.

4. *Care as organized response to opportunity and need.* William and

Christina found assistance through a variety of spontaneous acts by individuals. However, these individuals were part of larger networks of persons, institutions, and congregations that were trained and organized to respond to the particular needs of lesbian and gay persons. In subsequent chapters we will see the importance of organized legal and social services for adoption by lesbian and gay parents. We will discover ways of organizing for support, education, and healing in the coming-out process. The AIDS crisis will instruct us about the ways care is organized to ensure the availability of resources for research, education, prevention, support, and grief recovery for all who are affected, or potentially affected, by this disease. To be effective, care must be organized proactively as well as reactively.

5. *Care as strategic public advocacy.* Part of Christina's early self-care was the realization that she needed to affirm her lesbian orientation publicly. The form this took was wearing a button that said, "Gay love—it's the real thing!" and to advocate gay rights. She and others knew that to change the structures of heterosexism in our culture meant that the laws, public policies, and allocation of resources must not be directed exclusively toward heterosexual interests. We will later discover how important it is to the care of individuals, families, and couples to engage and change public religious and civil policies and practices that work against their full humanity. William and Christina both affiliated with congregations that are widely known for their activist stances toward lesbian and gay inclusion, as well as toward other forms of social justice. It is critical to their care for lesbian and gay persons to know that heterosexuals are joining with them to oppose unjust laws such as Amendment 2 in Colorado,[4] and working against religious policies that exclude them from full participation in the life of the church.

To embody these five dimensions of care is, in effect, to "come out" as religious individuals and communities for and with lesbian and gay experience. As we will see, because these dimensions are grounded in a God who stands by and with humanity, they are the structures of care by which God's being and intentions are disclosed. They are the means by which God "comes out" of the closet too, and by which God's image is reflected in human experience. Because coming out is such a central part of lesbian and gay caregiving, we will examine its processes more fully.

2

BREAKING THE BUBBLE

Care and Coming Out

David Wilkonsen said that coming out of the closet in his late twenties was like breaking a bubble. He had been reared in an affluent suburban environment. His family was active in the Episcopal Church, and his father was a highly successful businessman. David had five brothers and sisters, and his mother was positively involved in his life. David reported that his family was close. This family was at the apex of privilege in our culture. Life began to unravel when David was in law school. He had a nervous breakdown and spent several months in a psychiatric hospital. He discovered in this crisis that he had a bipolar depression and that he was gay. The "bubbles" of normality and white male heterosexual privilege were irretrievably broken.

David went back to church to "get fixed," stating, "if the psychiatrist can't fix me maybe God can." He said that every time he heard the word *sin* in church he thought of the homosexual part of himself. Religion was "the lightning rod for evil, life-defiling, and necrotic things to constellate around inside me." Through priestly help, he was able initially to face these terrors and to begin to come out to himself. He said that the psychiatrist helped him in many ways, but the "priest's help went right to the soul. The priest communicated, 'I hear you. I believe you. I am with you.'"

David recounted a profound spiritual experience that was the turning point in affirming his homosexuality. "In actively accepting that part of me, not just regarding it as something rattling around inside me that I could push out the door when I wanted to." He had come to the point where he thought that he had successfully repressed his homosexuality and that it had gone away, when this crisis emerged. "In this crisis, I had an image of Moses in a basket floating down the river. I knew I had to grab that basket or Moses would be gone. I reached out and grasped it, and suddenly I knew that this is ME! It was a seminal turning point in my life." David said that he just "knew" the truth that he must actively grasp and accept. He does not know the source of this experience, but regards it as something that just came from deep inside him. It was "something greater than myself coming through. I knew, 'this is me!'"

For David, this pivotal experience was an anchoring event for the rest of his life. "The journey has been entirely different since that time. Now that I have embraced this, how do I accept this thing I have been trying to annihilate for twenty-five years?"

David began actively to seek and find support. He took the initiative to find gay people he could talk to and groups of gay persons to be among. He immersed himself in gay circles and read gay literature. "I realized that though I was a white male, I was really on the outside of the power bubble. I was socialized as a heterosexual white male, so I now have to embrace that I am an outsider. I had to question the old way of life and figure out new values and identity."

The major source of care in this time of vulnerable transition was gay friends. "Once you have been expelled from the big heterosexual bubble, you are just out there, and God only knows how things will come out. You also need sources of care that are not gay—they are just as important. But there are some things you can only talk about with gay persons, so your world is more fragmented and differentiated."

David's coming out has changed his relationship with his family. He said that he wanted "them to have some idea of what I had been struggling with, and to put an end to the lie about when I was going to be married, and so forth. It was a tremendous risk, because you do not really know what will happen." He has become much closer to his mother and to all of his siblings, with the exception of one sister who can't accept his orientation. For a time, his father wanted to be with him as frequently as possible, just to be together. But now the relationship "is like it was before: we are in each other's life, but there is not a lot of interaction." On the whole, however, David feels grateful for the way he has been accepted. "Last Christmas it was an added joy to be with them because they knew. I didn't have to hide. When people look at you, they see *you,* not a mirror of themselves. Now I can see myself as I am, and I can make sure that others do too."

David has continued taking medication for his depression, and he has been in recovery from alcohol addiction with the help of Alcoholics Anonymous. He also continues to find assistance from an active relationship to his church. He sees all of these areas as places where "light" can shine. "You are only as sick as your secrets. I am trying to become whole and find healing. When I went back to church six years ago, I was a fractured person trying to get rid of something. Now I am back as a whole person. I came back with a friend who was a guide. Before, I was alone."

David's journey with God is in flux. Freud's view of God as a projection of a father figure influenced his belief system. "I went through a period not using the word *Father*. Father-God was austere, distant. I used other images. God was like the Wizard of Oz, turning the crank to move crap out of the system. But this has spots where it doesn't work for me either. If you just trust sometimes, things work out. I realize that faith in God is a journey, and not just one journey. I have free will and I can turn away. It is like a dance; if I turn away, God has to take a better move to stop me."

A year ago, David's relationship with God deepened after an unsatisfactory counseling session with his interim pastor. He went to the pastor because he did not feel comfortable with some of the religious content of the church. "The pastor was not equipped to deal with it. I was angry and went back a second time. It didn't help. I felt I abused him in my anger, and I felt guilty. I wondered if the church hadn't given all responsibility for healing over to psychiatrists. In all my visits to psychiatrists—and I go monthly now—I realized that I had never talked about my deepest beliefs with a priest. It then dawned on me that God was there and listening. Even though my priest couldn't hear me, God did. When I realized this, the anger went away. Then I remembered the first priest and how helpful he was when I was in crisis. All he did was affirm me. I didn't know it at the time; it just took some time for the understanding of what was happening to emerge."

The care that David received in his coming-out process was integrally tied to the psychiatric and family support that he received for treating his mental illness. Initially, his bipolar depression and his unassimilated homosexuality obscured one another. With sustained investigation and diagnosis, these were separated and responded to accordingly. David described the relationship between his illness and his orientation this way: "I don't think the repression of my homosexuality caused my bipolar illness, but fueled it. But bipolar illness is a metaphor for a lack of wholeness and integration, of 'man against himself.' I am much healthier now, more integrated. For my parents the diagnosis of bipolar depression was a relief. I resisted it because I thought that I had a spiritual problem, not a medical problem. I have had to build a bridge between them."

David's narrative is very instructive for understanding some of the critical elements of care in the coming-out process. First, coming out constitutes a crisis for the lesbian or gay person, as well as for his or her social network. In David's words, it is "breaking the bubble" and being "expelled" from the structure of heterosexual privilege. It is risky, often attended by frightening internalized messages connected with evil and death. For many it can be lonely and potentially isolating. For others it can lead to attempted or successful suicide. The caregiver must be very sensitive to this acute vulnerability and, like the first priest David talked with, communicate "I hear you, I believe you, I am with you, I affirm you."[1]

Second, it is clear that hiding or obscuring homosexual feelings is a common experience for many lesbian and gay persons. To come out is to "break the heterosexual bubble" and to be exposed to a frightening, indefinite future. It is sometimes easier for lesbian and gay persons and their caregivers to attend to the "nonsexual" elements in a crisis—such as David's mental illness—than to explore more deeply about matters of sexual orientation. Fortunately, David's priest and doctors did not make this mistake, but helped him gain a true picture of his situation and to respond fully to it. Both his doctors and his priest were able to affirm his homosexuality and not treat it as a symptom of sickness or sin once it was recognized. They provided a context in which he eventually could overcome his own self-hatred and rejection and affirm in himself what he had been trying to annihilate. Simultaneously, they did not assume that his mental status was only a result of his sexual conflicts and that it would resolve itself as he integrated his homosexuality into his ego functions. Differential diagnosis by gay-affirming helpers was essential for David's care as a mentally ill person who was seeking both psychological health and clarity about his sexual orientation. Coming out ultimately has to do with greater truthfulness at various levels of personal and social experience.

Third, the religious and spiritual dimensions of David's coming out are emotionally charged and acutely ambiguous. They must be treated in their own right. They cannot be subsumed under some other category, such as mental illness or delusional thinking. They are complicated and nuanced, and must be responded to as an inherent part of the lesbian or gay person's personality. Because they are so "primitive," difficult, and sometimes bizarre, it is easier to ignore them or hand them over to the psychiatrist for response. Yet for David it was important that a bridge be built between his sexuality, mental illness, and religious struggles. It was to his enduring benefit that this bridge was built and that the positive and negative elements of his spiritual life were treated as an authentic part of his healing.

David's imaginative "waking dream" about baby Moses was the transforming event in his coming-out process. Before this event, religious ideation had largely been connected to evil and death. In this "salvific moment" it was transformed and connected to life. In this situation we see how a personal crisis of health and identity eventuated in a genuine spiritual gain.[2]

In David's case, the spiritual crisis is connected with his sexual orientation and whether it will have a liberating and life-affirming place in his life or whether it will be connected to death. He knows that he must choose and that his life will be lost if he does not. Something within him empowers him to save himself by affirming himself; by saving "Moses" he is saving the part of himself that will liberate others and be a medium of

God's law to the larger community. Affirming his sexual orientation was not narcissistic self-indulgence of something despicable or evil in David, but a grace-full spiritual discovery of his true selfhood under God. It is a situation in which fundamental estrangement from his true self was healed and overcome, and the basis for a divinely empowered ministry of liberation for others.

Not all lesbian and gay persons, or heterosexuals for that matter, have such powerful and dramatic spiritual experiences as a part of their crisis of sexual identity and development. For them their spirituality and sexuality interconnect in other ways. But the caregiver must be attentive to a surprising interplay of the care-seeker's religious heritage in the context of sexual self-discovery. The caregiver cannot assume that it is either only negative (even though that may appear to be the case for a time, as in David's situation) or that it is only positive. Rather, there is much to be gained in terms of care to particular individuals by attending to the ambiguous dimensions of their spirituality, with the belief that in due time there is the potential for a transforming reconfiguration of their religious heritage. The spiritual dimensions of David's life ultimately provided the basis for him to affirm his orientation as a core part of his personality and to affirm rather than annihilate his life. The final decision at the apex of this crisis was David's. However, without the resources of a heritage taught to him as a child and without a wise and available environment to support him in his crisis of coming out, it is quite possible that Moses would have been left to the river and perhaps lost.

Another dimension of David's spiritual coming out is his developing relationship with God. Like most of us, his belief in God is ambiguous and developing as his self-understanding changes through interactions with others. In the midst of his crisis, he returns to church looking for healing, perhaps with magical and childlike expectations. Under the influence of Freud, he goes through a process of identifying God with a remote father, and separating himself from each one. He develops a temporary, transitional fantasy God, characterized by the Wizard of Oz who from a hidden position cleans "crap out of the system." He realizes that this is inadequate to his experience and that some things just have to be lived through and they turn out positively without divine intervention. He also began to realize that his own agency was a part of his relation to God, that God in some ways was a dance partner who sometimes had to creatively move against him rather than merely a magical "fixer of brokenness." Lately he has recognized, through a frustrating experience with a priest, that God's reality was most clearly communicated to him—without his realizing it at the time—by the first priest who affirmed him, believed in him, and said that he was there for him. David now senses that God understands him and listens to him in a supportive, affirming, and empowering manner.

The way David images God has been profoundly changed through the care he has received in the coming-out process. It is not too strong to say that the image of God has been disclosed in new and promising ways for him. From the care he has received for his mental illness and coming out, God is disclosed as healer, dance partner, relentless pursuer, liberator of the liberator, sympathetic listener, and the one who understands the depth of his personality. These spiritual and theological convictions were not so much "taught" as "caught"; though without childhood religious education and ongoing liturgical and homiletical influences mediated through the congregation, the resources of his various caretakers would have been severely limited. We will later examine more fully how the images of God that have become spiritually vital for David as a consequence of the care he received in his journey of healing and coming out link theologically to an interpretation of what it means to be fully human in the image of God. For now, it is enough to suggest that as David and others find healing from illness and the ability to affirm the truth about their sexuality through the medium of care, the image of God is disclosed in significant new ways.

Finally, David's narrative illustrates again how important it is to have a reliable environment for care to be effective. *Coming out* as a lesbian or gay person in our culture means to "break a bubble" of privilege and protection, and to open oneself to internal terrors and social risks that literally can be deadly. Lesbian and gay persons are not simply fighting to understand and accept the inner meaning of their lives; they are fighting against an external system of hatred of their core humanity and an internalized self-denigration emerging from this culture of "homo-hatred." To affirm one's homosexuality and live openly and joyfully with it is to lose status and to launch into a perilous future. It is not possible to face these losses alone. In addition to enormous personal courage, considerable social support is required.

David's metaphor that coming out is "breaking a bubble" says more than something about the courage and risk involved in leaving the dominant heterosexual culture. It implies that that culture is itself vulnerable and illusory. It is a bubble rather than a foundational structure of creation ordained by God, in spite of its self-understanding to the contrary. Those who break the bubble threaten its status as well as their own. If persons break the bubble, survive, and through care and solidarity find new and transforming dimensions of relationship with themselves, others, and God, then much of the assumptive world of heterosexuals is threatened. David's metaphor discloses that heterosexuals live in a bubble that can be easily broken; the heterosexist structure of experience is ephemeral, costly, and illusory. It can "pop" in an instant, and that is terrifying and infuriating. Thus care in the coming-out process requires attention not only to those leaving the bubble, but assistance to help those within it to think differently about their own situation. David's metaphor therefore leads to the question, How do we construct environments that not only assist lesbian and gay persons to find new potentials for loving relationships and divine vocation, but that also free straight persons for expanded images of human relationality under God? What might human solidarity look like once we break the bubble of heterosexist privilege and domination?

Coming Out at Seminary

Many of the lesbian and gay persons I interviewed had been to seminary or theological school. Nearly all found that the seminary environment was positive for them and either initiated their coming-out process or enabled them to feel more secure out of the closet. They found support and solidarity in the seminary and an ability to have their experience normalized in chapel, class assignments, and the governance structures of the seminary.

One of the more memorable examples of coming out in seminary was one I observed firsthand and in some ways participated in. This took place in a class on ministry and human sexuality taught by theologian Sheila Greeve Davaney and myself. One of the ground rules of the course was that each student was free to disclose his or her ideas, feelings, thoughts, and experiences about sexuality at whatever level he or she chose. We agreed that there would be no pressure on class members to disclose a great deal of personal material. At the same time, the class agreed that those disclosing more fully would be respected and that confidentiality would be honored if requested.

Several weeks into the course, Sheila and I received an anonymous letter from a member of the class. The student stated that he had long suspected that he was gay, but that his mother's warnings against the evils of homosexuality prevented him from admitting to himself and others that he was gay. He also did not want to lose status within his evangelical religious community. He acknowledged that he felt conflicted and that it would be some relief to him for the class to know that there was one among them who was struggling at a personal level with the issue of homosexuality.

We agreed to read this to the class, as requested, because we felt obligated by the group contract to honor each student's mode of self-disclosure. After reading the letter, the class was fairly silent. We asked for responses to the letter. It became quickly apparent that the members of the class were touched, even moved, by this disclosure and wanted to take great care in responding. The dominant tone was respect for the courage it took to share this struggle, and compassion for the discomfort and anxiety the person must be experiencing as he anticipated and received the class's response to his letter. A number of class members expressed empathy for how lonely the student must have been, living with this tension, and how relieving it must have been to let others in on his secret struggle.

One of the more memorable dimensions of this discussion was that no one expressed criticism or negative feelings toward the letter or the student, although from earlier class discussions it was clear that not all members were gay affirming. Although some members were more or less militantly "out of the closet" gay and lesbian persons, and there were gay-affirming heterosexuals in the course, some of the students had candidly stated that they did not think that gay and lesbian sexuality was compatible with Christian teaching. There had been some sharp—even vigorous—disagreements, and the tone was not always respectful. However, when the topic of sexual orientation became an expression of a concrete human being's spiritual struggle and search for honest self-expression, all members of the class demonstrated compassion, care, and respect. The discussion had moved from an abstract issue to the anguished struggle of a living person with whom each member of the class had some kind of prior relationship. The class as a group, consequently, moved from analysis to care without thinking very much about this transition.

Subsequently the student made an appointment to reveal his identity to Sheila and me. His name was Jack. He was a fairly quiet person and one of our stronger students. His appearance was somewhat unkempt, and he had a kind of slouching posture. He had a good sense of humor and occasionally contributed satirical pieces to the community underground newspaper. The purpose of the appointment was to seek our advice about identifying himself to the class as the author of the letter. After some exploration, he decided to do this, recognizing that a few members might feel that they were morally obligated to disclose his orientation to the denomination that they held in common.

At the next class meeting, Jack told the class that he had written the letter. He expressed his gratitude for the care with which it was received. He said that he felt affirmed and empowered to keep looking honestly at his identity. The class expressed its appreciation for his disclosure. Some members offered themselves as friends and conversation partners if Jack had need of them. There was a general good spirit in the class and a sense that the class was not just teaching about ministry and sexuality, but was a context in which real ministry was taking place in a surprising and grace-filled way.

In the remaining weeks of the course there was a notable change in Jack. He got a new wardrobe and changed his hairstyle from what one might call "student unkempt" to "fashionable professional." He began wearing coats and ties rather than jeans and T-shirts. His posture was upright, and he carried himself with a sense of pride and vitality. His previous slouch was gone. Several members of the class commented to us and to one another on how much more vital and alive he seemed; some used the word *transformed* to describe the changes they perceived in him. At the end of the class we learned that he had come out to his father on a recent visit home and that his father had been accepting. (He was regretful that his mother had died before she could learn the truth about his sexuality.) He thanked the class for its care and acceptance and for the opportunity it afforded to take this critical step in his life. The class expressed appreciation for his courage to trust them with this vulnerable aspect of his life and noted how good they felt at the positive changes that took place as a consequence of his coming out and accepting himself for who he was. This class, unlike any other we taught, concluded with a ritual of celebration and sharing of gifts to commemorate what we had learned and experienced.

This episode of care anchored in a new way the transforming power of acceptance, especially when this acceptance is based in a reliable community of care and is empathically connected to the vulnerable striving for truth at the core of one's personality. Deep human compassion and solidarity across lines of sexual orientation emerged in a surprising manner through Jack's coming out in this course. The heterosexual bubble popped for all of us to some degree through this shared experience of care. Persons with strong theological differences about the nature of homosexuality somehow found a unified compassion in the face of a real person who was reaching out for assistance and affirmation. There is no question that this unfolding represented a narrative of care that encompassed, yet transcended, the ideological commitments of each of us. We all sensed that we were caught up in something bigger than any of us and that its unfolding was truly an unfolding of grace in our life as well as in Jack's. Rather than a classroom of learners and teachers, we were also a community of caregivers who discovered aspects of one another that enriched us all.

Another significant outcome of this event was the recognition of the extent to which persons who had oppositional theological and ethical attitudes toward lesbian and gay sexuality were capable of genuine empathy and understanding when in the presence of particular lesbian and gay persons. The act of caring itself became a kind of critique or window through which to examine beliefs that on one level would not support such compassion and solidarity. When compassionate involvement leads to the gracious unfolding of a more active, open, and fulfilled life as a gay person, how does one regard belief systems maintaining that to be fulfilled as human beings, gay persons must be something other than openly and actively gay? Does not the coming into wholeness and overcoming estrangement as illustrated by persons such as William, Christina, David, and Jack disclose something deeper about the relationship of our sexuality and spirituality than earlier recognized? Do not these experiences push us to ask what it means to be fully human as sexual beings in the image of God? It was in the context of the narrative of Jack's coming out that the pastoral-theological issue of the relationship of care to a transformed appropriation of our sexual orientation first clarified itself for me.

A Temple "Comes Out"

Breaking the heterosexual bubble and creating reliable communities of acceptance and solidarity are tasks that face not only the lesbian and gay person; they are challenges of care also for those inside the heterosexual bubble. Temple Emanuel in Denver, Colorado, illustrates how one religious congregation popped the heterosexual bubble and itself began to face the challenge of becoming a welcoming community for lesbians and gays.

Rabbi Steven Foster, a former Doctor of Ministry advisee and current friend, asked me to be a consultant to the board of this congregation as it faced the question of whether it would appoint a lesbian or gay associate rabbi. The congregation had "fallen in love with Karen," a candidate for the position, and offered her the job. Throughout the interview process, they had found her winsome, intelligent, and spiritually mature. They were enthused about her potential as their rabbi and were excited about the prospects of her joining the leadership of this large, affluent, and influential Reform congregation.

Before deciding about accepting the position, Karen shared with the Temple board that she was lesbian and that she would be living openly with her partner if she came to Denver. She wanted the board to know this beforehand, in order to give them an opportunity to withdraw the offer of the position if they felt it necessary. The board reaffirmed its decision, though some members had misgivings because of the timing of the disclosure. After considering the reaffirmed offer, Karen decided to take a position in another part of the country rather than relocate to Denver.

There was great disappointment that Karen did not choose to relocate, but on reflection it was agreed that the Temple had not really been prepared to consider an openly lesbian or gay rabbi on its staff. Their respect for Karen and the integrity of the search process mandated that they reaffirm their offer, but they recognized that more intentional consideration needed to be given to the question of their openness to other lesbian and gay persons who might apply. Karen's coming out to them led them to the challenge of deciding how they would regard same-sex orientation at the highest levels of leadership in the community.

In consultation with the twenty-five-member board, Rabbi Foster decided to have a one-day workshop to work through the issue of hiring a lesbian or gay rabbi. He invited me to help them design a process for the day and to provide relevant insights from my research. He also invited a man and a woman from the Rabbi Search Committee of the congregation in New York where Karen finally accepted a position, and a lay leader from a congregation in California that has had an openly gay rabbi for several years. We met for about six hours, including lunch, to explore attitudes and feelings and to see if the board could reach consensus about its direction.

From the beginning, there was sharp but respectful disagreement about appointing a homosexual rabbi. At one extreme, members expressed the fear that a lesbian or gay rabbi would molest their children and, short of that, send the wrong message to the community about the kind of family values the Jewish tradition supports. Some thought that a lesbian or gay rabbi would make lesbian or gay persons out of their children. Others thought it would decrease membership—that some would leave as a result of this action and others would not be attracted to the congregation. Some expressed their discomfort about being in social events with a homosexual rabbi, especially if he or she showed up with a partner and expressed affection openly. There was considerable discussion about whether Karen had been responsible in disclosing her orientation after the job offer rather than being "up front" from the beginning.

At the other extreme was the conviction that this congregation could not repeat the moral equivalent of the Holocaust on lesbian and gay persons and, short of that, could not renege on its public leadership in a variety of civil rights matters. On the positive side, it was expressed that most of the negative opposition was based on myths about what lesbian and gay persons are like, how they behave, and how most people react to them. These members cited their positive experience with Karen about how a lesbian person could in fact have the moral, personal, and spiritual qualities to represent Judaism in an appropriate—even impressive— manner. They saw it as part of the Jewish tradition to be open to "outsiders" and to welcome and protect the vulnerable. Some cited their positive relationships with lesbian and gay friends and colleagues. It was stated that to vote against a lesbian or gay rabbi on those grounds alone would be to give a negative message to lesbian and gay members of the congregation, especially to gay or lesbian Jewish children who would be hurt by the rejection inherent in such an act. Many were sympathetic to

Karen's late rather than early disclosure and linked it to their experience of job discrimination as Jews. They reported that sometimes Jewish persons know that if they initially disclose their Jewishness, no interview or job offer would be forthcoming. All pretty much agreed that in terms of their future decisions about considering a homosexual rabbi, the timing of Karen's disclosure probably helped them deal with the issue in a way they might not have otherwise. This conversation was thorough, heated, and inconclusive.

We then turned to the lay members from other congregations to describe their experience. It was clear that they were enthusiastic about the leadership of their rabbis, and they indicated that congregational life had been strengthened rather than weakened by their presence. The fears of some people in their congregations were not realized, but, on the contrary, their rabbis and congregations had accomplished excellent working relationships and mutual respect for one another. The retreat leaders answered candidly many questions about how difficulties were faced and how the congregations came to accept their lesbian and gay leaders.

During lunch there was informal conversation about the issues raised that morning and an eagerness "to move on with it," since the board members "have heard what people think." After lunch, I presented two pieces of information for subsequent discussion and response. First, I described four ways that religious traditions have assessed the status of lesbian and gay sexual orientation, drawing on James Nelson's well-known summary.[3] I emphasized that there was no consensus that I knew of in the Jewish and Christian traditions, but that we had to work out our understandings in the light of ongoing knowledge and experience, taking responsibility for the limitations implied in each position. I then presented the following assessment categories for religious and ethical status of homosexuality: rejecting-punitive, rejecting-nonpunitive, qualified acceptance, and full acceptance. After a very brief discussion, the group quickly reached a consensus. Their assessment category fell somewhere between qualified and full acceptance of homosexuality, while recognizing that they still had not answered the question about whether they wanted a lesbian or gay rabbi.

Second, I presented a brief description of the qualities of a gay-affirming environment, as reported by the lesbian and gay persons that I interviewed. I described care as active welcome and full affirmation. I shared that lesbian and gay persons reported being cared about when their participation was normalized and used in a community's life. I emphasized that care also was conveyed when there was an organized and intentional response, rather than neglect or haphazard attention to the concerns of lesbian and gay persons. Finally, I underscored the importance of showing care through strategic public advocacy, such as seeking just laws and policies and opposing legislation like Amendment 2 that had recently passed in Colorado. (This amendment renders it illegal for any legislative or judicial bodies in Colorado either to make or to enforce laws related to discrimination against persons based on their sexual orientation.)

In the remaining hour and a half, the tone of the discussion dramatically changed. After discussion of the characteristics of a positive environment, the board affirmed that it wanted to be a welcoming rather than rejecting or indifferent community. It believed that to be Reform Jews was to be open and affirming, and to take risks for the civil rights of the outsider. From this, it was concluded by most of the board that they would welcome an application from a lesbian or gay rabbi and would not let sexual orientation determine an applicant's suitability for the role. If the person demonstrated the personal and professional qualities that they were looking for in a rabbi, as Karen did, they would be open to hiring him or her. Not all agreed with this, and one or two persons were particularly opposed to this direction. The workshop ended on a positive note, with a sense of resolution and direction gained by the body as a whole. A few months later, Rabbi Foster told me that those who had left with strong negative feelings had come to him and said that they had changed their minds after further thought and conversation. They now found themselves at a place where they could, in conscience, support a lesbian or gay rabbi; they felt that the workshop and educational processes of the Temple had assisted them in changing their minds.

In terms of care, this proactive stance of Temple Emanuel is quite constructive. It eventuated in the ability to more fully fulfill the framework of care that I outlined in chapter 1 and presented to them. They were able to actively welcome, fully normalize, strategically organize and use, and finally publicly advocate an expanded role for a lesbian or gay rabbi. One key to the movement out of the heterosexual bubble was the rabbi's leadership and a congregational history of leadership in matters of social justice. The lay leadership in the Temple was extremely strong, and there was a history of normalizing conflict. People could speak their minds honestly and openly, disagreeing vigorously, but with a sense of respect and genuine attention to the opinions of others. Thus, to care for lesbian and gay persons in the context of a congregation requires the development of strong pastoral leadership, a climate of diversity, and a capacity to handle conflict constructively rather than divisively.

It was also critical to discuss these issues in relation to real persons: Members had met and loved Karen, a lesbian person, and they brought resources who had firsthand experience with the issues being addressed. Care was not abstract but grounded in real relationships with real people in real congregations. When the bubble burst, there was a breakthrough to a fuller reality instead of dissolution and demise as feared.[4]

Coming Out and
Cultural Challenge

Diana Sandoval, a twenty-eight-year-old lesbian, grew up with an Anglo mother and a Latino father. She and her family were active in a socially and politically liberal Protestant denomination in a North American city. In her youth group, sexuality was discussed fairly openly, and the adults were tolerant about boys and girls showing affection. "There was an okay given to many things about sexuality." Although they assumed that everyone was straight, if "someone had come out at that time the group would have been supportive."

When Diana was in high school, a leader in her denomination began to come out after forty years of marriage. Diana's parents were very close to him and had to come to grips with his sexual orientation. Diana believes that this helped them to be supportive of her, when she came out later. Diana said that she had a positive childhood, with little traumatic experience.

Coming out to Diana's parents was a "nontraumatic experience as compared to the experiences of others. My parents had a number of gay and lesbian friends in the church, and one of my friends came out to them before I did. They accepted her." Diana said that at first her parents' reaction was one of shock (not denial). Her father had more difficulty, until her sister approached him and said, "You are not behaving right. What's the deal?" Diana reported that "my coming out forced him to face his sexuality. He has been very supportive after he has gotten past his own."

When she came out of the closet as a young adult, she did not find a group or church that was supportive. "I went from idealism to the realization of how the church really is." She went abroad soon after coming out but was aware that some of her friends were actively trying to get her denomination to deal with homosexuality. They "tried to dialogue with the church, but they were getting hurt right and left. I was so angry that I couldn't talk about it.

"Initially, coming out was pretty isolating. Then I sought out other gays and lesbians. They were sources of care. The hardest part was doing the self-definition part. I needed someone to listen who had been through it, to give advice. My sister immediately accepted it and changed her whole language about me. I try to share my family with other gay and lesbian friends because it is so incredibly good. I have always had a close friend I could share with, and that helped a lot too."

Diana is not out to her larger family network. Her mother's Anglo family background is quite conservative and small. "One aunt is an extreme fundamentalist and sees everything as evil. The other aunt's big deal is to see me married."

Diana's father's family lives in South America. "It is extremely homophobic. I could be killed for my sexuality. Two people of the same sex could live together down there if they don't get caught doing anything. Lots of people don't have money, so it is not uncommon to share one bedroom and bed for economic reasons. But I am not close to my relatives in other ways. I lived with them for a while, but my liberal views gave people heart attacks. I am still family, even though I am all these things. But if they knew I was lesbian, it might affect my family standing. My father would take a lot of shit. There would be a crusade to save me—before they gave up on us. They would try to get me counseling, get me married, etc."

To receive care in the coming-out process meant for Diana that she had to be very selective about her disclosures. "In Ecuador, for the most part, I would not come out to my friends. I'm very out in this country. There is a guy I used to date who took it pretty well; I doubt if he told anyone. Most people I have told have not told anyone. They knew I would be shut out forever. I have thought of moving back, but being closeted would be difficult."

Diana reports that most of her support comes from friends with church backgrounds. "They are all around the country, and I keep in touch with them. For most of us, the church was a peace and justice church. Most of us have pretty strong justice stances. They left the church because it does not stand for justice in lesbian and gay issues. All of us keep challenging the church at times. I know a lot of the church hierarchy and how it functions."

Diana's religious upbringing has not only provided social support and role models, it has also given her a tradition of meaning by which to affirm that her sexual orientation is morally acceptable. "Growing up I had a New Testament orientation and probably a belief in the loving Jesus who was justice-oriented. I began questioning the male God before I questioned my orientation. Questioning was allowed in my church, as long as you believed in God. I did not have to overcome any teaching that if I am lesbian I am not loved by God. My belief was that God accepted all. My anger at the church is very high because so many of my friends had to struggle with this false belief that God didn't accept them, and they are deeply hurt. I did feel guilty about sexual things in general for years, but it would have been hellish if I had to choose between love of a woman and love of God."

Currently, Diana works for a gay rights organization and is fairly visible in the public advocacy carried out by this group. Her care needs are not so much focused on her status as a lesbian, for she receives much daily support for this in her work environment. However, she struggles with burnout from overwork in her efforts to promote a variety of cultural rights facing groups in our society. She says that she has been concerned about racism and sexism, and that she has "known people from other countries where oppression is greater than here." She said that she "can't imagine fighting for just one group's rights. Our rights are interconnected. If I had equal rights as a gay person, I would also expect to have equal rights as an immigrant's daughter or as a bilingual woman."

Diana does not experience very much support for her commitments to multicultural justice. She has one colleague at work who understands, but in many ways she finds that "there is a heck of a lot of racism in the gay community. People of color have their own bars and events. There is a great deal of segregation. In Dallas, the personals in lesbian and gay newspapers specified race. For me, the color of the person is not the issue. It is the cultural piece." In this difficult arena, she does not find adequate support in Christianity. "In the last few years I believe that my faith has gotten vaguer and vaguer, and more all-encompassing. I am exploring other religions. Christianity is not very holistic; it does not emphasize interconnections."

When I interviewed Diana, she was fatigued from the demands on her at work and from her volunteer help in two women's shelters. She was considering going back to school for a degree in social work. There were strains in her love life, and she was considering seeking therapeutic help for her situation. She knew that she had strong family support, good friends, and effective means of self-care. She also knew that she needed to be intentional about finding supplemental resources to help her clarify the next steps in her life's unfolding.

Diana's experience discloses that for many persons coming out of the closet is more than breaking "a white male heterosexist bubble," though it may certainly include that as well. It can put one outside of one's family, religious, and cultural heritage forever, and even bring the threat of death on oneself. Seen in the light of this overwhelming opposition to the core of one's being, coming out requires enormous courage on the part of lesbian and gay persons. To be sure, such courage is grounded in the self-esteem and personal strength of gay and lesbian persons themselves, but it is also made possible by positive religious teachings and reliable communities of support. Diana makes it especially clear that to be caring, these communities must be able not only to affirm and help her interpret her experience in positive terms, but they must maintain confidentiality so that she is not exposed to undue risk. The capacity for personal courage in the coming-out process, therefore, is mirrored by the community's ability to maintain confidentiality and "bounded knowledge."

Reflection on Diana's narrative suggests two additional dimensions of caregiving, along with those already noted. First, caregiving recognizes that coming out is a lifelong process that involves ongoing defining and redefining the totality of one's life over time. It is inappropriate for care-givers to push people to disclose prematurely or in ways that expose them to greater personal and relational risk. In many ways Diana lives her life at several levels of disclosure: She is a courageous public advocate for a gay- and lesbian-identified rights group, and she brings her lesbian and gay friends home to her welcoming nuclear family. Yet big secrets are kept from aunts and uncles, grandparents and cousins because the costs would be too great of disclosing the truth at this time because the extended familial and cultural systems are not able to receive it.

Caregivers must respect the tensions inherent in living at various levels of disclosure and assist lesbian and gay persons to handle them constructively. There are costs to living two lives, to be sure, and these costs must be explored and shared. However, there are also costs to disclosing fully before one is ready. Caregivers cannot responsibly determine when others should put their lives and relationships at risk. Caregivers share the costs but do not bear them through life and death. Hence, there must be great sensitivity and patience. If caregivers recognize that coming out is a lifelong process involving the totality of one's relational web, rather than a one-time act confined solely to a selected aspect of one's sexuality, such sensitivity and patience will be less difficult to attain.[5]

Second, effective caregiving recognizes that coming out is a dimension of justice making; it goes beyond simple tolerance and interpersonal affirmation. Diana's experience discloses that religious affirmation about divine acceptance of lesbian and gay persons leads naturally to claims of social justice for those who are divinely accepted. Religious teaching that affirms the value of persons also requires efforts toward ensuring that these same valued humans will not be mistreated ecclesially, socially, and culturally. Affirmation and justice interlock. Neither is optional. Sexuality is not a private and personal matter; it is embedded in social processes that may work for its fulfillment and beauty or that may deface and destroy it.

Diana's coming out is a matter, then, not only of personal affirmation and acceptance of God's acceptance of her sexuality in its fullest sense. Her coming out is also an embodiment of a relational justice that seeks means by which every human being can be on constructive terms with every other human being. Relational justice, when connected to the coming-out process, involves courage and truthfulness, and challenge to ignorance and prejudice. It works toward the mutual fulfillment of equal partnerships between unique persons and communities. Relational justice will be discussed more fully below in connection with what it means to be in the image of God. For now, it is enough to suggest that Diana's narrative helps the caregiver to link the concept of relational justice to the dynamic and positive interplay of the personal and the social, the sexual and the spiritual, and the divine and the human in the process of coming out.

Conclusion

From these narratives, it is possible to discern a profile of care in the coming-out process. In most cases, coming out is a crisis for the lesbian and gay person, and the surrounding environments. It is a crisis for families, congregations, the work environment, friends, and the larger cultural setting. It is a "shaking of the foundations" of reality. It is an awakening to powerful hidden forces that will cut new paths in the bedrock of self-understanding, social connections, and religious experience. Coming out requires individuals and communities to accommodate new dimensions of truthfulness and to develop richer patterns of justice.

To provide effective care in the coming-out process, caregivers must understand that coming out takes time and that there are enormous risks involved for the lesbian or gay person. Patience, support, and empathy are essential. There must be a variety of settings for unending conversation so that the person coming out can fashion a new core definition of selfhood. There must be "practice and rehearsal" of one's encounters with significant others as the coming-out process unfolds. It is essential that confidentiality be preserved in a trustworthy and safe caregiving framework. Allies in the family must be developed to help interpret the coming-out process to more resistant or hostile family members. Links to support and advocacy groups in the lesbian and gay community and to supportive religious environments are critical.

The caregiver needs to be attentive to the ambiguous, and often negative, place that religious, theological, and spiritual factors have in the coming-out process. Although religion has been a positive resource in formulating a healthy lesbian and gay identity in all cases previously described, each individual affirmed a homosexual identity after a considerable effort in overcoming negative religious influences. Some are still struggling to find an authentic and transformative religious orientation that is congruent with their sexuality. If caregivers are to be helpful in the coming-out process, it will require them to be both realistic about the negative influences of religion as well as open to surprising novel configurations of religious resources.

All of the narratives of coming out indicate that coming out is a challenge to the "white male heterosexist bubble." That is to say, although coming out is a crisis for the lesbian and gay person, it also requires new ways of thinking about the dominant structures and values of our culture and religious traditions. To create reliable social environments that support and actively welcome lesbian- and gay-oriented persons as a normal part of communal life will require intentional action, as indicated by the experience of Temple Emanuel. It is also imperative to understand that heterosexist-dominated environments, even when welcoming and normalizing, are not sufficient to meet the full array of social needs for lesbians and gays. As much as possible, there must be support for participation in gay-dominant and lesbian-identified communities of study, recreation, service, worship, and healing. To promote and celebrate human diversity means in part to contribute to the development of diverse subcultures and unique experience, while at the same time expanding opportunities for persons with diverse experiences to collaborate in creating fuller communal experience with one another.

Caregivers will need to learn to take initiative in creating larger communities of acceptance and participation. Rabbi Foster's leadership with Temple Emanuel was critical for it to "come out" successfully as a gay- and lesbian-friendly Jewish congregation, but lay participation and leadership were also required. There needs to be, in addition, the ability to engage strong feelings in a positive manner and to utilize conflict as a source of enrichment rather than as necessarily divisive or destructive.

Above all, for coming out to be a transformative experience for lesbian and gay persons and the surrounding environments, one must deal with real persons, not with ideas, issues, or points of view. When Jack disclosed his concrete conflict between his Christian faith and his homosexuality, he elicited compassion and solidarity rather than a discussion about ideology. People moved beyond stereotypes to an authentic engagement with a complex human being with whom they had a prior relationship that was important to them. In the unfolding of the coming-out process, they discovered new depths in their own experience and contributed to the emergence of a fuller human being whose life took on depth and richness. Everyone became more "real" as a consequence. Life and faith become more complex. At the same time there was a freshness and simplicity that had not existed in Jack and the class before his coming out occurred. In the caregiving process, all are changed in a reciprocal interaction that potentially transforms the circumstances of living. Diana realized the need to work harder for relational justice at all levels of society and culture. Temple Emanuel expanded its communal boundaries so that lesbian and gay leadership might become a reality. David gave himself definition by grabbing the real "me" represented in the baby Moses in the basket in the river. When he stopped trying to annihilate something he hated in himself, he was able to become real by finding reconciliation with his true self and with the God from whom he had been estranged.

The process of overcoming estrangement from self and God and creating new forms of truthful and affirming community are theologically significant dimensions of the coming-out process. When we move beyond ideology, stereotyping, and abstract debate about the biblical status of homosexuality and look at what actually happens in the lives of those engaged in the coming-out process, we find ourselves shifting the theological axis of the discussion. We see self-acceptance, healing, and qualities of relational justice and human solidarity. We are now faced with the challenge to put these positive outcomes into constructive theological terms. As the coming-out process eventuates in fuller self-affirmation, richer human community, and a spiritually enlivened relationship with God, we see people becoming more fully human. To be fully human, in theological terms, is to move toward realizing the image of God. We will return to this discussion in chapters 7 and 8. For now it is sufficient to suggest that an examination of the dynamics and outcomes of care in the coming-out process provides a foundation for thinking of lesbian and gay orientation as a means of understanding and partially fulfilling the image of God in human experience.

3

Partners and Lovers

Bridging Eros and Agape
Through Care

There is a popular colloquialism that states, "Sex may not be the most important thing in life, but it is way out in front of whatever comes second!" Whatever is meant by "sex," this colloquial joke suggests that our embodied attractions toward one another are more than casual or neutral. They have very high value in relation to other dimensions of human experience and constitute a major basis for making decisions about what is most important to us. We order our lives in large part by the degree to which their sexual dimensions are fulfilled.

The colloquial joke not only affirms the primacy of sexuality in our daily experience, but it also suggests that sex is a source of anxiety and potential danger. Joking helps to moderate anxiety and threat. Joking builds bridges between adversaries; it mediates animosity. Joking weaves affection and hostility into new configurations. Joking softens taboos and "transvalues values."

In this case, the colloquial joke suggests that there are both wide differences and inherent connections between sex and other values in human experience. The laughter of recognition evoked by the joke makes it possible to affirm without undue discomfort the pervasive degree to which sex and sexuality are indeed central in human motivational systems. Yet the joke implies that something radical or unconventional is being suggested. There is a presumed disjunction between sexuality and other values, and some discomfort implied in the disjunction. The joke eases the tension and makes the disjunction bearable and even potentially creative. Thus the colloquial joke discloses an inherent perception that sexuality and other experiences are in conflict and suggests that some danger exists in affirming that sexuality, which has largely been a taboo subject, is now elevated to the apex of a hierarchy of motivators.

Jokes not only soften conflict between values; they suggest something about the nature of reality. They invite analysis and conceptual reformulation of experience. This particular colloquial joke gives rise to several questions about our sexuality and its relationship to what it means to be fully human. How do we account for the pervasive influence of our sexuality, especially its bodily passions and relational expressions? How do we understand and accommodate its taboos? How do we interpret and moderate the dangerous juxtaposition of sexuality and other dimensions of experience that struggle against one another? Can we create an "order" of value that fully affirms our sexuality while at the same time vitally connects it to all other dimensions of experience? Is it possible to find a systemic rather than hierarchical ordering of our sexuality and other motivating values? Can sex and sexuality be positively linked to our most primal bodily instincts as well as to our highest spiritual aspirations?

The largest questions, underlying these other questions arising from the colloquial joke about the relationship of sex to human experience, are as follows: Why do human beings come together at all? and How do we evaluate and regulate the multiplicity of our connections, including the sexual, within the web of life? The first two chapters have begun to address the second question. In those chapters, we have suggested that relationships are evaluated positively by the extent to which they overcome estrangement or alienation and serve the goals of truthfulness and creative, loving communion with God, self, others, and nature. We suggested also that we regulate our relationships through relational justice. It was implied that a variety of caregiving relationships assisted in the movement from alienation to affirmation, distortion to truthfulness, self-hate to self-love, isolation to communion, and relational injustice to justice.

Until now, we have not explored the fundamental question of why human beings come together in the first place, and the role of care, sex, sexuality, and love in answering this larger question. We have argued in earlier chapters that lesbian and gay persons provide a window into understanding more fully the power of care in bringing about a richer and deeper humanity characterized by positive loving and just relationships infused by sexual feelings and activities. We have made preliminary suggestions that in these positive experiences the image of God is being more fully realized in concrete human relationships. In this chapter we explore the degree to which lesbian and gay sexuality, understood through narratives of care, shapes an answer to the fundamental question of what it means that human beings are so pervasively drawn to one another through bodily passions and relational intensities.

Katherine Bowen:
The Erotic Discovery of Truth

Katherine (Katie) Bowen is the assistant to the president of a prestigious graduate school in New York City. On the whole, she finds support and care as a lesbian in her work environment. Her colleagues have been open and affirming, and it has been healing for her to take part in planning events directed toward gays and lesbians.

Katie was raised in a Christian home. Her father was an Anglican from England; her mother, a Roman Catholic immigrant from Italy. Her father's Christianity was oriented toward social activism. Her mother left the Roman Catholic Church, converted to Anglicanism, and raised the kids in the Episcopal tradition. "I learned from her that the church can come between God and people. Families have to overcome that. We have to share resources and work together. God has rescued us from poverty, war, and lack of opportunities in Europe. We are now privileged, so we must share it."

Katie was popular in school and active in church. Yet early on, she knew something was amiss. She wanted to be an acolyte when she was ten and present a program in her Episcopal Church when she was thirteen, but she was refused because she was a female. "There was this perduring, always present sense, that I don't belong. I used to wonder what it was about. Now I know that it was about a lot of things, but sexuality was one of them. Even at age nine I knew that I was on a different track, but I didn't know what it meant. Later, I dated because I thought that was what I should do. I was happy when I could be friends with boys and play touch football and ride bikes, but not when I dated. But I did it, and surprisingly, I was quite popular. I never understood that. By high school I was very aware of my attraction to women. I went to an all girls' school. You hear locker room stories. I thought, 'Wow, some of these girls are really beautiful!' My schedule put me in a gym class with seniors when I was a freshman. And so instead of my bony little classmates, there were voluptuous seniors! I would dress in the shower. People thought that I was very shy, but I was afraid that someone would see me looking at them. I knew that women were more beautiful, but being with men was your duty. And I always wanted to have children."

Katie married young. Her husband completed seminary and became a priest and religion professor. She said that her husband was "not macho and was extremely bright." They had children together. "I loved my husband, and he loved me. There were many good, strong points, but it hit a crisis. And because eros was not there for me, and not returned for him, there was no glue. This crisis could not be navigated. There was no longer the passion to make it work. I didn't realize that until I tasted eros. I would have broken my back to make this marriage work. But I wasn't home, and tension built up until it finally exploded."

A series of crises involving the death of her parents and the illness of one of her children led Katie to therapy with a heterosexual male. After settling these things, the therapist touched on Katie's lesbian issue. "God didn't give me everything to deal with at once! The therapist finally suggested that I try to understand my sexual orientation. He said, 'You know that you are never going to solve this until you try.' That was all the permission I needed. I came back a week later, and I told him that there was 'no question that I am a lesbian and I hardly have time to sit here and talk to you! (Laughing) There are so many women and so little time!' He said that I should see a lesbian or woman therapist, and I still have great respect for him."

Katie said that "to be gay and out was like coming home!" She had never before sensed that she fully belonged or had ever experienced eros, or passion. "Until I fell in love with a woman, I never knew why wars had been fought over love, poetry written, and the Taj Mahal built! I had known pleasure before this, but never intimacy. Never coming home. I went to bed one night thinking I was an unhappy celibate straight woman; I awoke knowing I was lesbian. Over and over again I had a sense that I was home. I was not a miserable heterosexual, so it took me a year to integrate this."

Katie said that she "found a family. I found my children again. Even if it meant losing their love, I would come out. I burst my way out of the closet. I didn't wait to open it. I karate-chopped my way through. It was a pretty disruptive period. But it was a disruption that I knew was good, and I was willing to live with whatever happened because of my need for wholeness. Unlocking my sexuality was the final key to what was keeping me from growing and being happy. It's like giving birth; it's both scary and exciting."

Katie discovered new depths in her relationship to God through her newfound erotic connection to her lover. "I never thought that God didn't love me. I was just puzzled at the human family that God created in the church. I had a sense that God was leading me. Everything that happened then had the ring of truth and spiritual authenticity. It was not an earthquake I had created in my own life. It was a movement about my life and affecting my life, but I was not the author of it. I had not been living truthfully; I was creating dramas to substitute for real passion, for real fire. I believed the evangelical hymn: 'I don't feel no more afraid. . . . God hasn't brought us this far to leave us.' I really believed that if God created me, I was God's own. As a parent I know that nothing can separate me from my love for my children, even if they reject me. So how could God, who is so much less complicated a lover, ever reject me?

"My coming out was more a coming home to God: 'You made me this way, you love me this way, I am lovable, and I will find love in my life.' I used to pray very simplistically, like a kid praying for a ten-speed bike. I once prayed, 'Lord, let me be with a woman before I die. Just once, let me taste heaven on earth before I die, and I'll do anything.' I was bargaining. 'Just give me one special moment!' Instead, I found a relationship that is truly what I wanted. So even in those moments, God's abundant love was evident. All I wanted was a one-night stand, and I got a land flowing with milk and honey! So, God was very much at the heart of this, giving me the courage to go ahead."

Her erotic connection to her lover unlocked the door to a new life of loving communion for Katie. She found a lesbian therapist who helped her explore her new identity. "I found a model in her. She helped me get connected to lesbian mothers' groups and coming-out groups. I began listening to all women/lesbian music. I began reading only lesbian writing. It was a coming-out process, and I knew that I would go back to other interests some day. Now I would go to a good nongay therapist as long as she was lesbian-friendly, but then I needed a lesbian therapist."

Katie and Cynthia had a lesbian union officiated by a Metropolitan Community Church (MCC) minister. The event took place in an Episcopal Church. Afterwards, Katie had to leave this congregation because she felt that she didn't belong once she came out. "There were many slights. I wasn't asked to present the programs I was responsible for. I was no longer asked to assist with liturgy. Some women didn't extend the kiss of peace like they used to, and the rector said, 'You might be happier in another church.'" These messages heightened the conflict Katie felt between God's acceptance and the church's rejection.

Katie became active in Cynthia's MCC congregation. She said that she is working to heal the split between her relationship to God and her relationship to the church. Yet she says that "the church is still an albatross around my neck; I can't get free from it." In her new church, she sat in the back pew and cried for three Sundays. Over time she has had a sense of regaining some trust and finding her call as a lay minister. "I am called to a ministry of teaching and a ministry to parents." In spite of some tensions connected to being the "pastor's spouse," Katie has found a lot of communal love in her congregation. She could preach and teach and try out her ministry in a way not permitted in her Episcopal congregation. "My new church has also given me models of a gay and lesbian Christian life and an ecumenical experience that I never had before. There is excitement in sharing a vision."

Eros has created for Katie a new relationship to herself, to God, and to the church. It has also created a "good disruption" in her family. When she and Cynthia set about establishing their life together through a public commitment to their relationship, there was the challenge to build a new family system. She says, "My children have gained a sense of the value of the individual; there is room for everyone here. It's a big table. We have asked that they give that acceptance to us, and we have also given it back to them. It is not a superficial tolerance, but an honesty. I underestimated my children's love and the supportive role that their father would play. He was supportive throughout."

When the family needed therapeutic assistance, it was critical to find a therapist who understood and affirmed the unique features of lesbian unions. "Some therapists say they understand, but they don't. One of our children was acting out at school. The intake supervisor asked many inappropriate questions about our family. We try to have an open family system, and she couldn't 'get it.' This assumption of our secrecy destroyed the helping process. I called a gay and lesbian family therapy center, and they got it right. My daughter's father had just started a new relationship, and I had just had a holy union, she was a preadolescent and not well matched in her school. We needed someone who could recognize all these issues and not get sidetracked because we were lesbians. Lesbians and gays have a tremendous fear that a therapist will sabotage their families. We needed help, but we needed help that would protect, not destroy, this family. I see other gay and lesbian families needing this but not able to find it. I am very aware of how our social and economic privilege helped us find what we needed. Tribute must also be paid to the children's father, who supported our relationship and our children in their adjustment. God's grace was clearly there. And there was a *lot* of grace. My divorce was not a lifelong battle. We tried to understand that sexuality can be fluid. What matters to families is commitment, honesty, and love. I found out later when I read books on coming out that I had broken most of the rules in coming out to my children. But now they know that we are all individuals and that our family will endure."

Katie and Cynthia and their children have built a rich life together. They have friends, challenging vocations, and a stable relationship. They have a sense of God's grace: "Where we have found what we have needed, I know the role of privilege; and where we have found more than we deserved, I know the role of grace. I know that grace is available to everyone, but not all of us can draw upon it. So we try to give some things back."

Katie says, "We are a 'model' lesbian couple, but we have to go outside our network to live a full life." Because of church dynamics and Cynthia's long hours at the parish, they find it difficult to have a church life together as a couple. However, they are able to nurture their relationship and care for one another in positive ways. "We do not have economic worries or family tension. We greatly enjoy each other's company. We don't go to sleep angry. We are both stubborn, and we want this relationship to endure. We try to help other couples who are struggling. We are glad to see each other at the end of the day. We share core values, but we are very different in terms of age, background, and personality. I think that this acceptance of difference is a gift that lesbians and gays have to offer others. Because we break the big rule of partners' gender, we are freer to break rules about age, social class, race, etc."

Katie's narrative helps us to address one of the questions we posed at the beginning of the chapter. What accounts for the human capacity to relate to the world and to one another? Katie's narrative suggests that "eros" is at the center of human motivation and fulfillment. Her attraction to the beauty of female bodies and her passion for sexual and relational intimacy with another woman are founded on an exhilarating and sometimes frightening erotic passion. For Katie, this erotic passion was the human and divine force out of which true communion and positive disruptive creativity arose. For Katie, eros accounted for an increase of appreciative human affiliation in the broadest sense, as well as for sexual passion and relational intimacy with particular individuals. It was grounded in her sense of God's love for her and led to more truthful, vital, and caring relationships at all levels of her experience. Eros, divine love, and human care are linked in a mutually enhancing rather than competitive or linear manner.

Katie's experience with eros suggests that all one's loves can be ordered in a systemic rather than hierarchical fashion. Eros created an "order" of value that fully affirmed her sexuality while at the same time vitally connected it to all other dimensions of her experience. To be more spiritual and loving, she was not required to be less sexual and erotic. On the contrary, spiritual vitality and "servant love" increased as she was able to be truthful and expressive of the erotic passion she felt toward women. She discovered a deeper relationship and coming home to God in her coming out to women. Her story reveals that sex and sexuality can be positively linked to our most primal bodily instincts as well as to our highest spiritual aspirations. All of her relationships were reordered in a vital reciprocity. When she was able, through erotic passion, to move to communion and intimacy with Cynthia, she was in a position to assist all in her relational network to gain freedom and find a "place at the table." The relational network as a whole, and each person within it, found new freedom and new sources of nurture. To be sure, there was disruption. Eros is scary. But it was good disruption, because it eventuated in egalitarian and mutual communion rather than isolation and emptiness. Eros is fulfilling and enlivening. It is the force that brings humans together and is the basis for infusing all our relationships with grace and life. It is connected to God's grace and plenitude, leading persons "home" to God, self, and neighbor in fuller terms. It is the energy behind our capacity for care, as well as the energy driving sexual passion and community-creating, self-giving love.

The Sacrament of Eros

Katie found eros to be a "means of grace." Eros made the table bigger and unlocked the door to a happy life. It enlivened her relationship to

God. It overcame her estrangement from the truth about her own being and eventuated in an increase of self-regard. It compelled her to the world in redemptive passion and service. It expanded her capacity to be "truthful" about herself and opened to her a fuller grasp of the communal nature of life. Through the multiple forms of care that she received, Katie was able to discover and express the erotic passion at the core of her being as a lesbian woman. In turn, the liberation of her erotic passion made possible a greater loving participation throughout the interlocking matrices of her life. Care evoked passion, and passion was given expression in an enlarged capacity to care. All of this was "suffused with grace" and gratefully received and shared.

Katie's experience of the transforming power of eros was not an idiosyncratic event. It was remarkable how the breakthrough to eros was experienced by so many other lesbian and gay persons as a disruption of grace that allowed them to burst through the closet door into new vitality and freedom. In chapter 1, William Carroll discovered twenty-five years before he came out that "such a forbidden kiss could be an act of care" that surprised, pleased, and startled him. It brought joy and a sense of hope, along with ambivalence about its origin in same-sex passion. Christina Troxell suppressed her erotic passion as a new Christian and found herself diminished and estranged from her human vitality. When she was able to break through to passion and connect it intimately with another woman whom she loved, her life took a new direction. Now, in her one-flesh union with her partner she experiences personal wholeness, relational fulfillment, and a sense of the kind of love that Christ has for the church, and that Father, Son, and Holy Spirit know internally in the Godhead. Rather than being opposed to "the highest and best" of Christian spirituality, William, Katie, and Christina witness to the degree to which erotic pleasure and the intimacy of bodily mediated communion are vehicles for God's gracious affirmation and transformation of all dimensions of living.

The joke with which I began this chapter playfully suggests that erotic sexuality is pervasive and important. It doesn't really say why this is so; that is left to us. Here I am suggesting that erotic sexuality is so important because it is a means of divine and human grace that makes life fuller and more loving. Indeed, it infuses life with vitality and harmony; it overcomes triviality and discord. Robert Parkin, a psychiatrist whom I interviewed, said that as a young boy he knew that he was "a queer kid." He soon discovered that he could not suppress or deny this truth about himself, because "if it had to do with [his] sexuality, it had to do with [his] survival." To be real, to be natural, to be in touch with life, Parkin knew that he had to go through, not around, the erotic passion driving and drawing him to other males.

Gary Johnson, a closeted Lutheran pastor, struggled for years with his sexuality. Finally, he knew that he could not deny his sexual feelings any longer. "I couldn't know my feelings about anything until I felt my gay feelings," Gary said. Eros was the path to self-knowledge. Eros made it possible for Gary to orient himself to the world truthfully. Acknowledging his erotic feelings for men expanded and focused his life. He developed clarity about who he was and what he was called to do and be as a gay Christian pastor, even if this meant selective withholding of information from those who would use intimate knowledge for harm.

One of the mistakes commonly made by "helpers" is to dismiss or attempt to change sexual feelings. Repeatedly, I was told of incidents where therapists, pastors, parents, friends, and even lovers negated sexual feelings toward members of the same sex. For example, when William Carroll sought psychiatric help for his feelings toward men during his engagement to his wife, the therapist told him that these were signs of anxiety about marriage that he would eventually outgrow. He was given antidepressant medication. It would have been more helpful if William's therapist had validated William's erotic orientation to men and helped him decide the course of his life based on an acceptance rather than suppression of his true sexual feelings.

In a similar vein, Ralph shared how his pastor and his therapist told him that his sexual feelings toward men were unnatural and that he would overcome them through transferring them to women. He said, "When I kissed a woman, it felt unnatural; when I kissed a man it was natural. This felt so good, there was no way it was wrong!" Fortunately, Ralph found a pastor and religious community that concurred with his positive interpretation of his sexual experience and helped him celebrate it as a means of grace rather than as a problem.

Ken and Barry, a gay couple in Atlanta, Georgia, recounted a poignant example of a sensual experience that carried sacramental power for them. They are active at St. Bartholomew's Episcopal Church, a congregation that is widely known for its gay- and lesbian-friendly atmosphere. The congregation and its priestly leadership have made them feel at home and have been fully available to them in times of serious crises, as well as moments of joyful celebration. In addition to being gay, Ken is paraplegic and uses a wheelchair. He has needed pastoral assistance for emergency surgery connected with his disability. He and Barry have found full acceptance and participation in this congregation: "God is where you are able to expose your total self to God, shamelessly. This congregation is a place where you can totally be out and be a part of a community that is affirming all the way around. Not just for lesbians and gays."

As part of pastoral care, their priest had helped Ken and Barry to see that it was important to care for each other and to nurture their relationship. On their six-month anniversary they decided to spend a night in a "very ritzy" hotel. "We had it planned out to have a romantic night. We got upgraded to a suite. There was a 'Queen' working behind the desk, and there was a little bit of the sympathy factor too, with Ken in the wheelchair. So they upgraded us for the same price. When the bellhop took us upstairs, he asked us if we wanted him to make reservations for dinner in an intimate corner of the dining room. When the maid came in to turn down the bed, she found us snuggled in our bathrobes on the couch in the living room. She turned down the bed, we said 'thank you,' and she left. When we went into the bedroom, she had turned down just one side of the bed and left the mints on that side.

"We were going to have a bath and then go to bed and have sex. We went into the bath, and it was all ornate. There was brass everywhere. We never made it to the bed. The best sex we ever had—ever!—was right there in the bath of that hotel."

Later, when Ken and Barry had a holy union in the Metropolitan Community Church, they asked their Episcopal associate priest to do the homily. "He couldn't do the holy union because of church policy. But his homily was care to us. It knocked everyone's socks off. We picked the Gospel Scripture on agreeing and touching, based on Jesus' saying that when two or three are gathered in his name. The priest said, 'When just two people touch, God is there. And, Ken and Barry, when you fight battles all day against prejudice and stereotypes and homophobia, at the end of the day when you draw the bath water remember that there are erotic touches too!' Everyone's mouth just dropped open. It was wonderful! The priest didn't know about the warm bath at the ritzy hotel when he gave the homily that when two are touching Jesus is there! He talked about a warm bath, but didn't know about our special warm bath when he gave the homily. By the grace of the Holy Spirit, his illustration helped us to remember our story."

Barry said that as important as this erotic experience was, "the ultimate act of love is not sex alone. It is sleeping together at night and holding each other." Ken agreed and added that "there is something special about being present to each other that can include sleeping together. But it is more. It is experiencing things together and building our memories together—like our business trips and church activities. Love and care are built on experiencing things together and then being able to talk about them, like the warm bath at the resort."

For Ken and Barry, sex wasn't "way out in front of whatever came second." It was an integral part of a rich life and functioned as one means of grace among many. The associate priest unknowingly tapped their story about the warm bath and tied it to Scripture when he participated in their holy union. The congregation has provided a welcome acceptance of their gifts as gay individuals and a committed couple. They have worked through the initial rejection by Ken's family and have found reconciliation and acceptance. Their business venture is successful and gratifying. Life is graced and vital for them, in spite of ongoing physical and societal challenges for which care is necessary. The memory of the warm bath as a sacrament of eros—the place where they connected God's presence to the totality of their lives—provides an organizing center by which to interpret their blessings and face their challenges.

Eros and Oppression

The narratives so far have disclosed an essentially positive relationship between eros and human fulfillment. Frequently, however, the interaction between eros and other dimensions of human life is more mixed. It can even be conflicted and negative.

Don Cheeks is a thirty-five-year-old African-American gay man who pastors an African-American church in which he does not feel safe being entirely "out" to all of his members. He was reared by his mother and strongly influenced by his grandmother, who was his babysitter as a child. He said that his mother gave to him a faith and a "sense that I was rich in spirit. If I am God's child, I am rich in spirit and nothing can take that away. My sister and I were raised to think that we could achieve because of this! We were told by our mother and our church to dream of whatever we wanted. We felt protected and positive. Through faith in God, we felt that we could achieve our dreams, no matter what difficulty or oppression stood in our way. Our church communicated this kind of faith, particularly through music and sermons. Faith in the spirit was very real to me."

In addition to his rich spiritual awareness at an early age, Don awakened erotically and discovered when he was four or five years of age that he was gay: "Some people found out that they liked vanilla ice cream; others that they liked chocolate. I found out what I liked! (Laughs) It wasn't good or bad; it was just there."

However, a lifelong journey of conflict between Don's natural erotic feelings and the social prejudices of others also began very early. "In kindergarten, I was touching another boy, and the teacher scolded me. The boy was white, and I was black. I didn't know if I was scolded because of our racial difference or because of my sexual attraction to him. Two white boys were doing the same thing, and they weren't scolded. I was touching a white boy's hair, and she told me to stop and go sit in the corner. It was a strange feeling. I said, 'Something is wrong.' But I didn't know what it was." Not long afterward, still at age 5, his grandmother found him and another little boy kissing in the backyard. "She told my mother, and I got a spanking. I was told, 'Never do that again!' I said, 'Okay, I won't do it.' But I thought, 'I'll do it, but I just won't tell.'" Don grew up with two messages in his church and family: "You can be who you want to be, but the message at the same time was 'don't talk about who you are.'"

The climax came when Don became active in the church. "I found a lot of support there, especially within the youth department. I was also becoming increasingly aware of my sexuality. The more I tried to avoid it, the more it appeared in my dreams. I wasn't sexually active; in fact I was celibate until I was nineteen. But the fantasies and attractions to men were there the more I tried to bury them. I think that one of the reasons that I went into ministry then and began preaching was I thought, 'O God, if I am so sinful and this is so bad, and I am so wrong and ugly, then I must give my life to you in service. Please, God, take it away from me.' I thought if I gave myself to preaching it would go away. How could God condemn me if I preached God's Word?

"I asked God to take away my sexual attraction to men, the crushes I had on so many schoolboys. I prayed that when I woke up from sleep those attractions and crushes would be gone. I woke up, and it was still there! I still thought of men. I decided to avoid it by preaching. The church was a haven to escape and a place to avoid dealing with who I was. Spirituality became an excuse for not dealing with my sexuality. Family and friends at school would say, 'Don doesn't have a girlfriend because he is religious.'

"But I did find a way to express my attraction in childhood games boys would play at school. We would disrupt class by having foot fights, kicking each other's foot underneath our desks. When asked by the teacher to stop, I would quietly relax my foot and occasionally rub it on the foot of the other boy with whom I had just engaged in the foot fight (male aggression seems to be often an expression of the male need to touch each other). It never ceases to baffle me that the other boys with whom I experienced this contact would never move their feet. I still wonder if they were aroused and enjoyed it as much as I did. They would keep their eyes focused on their books, and although I think that they too knew that something sexual was happening, they would avoid eye contact with me. I remember those days with great pleasure and a thrill. If the guys didn't know what was going on, at least I did! (Laughs)

"Certain guys at school were accepting, curious heterosexuals or perhaps gay themselves. There were nonverbal communications and hand gestures that were very suggestive: a certain wink of the eye, long staring glances, scatching of palms during handshakes, slow nods of the head—saying yes and agreeing to perform something we dared not to speak or to act upon—and so forth."

Don continued to use religious ministry to suppress his erotic feelings and sexual orientation. They soured and turned negative. "When I was about twenty-one, I was becoming a little sexist and homophobic preacher. I was a pretty widely known preacher at the college I attended. I carried my Bible in my back pocket. I preached that there should be no women preachers and that gays were condemned. At the same time, some of my role models were gay members of the church. We spent a lot of time helping many kids like me. There were some church and community choirs that were made up of gays and lesbians. They were powerful choirs, singing with a lot of joy and praise."

It was during his own coming out at an African-American university that Don began to shift from negative suppression to tentative welcome and integration of his erotic feelings. "As I became more comfortable with my identity as an African American, I seem also to have become more accepting of myself as a gay man. I found in college a wonderful African-American male role model about this time. I thought sex was bad, so I would find the most repulsive way to express it and then hate myself afterward. I would find the person I was most repulsed by, the dirtiest and scummiest person I could find. In the morning, I would hate myself and read 1 Corinthians 6, which said, 'Flee fornication, for your body is a temple of the Holy Spirit.' When I came out to my role model, he said that he had known for three years. He helped me not feel guilty or hide it from myself and others. In college, when gay guys found me attractive, I would say that I had a girlfriend. This was because some of my male friends at school, who identified themselves as heterosexual, would hurt me by flirting with me and then telling me they had a girlfriend when I fell for their trap and came out to them. They seemed to always take pride in letting me know that they were not like me. My mentor taught me to be 'grand,' private, and wise as a serpent. He taught me to be proud of my racial heritage and sexual identity and not to let others play mind games on me, not to let them pick my mind about my identity. I learned from him that as an African-American gay man I might not have the same power and prestige of white gay men. Therefore, I had to practice discretion and define the time, the places, and the ways in which I would share my own identity, when I felt safe to do so. More important, my mentor taught me to respect and avoid this type of sexually confused male."

In addition to the care and understanding that he received from his mentor, Don was affected profoundly by a spiritual encounter with God. "What changed me was a revelation I had from God. It wasn't what the Bible was saying, or what the preacher was saying, but what God was saying which became important to me. When I was twenty, I had a dream. I was walking this road. I had a passion for streets, like a calling to street life. I was walking down this road with a friend. Up ahead was a bright church, like a castle up on a hill. To get there I had to walk down this really dark road. It was a really dangerous path. I said, 'No, I am not walking down the road! It's too dark and sinful.' I heard the voice of the Spirit, which said, 'You have to or you'll never reach that beautiful church on the hill!' I knew that everything and everybody whom I had called sinful, or bad, were not as I had judged them. Everything I called sinful in my- self had the potential to make me a beautiful person, if I learned to em- brace my struggles and to love myself as I was. I knew I could not reach this beautiful temple of light and brightness, develop the ministry, or be- come the pastor that God wanted me to be until I walked this lonely, dan- gerous, and seemingly sinful road. My grandmother's words of spiritual wisdom came back to me: 'We all got crosses to bear. No cross, no crown.' I knew I had to follow this call and see where it led. It was so real. I told my mentor. The first thing he said to me was, 'Don, God loves you!' I had heard this in church, and I preached it, but here it made sense to me. It was not a preacher but a black college professor who taught me more about God's love than the church itself. He said, 'Don, God loves you, and you must love yourself.' His office became a haven for me. He taught me to respect myself and to recognize and avoid falling in love with game- playing, sexually interested but sexually confused men. He helped me not to give my power away. He helped me realize that sometimes homopho- bic preachers ministered to me. For example, a preacher who was terri- bly homophobic preached about Paul's thorn in the flesh, and through this sermon he came to see that God's grace is sufficient in the face of things that don't go away."

Another source of care that assisted Don to bring together his erotic feelings and his spiritual life was the gay men's club. These clubs are places gay men congregate for protection, pleasure, and information about the gay scene. "The club life has a lot of down sides, but there is a strong spiritual side too. A lot of affirmation and safety. A seminary friend of mine was dancing by himself, and I went out with him and asked why he was dancing alone. The music was, 'I am never going to make it with- out your love.' He said he wasn't alone, but God's love was with him, and he was going to make it. His theology was not just developed in the sem- inary, but was also developed in the celebration of the club. He had gone through a lot of physical handicaps, so this meant a lot. I saw God's love in a new way. He said, 'When I think of the love of God, I just want to throw up my hands and dance.' I had never thought of it that way. He didn't care if he danced without a partner or who was with him. He wasn't out there for anyone; he just rejoices when he is on the dance floor. Even in club life where there is a lot of loneliness, a lot of despair, and wanting to belong (and wanting to 'be bad'), my friend realized that 'God is here and he affirms me, and I am going to have a ball! I am going to have the greatest time, because I am alive!'"

The physical act of dancing one's affirmation constitutes a spiritual and erotic unity for Don now. He has come to share the feeling that he learned from his friend in the club. "Whoever I am with, whether it is a gay or straight person, I am going to dance because life is a gift of God. I am going to enjoy that side. God was teaching me that there is a lot of affirmation in the clubs—a lot of dialogue about life in community and information about how to survive and cope. It has done for me as a gay man what the church has done for me as an African American. It has helped me understand the world that I live in and how to deal with it." I have observed Don's pastoral leadership in worship services in his congregation, and I was quite impressed with how expressive he is as a worship leader. He "danced before the Lord" and clapped his hands in praise of God. The congregation responded with vigorous participation.

Don has discovered other links between the club and the African-American church. For example, there are a number of black gay men in church choirs who bring club life into the church and vice versa. "Consider the kinds of things we do on the dance floor—hand clapping and all that. In some black gay clubs one will occasionally hear a gospel song and watch dancers dance to interpret it. Like many of our African-American ancestors, we do not separate the sacred world from the secular world. It's related to African-American spirituality.[1] Certain hand claps and dances of praise are sometimes taken from the church to the club, and then from the club back to the church. It links the two."

Don shares one particularly instructive story about how there is an "underground link" between eros and spirituality and a subculture among gay men in the African-American church: "When a fine brother (that is, an attractive man) joins the church, in some black churches the organist will play chimes! Finger snapping is also code that we've learned from African-American women and which we share with one another. Something profound which is stated from the preacher deserves to be accented with several 'finger snaps.' Sometimes the words of gospel songs are interpreted to have a double meaning to us. At one choir rehearsal, the choir was singing a song without any emotion, like they were spiritually dead. A musician told the choir why the song was so important to him: 'I was in the hospital and a woman brought me flowers, and another read the Scripture, but then God brought me my 'perfect piece,' and after he came I just kept thinking about my perfect P-I-E-C-E stayed on me, ooh glory, I rejoice.' While many of the heterosexual members nodded their heads about God's perfect P-E-A-C-E, the gay and lesbian members of the choir knew that the P-I-E-C-E about which he spoke was not the P-E-A-C-E of the spirit, but some fine, terribly handsome man sent to him from God. Many of the gay members of the choir whispered to each other, 'Ooh chil', I don't believe he went there. I don't believe he said that in the church.' He had them rehearse the song again, and although there was some objection among the gay men for his mentioning of sexuality in the church, yet they sang with a bit more feeling. When the choir came to the part of the song which said 'perfect peace,' the gay men smiled, closed their eyes as if they were meditating, and sang 'purrfect pieece.' The song became more alive. The gay men were smiling, not only because they were probably meditating on some man whom they considered their 'piece,' but because here there was a disguised connection and a double meaning about sexuality in the music. And that helps the church become a more lively, liberating, and humorous place. Under the guise of the church's homophobia, they had transformed the rehearsal and made the church a safer place for their expression of self and their creativity. Or sometimes there is the same kind of double meaning which provides some space to express ourselves in traditional church hymns like 'How Firm a Foundation.' When we would come to the verse that says, 'Fear not I am with you, O, be not dismayed, for I am your God and will still give thee aid.' With that last statement, 'I am your God and will still give thee AID,' in one church the musician, who in most of the African-American congregations is more than often the freest agent among the gay men to create the language of our subculture (indeed, he is our 'grand diva' and the head 'queen' of our clan, or so 'she' sometimes thinks), turns around from the organ with raised eyebrows and a frowned mouth, looks out into the congregation, particularly to find the faces of other gay men, and as the gay men frown back, they whisper to one another, 'I will still give you AIDS? Thanks a lot God!'"

Don finds that much of what goes on in the African-American church between gay men and sexuality "is fun and affirming," but at the same time isolating and repressing because it is largely underground. "In some ways that which the gay men enjoy in the African-American church perpetuates the very silence that many of us are trying to get rid of." Yet in the midst of repression and being silent about the experience, Don struggles to use language from the underground church culture to affirm those who have been silenced. He was preaching in the pulpit and "told the young people that they might think life is boring until they have sex, but then they might find that they have sex and life is still boring. I snapped my fingers, and the women in the church double snapped back! I think that they enjoyed it. The snapping was signaling. It is one of the codes which African-American women and black gay men use with one another to make a statement as a matter of power. I told a gay brother about this and he said, 'What, you snapped your fingers in the pulpit! I don't believe you! You are crazy! The people are going to crucify you!'"

Don knows, as do his gay brothers who are in the life, that there is danger in linking eros and spirituality in the church and culture. Because of powerful taboos, much care must be taken. Yet there are underground ways to do this that mitigate the danger, like the joke with which this chapter opened. Don has used preaching, videotapes, and community alliances to help expand the horizons of linking spirituality and sexuality in positive ways. His personal therapy and his friendship with some heterosexual people have provided assistance in more fully integrating all sides of himself and in turn influencing his capacity to challenge some of the estranging sexual practices of both straight and gay persons. "It is hard to integrate all sides into a whole. I need to go into counseling to integrate my selves better. When I take care of myself, I can take care of my congregation better. I need to hear and affirm all the voices inside of me and have them integrated into a better, truer self. My straight friends help me with this, because sexual attraction is a possibility. It might be an issue, but we can deal with one another and learn from one another in positive ways, without sex getting in the way. We can affirm each other and talk to each other. We can talk about relationships and keep each other accountable. We can touch each other without being misunderstood. We can be honest with each other. I have enjoyed their support."

One of the largest impediments to affirming and integrating his erotic energies into the rest of his life is the negative messages given by both the white and black culture to Don as an African-American male. "White culture has attempted to dehumanize African Americans and rarely highlights the positive images and contributions of black men. In reaction, black Americans have attempted to create a superficial image of what black men are supposed to be and what they should not be. African Americans say that there are no black men to marry black women because black men are in jail, married to white women, uneducated, on the streets, or gay. A lot of African Americans will say that white America has weakened black men and made them gay. So, when you're black and gay, you're dehumanized by whites for not being white enough, and you're excluded by blacks for not being a real man. You're looked at by both communities, and sometimes by the entire world, as being less than others. African Americans blame gay men as one of the reasons for the loss of black men, lessening the possibility for black women to find mates, and we don't talk about the black women who are lesbian who are not looking for men to marry. With black gay men and black lesbian women in the community, perhaps everything will balance out! The image of masculinity for men 'in the life' (that is, black gay men) is very important.[2] This is true also for gay men who are Latino or lower-class whites, because of what society has done to dehumanize us and make us weak images in our community. You still have to identify with your culture as a man. Like other black men, black gay men suffer with rage due to double oppression and have learned that they must be tough. Don't get into a fight with a gay man of African descent, because we are becoming more determined not to be kicked around in the black community. You've never seen real, untamed rage until you've seen the anger, due to racism and homophobia together, in the eyes of a black gay man. Street experience learned from hanging out on the streets while going to the clubs teaches one to be tough. You have to keep an edge around others: 'I am tough, don't mess with me.' The masculinity side is very important, especially when you are maligned by your culture as not being a man. You have to stand up for yourself."

So, alongside the erotic celebration of sexuality and spirituality that is largely underground in the clubs and the church, there is also what Don describes as "viciousness" between gay men. "In the gay community as a whole, it seems to be against the rules of masculinity to say 'I love you' to another man. The person first to talk about love often scares the other man away and is thrown out at first base. Love and intimacy is not a behavior men learn well. Relationships between men who love other men may sometimes be quite impersonal and vicious." Don also believes that "viciousness exists between black gay men because of the great deal of internalized homophobia and hatred of self they have received from society and the church. This is particularly true for gay men in the African-American church. Because they have been told for so long that they are bad and condemned, they act out the part in relations with one another. This self-hatred turns to viciousness and lack of intimacy and respect for themselves and for each other. It's not unusual in some black gay clubs to see a fight break out and for someone to pull out a weapon. Sometimes fights break out between younger black gay men and black lesbian women who are trying to sport a gangster look. Violence seems to permeate every aspect of the African-American youth community. There are certain clubs I do not frequent because there are vicious members of the black church gay community who feel condemned by their own sexual identity and think I should feel the same about mine. Out of misunderstanding and sometimes jealousy, they would try to out me and use my sexual orientation against me."

And even when there is not viciousness, there is unfortunate ongoing conflict between erotic pleasure and images of spiritual purity. Don described a relationship that he was building with another black professional his age. There was a great deal of mutuality and common interests. They were friends. They became lovers and were beginning to see one another regularly. When Dion went to church with Don and heard him preach, he was stunned at what he saw and abruptly withdrew from the relationship without explanation. When Don confronted him, Dion said, "You are really serious about this church business! I am sorry for doing all those things to you! I shouldn't have done that. You are a minister!" Dion could not overcome the estrangement in himself between his erotic attraction and stereotypical thinking about sexuality and spirituality. In Dion there was little recognition that sensual erotic pleasure with a cherished partner could be a means to a joyful spirituality characterized by gratitude to God for life's delicate richness. For him, somehow, "sex was way out ahead of whatever came second," but it was basically evil or dirty in comparison to the purity of religious devotion. Rather than a synergistic or system relationship between sexuality and spirituality, there was a conflictual and hierarchical order of value.

Don's narrative suggests that erotic pleasure and spiritual fulfillment are not inherently opposed, but that under social conditions they are forced into conflict. Eros may be driven underground, repressed, become vicious, but it will not be denied. God, through a dream, set Don free from internalized oppression and enabled him to draw on a variety of forms of positive care to bring about wholeness. The care that he received through mentors, friends, the liturgical, musical, and spiritual heritage of his African-American Christianity, and the social milieu of gay men's clubs, both black and white, are bringing about a greater integration of his religious faith and sexual orientation. It is an uphill battle, and in our last conversation, Don was fatigued but not discouraged. In spite of ceaseless assaults on his identity and integrity as an African-American gay male Christian pastor, he was still "rich in spirit" and confident that things can yet be better. God has called and is empowering him to be "on this really dark road," and he has answered the call. There is brightness promised at the end. He struggles to discover an integrated systemic wholeness of his erotic and spiritual energies that works against oppressive taboos and hierarchical thinking, both in terms of race and sexual orientation. In Don we see that eros is an enemy of oppression; it affirms and empowers the celebration of pleasurable bodily expression. Because God affirms him, Don is willing to walk by faith to struggle with his many voices, but through it all he is going to dance and have a ball!

Eros, Monogamy, and Multiplicity

Eros is the basis for intense human connection and a means of graceful connection to God and the world. It helps us answer the question of why human beings have the capacity and drive to come together in the first place. But all the narratives we have examined also disclose eros as an ambiguous reality in human life. The relational expressions of erotic energy invite moral assessment in the caregiving context. Eros can be the basis for grace and communion in living; it can open persons to mystery, depth, blessing, and honesty. Yet because of its ambiguous nature and its connection to powerful social taboos and oppressive structures of experience, as revealed most clearly in Don's narrative, eros can be dangerous and bewildering as well. Katie's narrative discloses how eros can be disruptive of the status quo and can either temporarily or permanently destabilize existing relationships. We know that erotic fantasies can be linked to an obsession with death and evil, as in David's case (chapter 2). Don demonstrates that erotic feelings and actions can be driven underground and become transmuted into hostile viciousness against oneself and others. Effective caregiving requires sensitive attention to the dangers as well as the blessings connected with eros. Moral assessment of the quality of the relationships generated by eros is therefore inherent in any approach to caregiving based in Christian reflection.

Allen Windham helps us grapple with the ambiguity of eros, especially in the coming-out process and the sexual lifestyle of many gay men. Allen was referred to a pastoral counselor by his parish pastor to help him address several crises when he was forty-three years old. When he began counseling, he was burned out from overwork. He was out of touch with his feelings and had put his "emotional life on the shelf." He had not grieved his father's death. He was having physical difficulties with his prostate gland. He had just awakened to the fact that he was gay and needed to work out what this meant for his personal identity and for his relationship with the woman with whom he had been living for sixteen years. Allen sought out a pastoral counselor on the advice of his minister. Allen believed "that all things happen for a purpose." He thought that the pastoral counselor could provide a safe space to help him discern that purpose.

In order for Allen to work on these major life challenges, he needed first to confront his erotic attraction to men. "Actually, my awareness of that I was really gay was a result of therapy. I had some same-sex fantasies about a fellow classmate in first grade, but I put it all away. When I slept with my first man at age forty-one, I knew. A lot of gay men hate themselves, but affirming my core has helped me deal with all these other things." Allen said that affirming his gayness has "raised my self-esteem. I have been able to set boundaries in relationships. I have come in touch with my emotions. I have restored my physical health because I now take care of myself. I have become more fun at work. I don't manipulate. I am more direct and open, and less controlling. I have more awareness when I screw up. I am more emotional and forthcoming." Rather than fracturing his life or placing the erotic dimensions of his personality "way out in front of whatever comes second," Allen found greater aliveness and vitality in all areas of life when he was able to bring his negated sexual feelings into focus. He found systemic wholeness rather than hierarchical fragmentation in this reordering of the erotic dimensions of experience.

Over a two-year period of counseling, Allen's life took on depth and vitality. "I had a wonderful life before, but now it is something more. I could not have done all of these things without affirming my gayness."

Affirming his gayness led to many changes in Allen's life. With the help of their pastor and close friends, Allen and his female lover separated agreeably. "After more than two years, we are still not in communication, by her choice, and this is a source of pain for me. My relationship with my children is fine. Actually, with my twenty-three-year-old daughter it is better than it has ever been." His sexual activity diminished somewhat after the separation. He was supported by his minister and his religious community. He stopped going to church after the separation, but attended MCC when he traveled. Once, when he was first coming out, he brought a lover from Florida to church. Afterward, when he told the minister he was gay, the minister said, "I wondered why you were there with that big handsome guy." The minister said that he wasn't surprised to learn that Allen was gay. "He gave me a big hug and asked what he could do to be helpful. He asked if he could help my friends deal with this."

In addition to the affirmation of his gayness from his minister, friends, and religious community, Allen found affirmation in multiple sexual relationships with other men. "I would not have known I was attractive if I had not slept with a couple hundred people. I worked with two pastoral counselors over this period of time. One of them was quite uncomfortable with this; however, I could not have prospered without his weekly consultations. He thought I was being promiscuous and that I was putting myself in danger. I appreciated his concern, but it made me uncomfortable. Maybe I was being defensive, since in part I was being promiscuous. But straight people don't always understand how important it is for many of us to have a lot of sexual experiences. It isn't entirely promiscuity, but it has to do with identity and overcoming feelings that we are 'outlaws' because we are gay. It is a matter of learning how to communicate and to be direct about who we are. The counselor was right about it being dangerous. But it was also more than that. It was about socialization and honesty and coming to feel good about who I am. If straight people are going to be helpful to homosexuals—especially gay men—then they have to understand that having all these relationships is not negative. For many of us it is necessary to figure out who we are."

Early in his coming-out period, Allen fell in love with a gay man. But this relationship turned out to be wrong for him. "I was needy and inexperienced, which threatened him, and he became verbally abusive. However, I was not too inexperienced to be able to fall in love, for which I will ever be grateful. I have told him, and I hope to see him when I go to Florida in a few weeks."

For about two years after ending his relationship, Allen did not have a special lover, but multiple sex partners. "I was not planning on having a partner. I had a good life. I sold a big house, did lots of traveling, had good friends, and read a lot of good books. Then I met my current partner. He is a school teacher, having returned here from California where he lived and taught for many years. He is a handsome man. Now he is the center of my life. We are monogamous. We both feel like we have been given a second chance. I love my life with him."

In this narrative, we see that underground and unrecognized eros was connected to a diminished and even unhealthy life for Allen. He was in a relationship with a woman that could not fulfill either of them. His emotional life was constricted. His work relationships were limited and fraught with negative elements, in spite of general success; he was the director of a publicly funded agency related to the arts and was well respected around the country. His range of self-knowledge and self-affirmation was narrow. He was not taking care of himself physically.

The awakening of eros brought these elements into focus and created a crisis. The crisis led him to seek care, and the care he received through therapists, friends, pastors, sexual partners, and lovers assisted him to accept his erotic energies and their directions, and to find positive contexts in which they could be explored, understood, and integrated. As his life became more honest and whole, so his capacity to transform his larger environment and to live well within it has grown. When seen in the context of a larger unfolding of personhood and human communion, and allowed to be named from the standpoint of the participants whose lives are transformed by the experience, the multiple sexual relationships along the way lose their status as "promiscuous." They are rather fluid but valuable components of a larger complex process of self-discovery and self-affirmation. Their moral status is not ultimately determined by the nature of the acts themselves or even by their "fleeting multiplicity," but by the care, pleasure, and mutual affirmation that is shared by these sex partners. Eros draws together, but it also drives toward fuller as well as deeper relationality. It is a mistake to contain it to one form or the other. In some cases, eros may seek a multiplicity of fleeting sexual encounters. And although these may be ethically problematic at one level, the overall ethical value of these expressions is best measured by the degree of richness and integrity that they evoke in the totality of life. In any case, *a priori* negative prohibitions based on conventional heterosexist norms of erotic engagement may miss the positive spiritual and relational dimensions of multiple sexual experience in the context of gay and lesbian self-discovery and liberation.[3]

For many heterosexuals, same-sex erotic pleasure is assumed to be in itself immoral and negative, leading to dissolution and debasement. Don's self-limiting experience of finding the "scummiest" person to spend time with would be thought by many to be what gay sex is really all about. And of course, if this is the case it should be opposed on moral and psychological grounds. However, the witness of the lesbian and gay persons whom I interviewed found that homoerotic experience is not self-defeating and debasing. They found the opposite to be true. They found that the negative evaluation of same-sex eroticism was the diminishing factor and, when internalized as in Don's case, eventuated in dangerous and debasing practices.

When, however, lesbian and gay persons found the courage to name and act on primal erotic energies, they were enlivened and transformed. For them, the negative ethical evaluation was the immoral act; shared erotic love was the transformative and life-giving moral truth, even—and sometimes especially—when it was shared outside of permanent monogamous partnerships. Rather than leading to estrangement from self, God, and others, this multiplicity of erotic intensity was reconciling, healing, and profoundly transforming.

Perhaps Connie, a lesbian who recently came out in her late fifties, summarizes best the positive connection between care, erotic intimacy, and the grace of God when she describes the effect of other lesbians on her life. "Just like I can only learn about my intellect and intellectual life by being intellectual, so I can only learn about my sexuality by being sexual. I was sitting around in a group of three women, and we were all barefoot. You sort of find yourself being turned on by another woman's feet. It's like they cared for me by helping me discover my self, by being generous enough with themselves to let me discover my sexuality. Okay, I'm sitting there in the group and getting all . . . you know . . . by this lady's feet. And she was generous enough to give me a kiss. My lover, Judy, was loving and trusting enough to explore physical intimacy with one another. And that is really caring. It is real care, I think. This may sound a little crass, but if there was ever any doubt in my mind that I was lesbian, there wasn't any more after being with Judy. And there was also the feeling, 'Wow! That is what this part of me is all about.' It was wonderful healing and wholeness. St. Paul would probably turn over in his grave, but it was a wonderful sense of grace. A grace experience. It was like total affirmation of loving and being loved. Again, I feel like I have been very, very fortunate. People are people. There are lesbians who are abusive like anyone else. I have not been in an abusive relationship. Women I have been lovers with I have met through my church. I think that the best place to find partners is the church, even though I know that not all people in the church are positive about this."[4]

Conclusion

Martin Luther, in an obscure and overlooked passage in a document that has become one of the authoritative confessions of the Lutheran Church, indicated that one of God's means of grace was "the mutual care and consolation of the brethren."[5] It is highly unlikely that Luther would have thought that this "mutual care and consolation of the brethren" extended to lesbian and gay sexual intimacy. Yet Katie, Ken and Barry, Christina and her partner, Don, Allen, and Connie would instantly connect this affirmation to the sexual intimacy they discovered with same-sex partners. For them, erotic coming together in "mutual care and consolation" has served as a means of grace and healing rather than as a means of injury and demise. The care that they have received from one another and from supportive caregivers in the midst of their struggle to be more authentically human has helped them link their primal physical desires with their highest spiritual aspirations in relation to God and religious vocation. Sexuality and spirituality have become united in a systemic wholeness. Alienation and estrangement are being overcome. Life is taking on new energy and depth. Their relational network has expanded, and human communion and affirmation are overcoming isolation and self-denigration through the care and love mediated by erotically driven energies. Thus, if sex isn't the most important thing in life, it helps everything behind it to catch up and share a vital place in a reconfigured center of experience. It creates new forms of human communion and destabilizes taboos that diminish the divine call for humans to create and care for multiply diverse forms of loving relationships. We turn now to a fuller exploration of the diverse forms of intimate relationality that eros generates for "the mutual care and consolation" of God's human community.

4

THE ARK OF PROMISE

Caring for Lesbian and Gay Families

Judy Dahl, a former graduate student assistant and now a friend, is a minister in the Metropolitan Community Church. In her book *River of Promise* she details the struggle that she and her partner, Terryl Miller, had in trying to adopt a child as a lesbian couple.[1] In the face of enormous physical, legal, and cultural difficulties, their main spiritual sustenance was drawn from the Genesis account of Noah's Ark. The story of Noah was for them a "river of promise" against the deluge that threatened the integrity of their lives and their hopes for the future. The rainbow was God's promise of survival and generativity. It was a sign of God's ongoing presence in the face of surrounding destructive forces aimed against the fulfillment of lesbian and gay family life. When they were ultimately successful in adopting two lovely children (a boy and a girl) and establishing a family, God's faithfulness was underscored and an enormous sense of gratitude prevailed. Without the support and care of family, fellow Christians, social workers, doctors, and lawyers, the deluge would have prevailed. Their "ark of promise" would have been swamped and the rainbow disappeared under ferocious thunderheads or obfuscating mists. Instead, they were able to contribute to life's continuity and richness through establishing a family haven for children to be reared in love and safety.

One of the strongest challenges to caregiving with lesbian and gay persons is responding to family dynamics. There are nearly always difficulties in the family of origin when a lesbian or gay person comes out of the closet. These are usually exacerbated when partnerships are formed. They sometimes become intolerable when children are in the picture. Aunts, uncles, grandparents, and cousins from both sides of the relationship play out various combinations of opposition and support. Ministers and the larger religious community can play a role for good or ill. State and federal laws and local community norms have an impact on the nature of care. The medical community and social service agencies have enormous influence on whether lesbian and gay partnerships will be arks of promise and refuge or little boats awash and swamped by the deluge.

A simple concrete example of the complexity of family dynamics confronting caregivers arises in Connie's family. We heard some of Connie's story at the end of the last chapter. Connie has an adult son and daughter. Each is married. She has not come out to her daughter because her daughter's husband is very conservative. "My daughter would be accepting, but I don't want to put her in a possible conflict situation with her husband." Connie's son lives in another state with his family. He knows about his mother's orientation. He and Connie were uncomfortable with "the secret" being kept from his sister. Connie's son and his wife think that their youngest son may be gay. "They are concerned about how to raise him as a gay boy. They don't have resources or social support. They also worry about society's impact upon me as a lesbian. I consulted with friends. I counseled my grandson's mother and father to love him and to give him a sense of values and integrity." As mother and grandmother, Connie wants to help the family find supportive resources and strong values by which to navigate potentially treacherous waters. But because of conflicting values in the family and because of her sense that full disclosure would be disruptive of family cohesion, it is not presently clear just how to proceed. The conflicting "family values" in Connie's extended kinship network make the way ahead perilous for all. Great care must be taken, or irrevocable damage may accrue in this family.

Judy, Terryl, and Connie press the pastoral caregiver to investigate and expand the dimensions of positive care for lesbian and gay couples and families. There are complexities beyond the scope of this chapter and book, but a beginning can be made to explore some of the positive dimensions that care can take, according to the witness of lesbian and gay couples and families themselves. What, then, might care look like for families challenged by the reality of same-sex orientation among its members, especially when personal and familial survival seems to be at stake when "Christian family values" are considered?

Normalizing the Untypical

In the previous chapter we spent some time examining how Katie Bowen's awakening to her erotic vitality was a part of a larger transitional disruption in her family. She and her husband had decided to end their marriage before Katie was fully aware of her sexual orientation. They and their children had received therapeutic assistance to establish separate households with shared parental agreements. They were blessed with a reconciled relationship shortly after the divorce. In spite of severe loss and grief, they were on the way to recovery and rebuilding.

However, when the disruption of Katie's attraction to women burst on the scene, a new set of challenges occurred. The need for care became even more acute for all the members connected to this kinship network. Katie's former husband and his spouse were challenged with decisions about whether Katie's parenting as a lesbian could be normal and healthy. Katie's children had to come to know their mother in new terms and make decisions about how they were going to relate to her, as well as to their father's new spouse. Katie and Cynthia were challenged to develop their relationship at the same time that they had demanding professions and significant parental responsibilities. All of them had to make decisions about the religious setting in which they would live and in which they would educate their children.

When Katie and Cynthia sought therapeutic help to deal with these family transitions, it was essential that they find someone who could understand that the challenges they faced were normal, though in many respects untypical. Katie recognized that there were pervasive forces in our society pulling against the success of lesbian families. She could not accept a therapist who would not support this family structure and work for its success. She said that several therapists she contacted gave the impression that households headed by lesbians could be healthy families, but they also communicated that such families really were abnormal because of the sexual orientation of the mothers.

Through knowledge of the system and a sense of being "graced by God," Katie and Cynthia were able to find a therapist who could work with the specific needs of the adults and the children within the household and in the extended kinship network. All of the adults, both those who were straight and those who were not, were helped to be cooperative and supportive of one another in parenting the children. They were helped to grieve the ending of the earlier family structure and to establish relationships with one another. Appropriate educational environments were secured for the children. Katie agreed to raise the children in the Episcopal Church where they had been baptized. A forum was established by which the children could deal with their conflicted feelings about the disclosure of their mother's sexual orientation and new lifestyle.

As Katie reported it, the outcome over time has been positive. They have all discovered that their family is a "big table" and that there is a place for everyone at it. This outcome was not easy, and at times there were severely painful exchanges of words and actions. But with the help of supportive friends, the goodwill of other family members, underlying love for one another, and competent therapeutic help, the emerging family structure was protected, and each person and relationship within it has grown.

Upon analysis, the core factor in assisting this family was the extent to which its challenges could be normalized rather than pathologized. As Katie recognized, for care to be positive it must not be contaminated by those massive forces already working against the success of lesbian and gay individuals and families. Therefore, for care to be effective, the most positive message must be that these families are normal, even though untypical with respect to sexual orientation, and that each person within them can thrive when love, commitment, belonging, and respect are dominant. Reflection on Katie's narrative of finding positive care for the family that she and Cynthia were establishing makes it clear that the defining norm of family has shifted. In their experience, the normal family has been redefined by love, belonging, respect for difference, commitment, and honesty. Heterosexual male-female and parent-child relationships are no longer the measure by which the "normal" family is defined. Richer family values and relational options are emerging. These values are available to all, whether lesbian, straight or gay, or in "mixed-status" extended kinship networks like Katie and Cynthia's.[2] In a time when our culture is racking itself to discover viable forms of family, lesbian and gay persons may offer us a window to discover more promising definitions of the family and provide some guidance for increasing health in all types of families, including those "blending" same-sex and other-sex orientations. We will return to these considerations at the end of this chapter.

The caregiver who would help families blend heterosexual and homosexual energies must be honest about where they stand and be able fully to affirm that these relationships are healthy variants of human sexuality.[3] There can be no attempt to change, criticize, or convert lesbian persons and to alienate children from lesbian or gay parents. When lesbian or gay persons, like Katie, ask directly where the caregiver stands in relation to the ethical status of lesbian- or gay-based households, an honest and direct answer is required. The caregiver cannot withhold answering or ascribe the question to some "problem" in the one who asks it. Caregivers cannot assume that the need to ask the question reveals unhealthy paranoia, lack of trust, ambivalence about orientation, or the like. It is part of a reality-based obligation on the part of lesbian and gay persons to assess who can and who cannot genuinely support the development of a fulfilled same-sex personal and familial lifestyle. If the caregiver cannot answer the question openly and positively, care will not proceed effectively. Immediately, assistance should be sought elsewhere to prevent further harm to lesbian and gay persons or to the members of their vulnerable kinship network.

Negotiating
Family Transitions

One of the biggest needs of gay and lesbian persons and their families is for sensitive and effective caregiving to assist with the coming-out process. Coming out is not just a matter affecting lesbian and gay persons. It is a challenge for all members of the family of origin and extended kinship network. As Katie and Connie's stories indicate, parents, children, siblings, grandparents, and aunts and uncles often do not have an easy time coming to terms with a relative's same-sex orientation. Sometimes spouses have to become reconciled to the devastating news that their husband or wife is gay or lesbian. In addition, friends, teachers, and even the community of faith all have special needs for incorporating the knowledge that someone they have known and loved as a straight person is now lesbian or gay. Teresa Neal's story helps put many of these elements into perspective.

Teresa is in her early thirties. Her father is a United Methodist minister. She was reared in a loving home with a sincere and vital faith. She felt accepted by God, her family, and her church. Between the ages of ten and twelve, she began to deal with her sexual identity. Concerning this period, she said, "I kept looking for something positive, but could not find it." When she was sixteen, she came out to a pastor for the first time. "He would not serve me communion. I felt that God accepted me, but I was confused why the church wouldn't accept me. I felt called to ministry, but my denomination would not ordain people like me. The pastor was not able to deal with this. He was not able to say that God did love me. He was not able to say that the church was wrong."

Teresa was upset and angry with her family and church because they did not accept her sexuality. She felt enormous grief because of this. She found her way to other lesbian and gay persons. Here she found some relief, "but they only accepted my sexuality and not my whole personhood, especially my relationship with God." She discovered a Quaker Meeting that welcomed her as a total person. "I could participate fully. This was a whole community, not just a gay and lesbian community. There was no issue here of communion or ordination and therefore of exclusion from these sacraments for *any* reason. They accepted me fully as a person."

Teresa belonged to this Quaker Meeting for six years. She was a normal part of the community and attained leadership positions. She became Clerk of Meeting. "I felt empowered as a whole person. The Meeting dealt openly with gay issues. They helped me deal with anger and bitterness at being left out of my family and church."

When she was nineteen, Teresa sought a therapist to help her with her pain. "I looked hard for someone who reminded me of my mother. The therapist never suggested that I talk to my parents regularly, but I realized that I missed having a close relationship with them, and I didn't want to lose them forever. Even if they didn't accept me, I wanted to see them. This attitude was a combination of what I was getting from the Quaker faith and my desire not to be separated from my heritage. I have always kept a journal, and my journal at that time shows that there was more to me than just my sexuality. I also wanted to keep connected to God, faith, family (both nuclear and extended), and to knowledge that there were other parts of my life as well."

Teresa's desire for connection grew. Even though she felt that she was an important member of the Quaker community, "I felt homesick for my Methodist Church. I missed the ritual and liturgy. I missed the sacrament. My parents had begun to change during visits home. They were more accepting of me, though not as a gay person. I was less bitter, and that made it easier for them. The Quaker faith helped me to be patient with society and the church. I was sick of the fight. I think that my relation to my Quaker church and its respected and accepting Clerk helped my parents change their attitudes. My life also settled down, and I generally grew up. They saw my being gay as more than a stage. When I made a commitment to a partner they liked, this helped too. My parents gave me the sense that God loved me and would always be interested in hearing from me. My father was in prayer, in conversation with God. I give credit to them. It hurt them. I could see it in their faces. They didn't say anything. The message was not that they didn't love me, but that my choice was hurtful to them. They saw it as another part of my rebellion at the time."

After years of struggle and growth, Teresa and her parents have a reconciled relationship. "We maintain connections with our extended family, and our mutual concern for grandparents, aunts, uncles, and cousins has given us the means of maintaining respect. My parents have been especially supportive of my relationship with Marcy since they witnessed her nurturing me through a horrific bout of depression last year. They have never been so effusive with us as this January when Marcy and I treated them to a celebration of their wedding anniversary, along with our own fifth-year anniversary! Their support of our church and of our commitment to it is tremendous."

Teresa has found a home in a Methodist congregation in Denver, Colorado, that has assisted with this reconciliation. The woman pastor was a student of Teresa's father, and "in her, I could be connected to his vision of Christian faith." Teresa believes that "there has to be something in you to keep that connection to the church, even when the institution can't acknowledge you and doesn't want you. You need to have something in you to oppose that, endure it, and make you believe that the church can get beyond its opposition."

The congregation that Teresa attends is "committed to feeding homeless people and has a minister who is supportive of gays and who wants to be there, even though it is a low-paying and struggling congregation. The church has grown in mission and maturity. It is no accident that a church so active in ministry would have so many gay and lesbian persons. The congregation is committed to giving to others, especially to others whom churches normally do not give to. I have been in all kinds of groups filled with gay and lesbian persons, but this is the most positive. People are not there to find someone to sleep with, or to complain, or to fight oppression. I feel called to ministry, but the door is shut in my denomination. I can't beat my head against it. Pastoral care sustains me in the face of the closed door. The pastor's personal support means a lot. She can let me preach as a friend, but she is not empowered to do this on behalf of the church. If more people were fighting to change the church, it would make me feel more cared about."

Care in the context of the church has helped Teresa to strengthen her relationship with God and to link her faith to all elements of her life. "Pastoral care has assumed that I have a personal relationship to God. It has helped me talk about prayer, knowing that I want to talk to God. It has helped me with my ministry: in the world, at home at night, in the work place, to my gay brothers and sisters. It has helped bring my Christianity into my politics, such as fighting against Amendment 2. The pastor respects my personal relationship with God. That helps bring maturity. Feeling closer to God is a good way to deal with a world that doesn't want to be closer to you."

Teresa's partner is Marcy. Marcy has a teenage daughter, Meredith. They all live together. "It is wonderful to be a part of a congregation that takes my partnership with Marcy for granted. We can raise our daughter there. It is the only church in Denver like that. Our congregation is accepting, but we can use more than this. Meredith particularly has some insecurity because so much of her life can't be shared with others. She is sixteen. She knows that people can be cruel. I wish that she could hear people from a community say that it is okay to talk about her family. For example, since she can't in very many places acknowledge that she has a stepmother, it is not possible to talk about our relationship. All of her life she has been the child of a single mother who is a lesbian. She has an early negative image to overcome. She hears the story against us out there."

Teresa, Marcy, and Meredith are able to talk about these things with friends and with Marcy's family. For about a year they found a counselor to help them with relational struggles. "Learning about Meredith's childhood, what she was like, and what happened to her helped me understand both her and her mother. This was not just about being gay, but about family issues. The counselor made Meredith and me talk to each other and listen to each other. We went to help Meredith work out her grief over the death of her grandmother. The stages of grief were discussed, as well as different styles of communicating. Marcy's family is protective of her, the youngest of ten children. If you treat Marcy right, you're okay with them. The counselor helped me see Meredith as an individual, not an extension of her mother, and we discussed cognitive and emotional stages of teenagers. I didn't know her as a young child, so I had a lot to catch up on. Just *talking* helped."

In Teresa and Katie's narratives we see the enormous need for care that arises when lesbian and gay persons come out of the closet, on the one hand, and seek to establish authentic same-sex families, on the other hand. There is very little social support for this process, and outright opposition in most cases. For care to be effective, as we have seen, there must be an active welcome of lesbian and gay persons and their significant others. There must be a message and set of behaviors that normalize their experience as a healthy variant of human sexuality. A reliable community of faith and support is essential. Often there is the need for therapeutic help to work on relational dynamics inherent in any attempt to build and strengthen a family. It can be enormously beneficial if those seeking care are able to access their faith in God through prayer, communion, worship, and liturgy. It is evident that spiritual maturity has helped bring about a reconciliation between Teresa and her family of origin. It is also important to note the empowering outcome of enlisting the resources of lesbian and gay persons in their own healing and in the healing of society. Teresa was able to balance her legitimate anger at her rejection with a sense of patience and compassion for those who did not understand. She also has been enlisted in programs of political action to change the church and society. The transition from alienation to tentative reconciliation and fuller participation in the community of faith is an ongoing process for Teresa, Marcy, and Meredith, and their extended kinship network. But through strategic care along the way, they are moving to a richer humanity and a deeper love for one another. They also have found an expanded mission to God's world and church.

Celebrating Partnerships

The narratives of care that we have examined so far emphasize the coming-out process and the initial establishment of same-sex oriented family relationships. In a heterosexist culture, the coming-out process will never be completed. Yet there are a surprisingly large number of lesbian and gay persons whose commitments to one another have led to enduring long-term partnerships that warrant recognition and celebration. Because these partnerships are countercultural, with respect to both heterosexual and homosexual norms, their contribution to an understanding of care bears examination.

The forty-two-year commitment of Bill Weaver and Doug Johnson is a prime example of the relational wholeness to be found in long-term gay partnerships. It also bears poignant witness to the dimensions of care that we have identified as essential for life to be rich and full.

Bill and Doug are in their mid-to-late sixties. They are retired and live together in a comfortable ranch-style home that they built and own together in the Dunwoody section of suburban Atlanta, Georgia. Doug is a retired professor of pharmacy at the University of Georgia College of Pharmacy. Bill was organist-choirmaster at several influential Episcopal churches in the Atlanta area. They became friends as undergraduates at the University of Florida in 1947/48. Bill was sixteen; Doug was twenty. This was not a sexual relationship. Bill did not confide his gayness, and Doug had not accepted his own. Later graduate study took Bill to Eastman School of Music in New York, while Doug continued graduate work in pharmacology at Florida. "During that period we corresponded occasionally, but with no anticipation of a common future."[4]

In the spring of 1953 Bill and Doug found themselves employed near one another in the Atlanta area. "With our long-established friendship and both now self-identified as gay, we decided to live together. Our thoughts were for the immediate future, with little consideration for the years ahead. In 1954 we bought a small house together in Decatur. As a World War II veteran, Doug was eligible for a V.A. loan. We contributed to household expenses in proportion to our individual incomes. Still not sure of what the future might bring, we also kept careful track of who owned which pieces of furniture and other durable items." In 1960, Bill was appointed organist-choirmaster of St. Anne's Episcopal Church in Atlanta, and in 1963 Doug joined the faculty of the University of Georgia College of Pharmacy. "Doug rented an apartment in Athens, spent weekdays there, and we were together on weekends. It was not an ideal arrangement, but we made it work for twenty-seven years."

In 1966, they built their present home. "Once in our new home, we no longer kept up with ownership of household goods. We currently live on Doug's retirement income and will activate Bill's when living costs rise with inflation. Our present resources are about half of what we had prior to retirement. However, with the house paid for, we manage. For the first time, we have a joint bank account (in addition to individual accounts) that we use to pay common obligations such as church pledge, real estate taxes, and property repairs."

Doug and Bill realized that their relationship was unique and that it was important that they discover modes of self-care to ensure its continuation. Because of social pressures against the success of same-sex couples, it took almost eight years for them emotionally to count on the future of their relationship and to begin to pool resources. They also knew that they had to be circumspect without being false in their public activities as a couple. "Unobtrusiveness was essential. In presenting our public personas, it was important to include enough care to avoid disaster and enough honesty to maintain our own integrity. We decided to conduct our public life based on three principles. We would never express in public our affection for, or commitment to, each other. But we would never pretend to be straight, that is, there would be no fake heterosexual dating. And we would in most situations function as a pair, that is, no social invitations would be accepted for one of us alone." At home, they cared for their relationship by minimizing arguments about unresolvable issues, focusing instead on little things. They also learned to live apart successfully and to develop a rich array of shared interests when they were together on weekends.

Another source of care has been other lesbians and gays. "In our early life together, role models for long-term gay couples were not easily found, not because they did not exist, but because gays then were mostly closeted. We were fortunate, however, to know one older gay couple in Bristol, Tennessee, who showed us that life together could be happy and constructive. These staunch Episcopalians are now deceased, and we remember them with great affection. Of our friends today, about half are straight and half are gay. Among our gay friends long-term couples predominate, and many are a generation or more younger. It is good to have supportive younger friends. They say we are a source of hope for their futures together. Among our straight friends, we are accepted as a couple, and while they undoubtedly understand our relationship, this is not articulated."

Doug and Bill love the Episcopal Church and have found it a source of nurture. There have also been painful disappointments, as we will see. They have appreciated recent liberating interpretations of the scriptural passages about homosexuality. When they were young, these were not available to them, so that as part of their self-care they had to construct "a personal rationale for church affiliation and participation. This rationale tends to be primitive, but it was, and continues to be, nurturing. Essentially the thought is, 'I was created gay, I did not choose it. I am created in one version of God's image and am loved by God whether or not the church understands. I will live the best Christian life I can within the resources at my disposal. I will choose to do so as a member of the community of faithful as long as I am accepted. Like all Christians, I am a sinner who was, is, and will be forgiven, but I am not a particular sinner to be rejected for the nature with which I was created. This places commitment and trust in the love of God above commitment and trust in the organized church.'"

Bill and Doug's relationship with the church has had some difficult moments. Once when Bill was a lay delegate at a diocesan conference, the diocese adopted an antigay position under the leadership of then Bishop of Atlanta, Bennett Sims. Thus began a process of reexamination that led ultimately to Bill's resignation as organist-choirmaster. "After forty years as a church musician, I just walked away from it. I took another job selling furniture. The first year, I was filled with self-recrimination for giving so much to the church. I could not walk into the building. Under my leadership they had purchased a fine Dutch organ that I thought I would play until I died. But now I felt, 'If the church did not need me and my kind, I didn't need the church.' Years later I went to lunch with then retired Bishop Sims and told him of my feelings. This was pivotal in changing his mind. He recanted and wrote a letter to the deputies from his diocese to the General Convention in Phoenix, Arizona, in 1991. The letter stated that the church needed to move from exclusion of homosexuals just as it has stopped supporting slavery and excluding women. Bishop Sims told of the years it took him to overcome his fear of homosexual persons and to come to know them up close. He said that 'very real people stand forth now in the gay community for me. In many cases they seem more grandly endowed with the virtues of strength and gentleness than I find in myself—and in the Christian community broadly.' Bishop Sims wrote to me that our 'talk at lunch that day in Atlanta is a well-remembered and valuable piece in the long odyssey of change through which the Spirit has led me.'"

After Bill and Doug left St. Anne's, they found their way to the Episcopal Church of the Epiphany. "We decided to be honest with the rector, and she was very supportive. It was arranged that we would be considered a couple. There would be one pledge and one mailing to our address. After we had been there a few months, we were invited to be a part of a panel on 'Family Lifestyles in the Parish.' The lifestyles presented were nuclear families, blended families, interracial families, gay and lesbian families, and single-person households (divorced, widowed, never married). About fifty adults attended the session devoted to gay and lesbian families. Our presentations were warmly received; some of the questions were naive, but none were hostile."

The manner in which the rector welcomed Bill and Doug (and other lesbian and gay members of the parish) and the way in which the congregation used their wisdom to educate others were significant acts of care for Doug and Bill. They said that "this program was our first public statement about our intimate lives, and we did so with no expectation of change in our spiritual lives. Significantly, the experience has brought rewards. We now feel a serenity in church that we had not previously realized was missing. The Passing of the Peace has become more personally significant, for we are now warmly and honestly welcomed. We are invited as a couple to present the bread and wine at the altar. From time to time we are sought out by parishioners who wish to discuss concerns for gay or lesbian members of their families. Being 'out of the closet' within the parish family is a blessing we treasure, even though it has been almost our lifetimes in coming. Bill initially filled in for the organist who was diagnosed with AIDS when the organist was too sick to play; it was astounding to watch the whole congregation grieve."

Bill and Doug were asked to be a part of a video series produced by the Diocese of Atlanta for the Episcopal Radio-TV Foundation on "Moral Discourse and Homosexuality." In one place on the tape, Doug becomes uncharacteristically publicly emotional and is a bit embarrassed about it. On exploring what was so moving for him, he replied, "I was saying that the day is past when gay people can be ignored. We can be open people. We can be honest. We can't go back. My deepest feeling is that honest inclusion of all people is Christ's desire for his church. I became emotional then because I realized suddenly how important the acceptance of the church is for me. I never realized that before. After my statement, there was a long silence in the studio. Then the two priests came to me and hugged me. Later, when recounting the event to Bishop Frank Allan, the current Bishop of Atlanta, he did so as well. It meant a great deal to me."

Bill and Doug are members of Bishop Allan's Host Committee, a group of straight and gay persons who meet monthly "to let clergy get to know gay and lesbian persons as friends, persons, and individuals. Conversions have occurred. The group is very nourishing to us. It feels very good to be in that group and to know clergy who really support us." Their participation in this group has provided an active welcome and a normalizing of their experience as gay men in the church. They are able to use their sexual orientation as a part of the church's intentional strategy of ministry. Being a part of this ministry has been a significant source of care for them.

On Bill and Doug's fortieth anniversary, a very important event occurred in their parish. It is the custom of that parish to give thanks each week for marker events such as anniversaries. Bill and Doug wanted to be included in this practice but were uncertain about doing so. "We went to the rector with two questions: 'How can the church give thanks for the longevity of a relationship it would not bless in the beginning? How can the church bless our anniversary when our doctrine is not affirming?' The rector said, 'We will write a prayer that you like; the Prayers of the People are not doctrine.' She was very inclusive. Gays and lesbians were welcome here long before we came. When the partner of a gay vestryman died suddenly, the parish helped hold his survivor up unbelievably.[5] At the next public service, our rector gave thanks for our forty years together.

Perhaps more important to us, at each anniversary since, this has been repeated automatically."

Bill and Doug are actively involved in the life of the congregation and share its organized ministry of care to persons with AIDS in their community. They are proud that during one year their congregation has helped deliver over 500,000 Project Open Hand meals to AIDS patients in the Atlanta area. They are also involved in PALS (Pets Are Loving Support), delivering pet food once a month to sustain the pets of persons with AIDS too sick to do so. They also support a personal friend who is in AIDS hospice care. Bill has published poetry addressing the grief of AIDS and reports that the response he gets is a source of care for him. "My poems have touched others, and they write to share with me. One entire public school community used my poems to help deal with the loss of a principal who died with AIDS." For Doug it is heartening to know that younger people can share problems and seek support from them. "Bill is empathetic. People can talk to him. I have a more austere personality, but it is important to be in the background."

Bill and Doug's family has been a source of care. Bill's mother learned very early that Bill was gay. "She hoped that I would spend my life with Doug, even before she knew that Doug was gay! She lived with us for an extended period in 1990 because of health crises. Her response to that year was to make Doug her alternate heir. That was about as accepting as you can get!"

Doug and Bill credit their relationship as the greatest source of care over the years. "We are sources of complementarity. We support each other in whatever we do. Whatever one owns, the other owns. We have so many shared interests, besides our infatuation with each other. At times, we still fuss and fight, and demand more understanding than the other is able to give, but even so we are glad to be the people we are. We have had satisfying careers. We have many friends. And most important, we have the intimate, loving, and enduring companionship that not all in this world find."

As Bill and Doug "stop being younger" together, the strong motivating force in their relationship has become companionship. "From time to time, both of us still try to remake the other as we would like him to be (with no more success than ever), but neither of us can imagine life without the loving presence of the other. We are now in our sixties and are beginning to wonder what we will do when we can no longer live independently. Retirement facilities for the general population that we visit do not seem congenial to us. Presumably our need is years away, and we will do the best we can when the necessity arrives. With no contract comparable to marriage available, we have had to ensure our terminal wishes through other arrangements. We have mutually supportive wills and have executed durable powers of attorney for healthcare. Our lawyer believes the deed to our home should be redrawn to specify survivor ownership. This is included in our wills, but wills for gays are often contested by families. We doubt this would happen to us, but correcting the deed is something we plan to do."

From their concern about the future, it is clear that new challenges of care will emerge for Doug and Bill, and other lesbian and gay couples. The need for a reliable community will grow. The church and culture will be called on to provide resources that support the long life of loving commitment that Bill and Doug have shared, and to preserve the integrity of their relationship when their own resources become strained. For the moment, we can only celebrate the care that they have shared with one another over forty years of loving partnership and rejoice in the new dimensions of care that are only lately available to them in their religious community.

A "Two-Dad" Family

Katie Bowen suggested in the last chapter that because gays and lesbians have "broken all the rules" about sexuality, it is part of their gift to society to see that family life is more than age or status or narrow role definitions. This is perhaps nowhere more true than in adoptive families headed by two gay males. What kinds of care requirements exist in these situations? How do these types of families challenge and expand our thinking about families altogether? Giff, Dan, and Anthony provide some compelling answers to these and other questions.

Giff and Dan met each other in Puerto Rico and soon recognized that they "were like soul mates and knew right away that we had found something special." They were raised with similar backgrounds in the South. Each had strong connections to the church. Each wanted "to grow up and have a marriage like my parents had." They continued to be in contact with each other after they moved to San Francisco. After a period of exploration, they decided to live together. They said, "We are probably the straightest gays around."

Their mothers are the strongest sources of support for Dan and Giff. Their mothers also support each other, for it is not easy to feel affirmed by their friends and church in the South where each lives. "Our mothers are like sisters. We are all going on a cruise together."

When Giff's mother first found out that he was gay, she did not know how to deal with it. She went to a chaplain in Memphis who helped her. Giff's brother, "a flower child," also talked a lot to her. "When she met Dan and saw us together, she fell in love with him." That helped her to accept it. Her acceptance helped Giff begin to put his faith and his sexuality back together. His father was a Methodist minister before his death. When Giff realized that the church rejected his orientation, he rejected the church. "I knew that if the church was wrong about this, it couldn't be trusted on anything else. When mother found out that I was gay, I read books that said it was okay to be gay and to be Christian. We did Bible study with gay and lesbian people. We went through the Bible passages that were used against gays and lesbians. Then we looked at the positive things that Christ taught about relationships. We didn't have the kind of relationships that the Bible was against. In fact, what Christ wanted in relationships we had. That helped me re-embrace my faith as a gay person."

Dan's mom had pretty much the same experience as Giff's. Being from a small southern town, there didn't seem to be anyone that she could talk to. She did tell Dan's sister fairly early, and they were supportive of each other.

Since Giff and Dan have been in California, they have been members of three churches. "We still have support in each. We were lucky. One was a Southern Baptist, one an American Baptist, and one a United Methodist. We have been accepted as a couple in all of these. Part of it has to do with the area. In this area, most people know gays and work with gays. We don't have to educate them about being gay. This has really helped our mothers and families coming out and visiting us. They see normal, fine people in our church and workplace accepting us, and they say, 'Well, I guess it is okay.' Back home, unfortunately, gays are stereotyped as promiscuous and going to bars all the time. We just aren't into that."

Dan had always had a strong faith, and it was not shaken by his coming out. "My faith has not changed from the day that I accepted Christ when I was nine years old. I had parents who taught me a very personal relationship with God. And it still is. Prayer and my faith are just a part of my life. People at work know that I go to church, but I don't evangelize. But they know that it is my faith that keeps me going. When I came out at age twenty-nine, it wasn't a big problem with my faith. I know that I cried many a night not wanting to be gay. But I had a lot of friends who were gay Christians. I had immediate reinforcement that I could be both gay and Christian. It was not a big struggle for me."

In spite of his strong personal faith, Dan had long since given up faith in the capacity of the church to support its own. "My father was a pillar in the church. He lost his business, partly because he gave food to people on credit who could not afford to pay him back. In order to support us, he went to work for Jim Beam Distillery. I went to college on a scholarship from Jim Beam. My father was kicked out of the church. This was my first dose of hypocrisy. I realized that things are not as they seem. I never left the church. I get more daily nurture from the people I work with. I am a school teacher and out of the closet. Most are not Christians, but they are very giving people. It is a diverse group. We have been together so many years that we are really family. People at work support us. They gave us a dinner and $500 for our cruise!"

Dan is "a firm believer in prayer. I go to church to pray. It is very meaningful. There doesn't have to be anyone else in the church." He and Giff are very close to James and Franklin, another gay couple in the church, and find a lot of ongoing companionship and support from them. "They are there for us all the time. We are there for them too. We have strong connections through being Christians. We have similar values such as family and home, not the singles bar. They are our primary care. It helps our moms to know that they are there for us."

Dan and Giff decided to adopt a child. Anthony joined their family when he was four years old. He was ten at the time of the interview. Anthony was born to a Latina mother who was not able to care for him. He was born drug addicted, with hepatitis, and was mute. He was socially withdrawn when they adopted him. He lived in several foster homes before Giff and Dan adopted him.

Anthony "has a half-brother and half-sister nearby. We have taken him to see them and to visit the foster homes he lived in. We have gotten into and have become accepted by the Mexican community there. Their families and friends have no problem with us. We would take his half-brother and half-sister and their Mexican boy friends and girl friends out with us when we took Anthony for the weekend. They had no problem with us in spite of gay bashing in their area! Like it's always been said, when you know someone as people, there is understanding."

Anthony has two half-sisters in their fifties on his father's side. One of them came from another state to take Anthony to live with her. "The Social Services here came together on our side. They said, 'We have had him for a year and a half, and he has made progress like no one has ever expected him to. We can't sit here and say that it would be better for him to go off with someone he has never met before. That was the first time that two gay men had ever taken precedence over blood relatives. The director of social services had a problem with it, but the case workers and psychologist said it couldn't be otherwise. The director couldn't argue with the results. In school, Anthony was just as sharp as a tack. It took a while to get him to associate with other kids, largely because he was in foster homes with large numbers of kids. He stayed under the bed for months in one of them. He has many friends now."

Anthony was baptized in the Methodist Church. "We were accepted there as a family. The church was very open and caring. But there were only a few gays. There was no children's program. There were no groups for us to be in, either our age or gay. Our best friends, a gay couple, went to a more active church. It had a good gay group and a wonderful children's program. We go there now. That church has been extremely caring. Very supportive. It is a mixed-race congregation. Many of the people who go there have been through a lot of discrimination. Not all like the gay openness, especially some older African Americans. But they do understand what it is like to be discriminated against. The pastor is really pro-gay, and we can talk to him."

The adoption of Anthony changed them in many ways. Before the adoption, Giff's mother did not want to tell people that her son was gay. But "the adoption caused her to tell others. Everyone's ideas changed. We were now seen as a family; our relationship wasn't based on sex!"

Giff, Dan, and Anthony have a reliable community providing various levels of care, as we have seen. "When the adoption came through, our friends and co-workers gave us a big shower. We were having a baby! There were presents for Anthony. Anthony plays Little League, and we are in the parents' association. Some coaches have had trouble with two gay dads, but that hasn't lasted. They like it that we know baseball and can bake cookies for the team! There are a lot of other kids in Anthony's school who are being raised by gay and lesbian parents, so he isn't that different. This is a very accepting environment. He has gay teachers and a supportive environment. Anthony's sister, Angel, is proud that Anthony has two dads! A lot of kids wish they had two dads. Anthony says, 'My mom can't take care of me. I have two Dads who take care of me.'"

Anthony has picked other foster children as his closest friends. Timothy, one of these friends, is having a hard time in his foster home and has asked to come to live with Anthony, Dan, and Giff. He feels safe and welcome there and would like to have two dads too.

Giff and Dan have made some significant adjustments since they have become dads. Dan took a year off to be a full-time dad with Anthony. "When he first came to us, he had so many needs that this was the only way. Besides, I wanted to be with him. We have had to learn about each other. Anthony now sees me as the authority, and we have had to deal with the effect of that on Giff's role. Giff agreed that he was more confrontational as a dad, like his own father, and that they were working things out." Both agreed that being a family meant that they have grown apart from single gays and from childless gay couples. They don't go dancing or have as much fun as a couple "on the town" as before. "Yet it is nice to have our own family. I wouldn't want it otherwise."

I interviewed Giff and Dan, and I met Anthony, in their comfortable home in Oakland, California. They had put a great deal of effort into remodeling a two-story home in a working-class neighborhood. Anthony moved between the interview and his room, and bargained with his dads for an extension on his bedtime. He won a little, but not much, of the bargain. He took turns sitting on his dads' laps, moving from one to the other and at first wondering who I was and what was going on. He seemed comfortable with the conversation and heard it all, though he clearly did not want to talk into the tape recorder himself. It was apparent that this was an open and loving family unit, with all three persons having a high level of comfort with one another. They were very welcoming of me and quite forthcoming in the interview. Giff said, "We have had some marital problems, but we knew we could work them out. I didn't think there would be counselors who would understand. It took me a while to realize that we could really have what we wanted as gay people."

Not long into the interview, Giff disclosed that he had full-blown AIDS and was in constant treatment for it. His diagnosis had come as a shock, because he had lived a monogamous life for many years. Dan is Giff's primary caregiver, but they decided to be open with Anthony and enlist his help at times. Because Giff is unable to work because of the illness, he takes Anthony to school and picks him up afterward and supervises homework every day. This has helped them to overcome the imbalance in parenting. Anthony assists as needed with the medication. He and Giff have strengthened their relationship as a result. Giff said, "Anthony helps with the IV. He perks me up. Anthony never did reject me for being sick. This confirms that we have bonded."

When Giff and Dan discovered that Giff was HIV-positive, they went to their friends and Anthony's godparents, James and Franklin. "They were shocked because we had all lived a monogamous life. But they were there for us. They are our family. We knew that they would listen and understand. We decided to go to a counselor to help us break the news to Anthony. After two or three sessions, she said, 'You have it together. Give each other love and support.'" The Meadows-Douglas family finds a great deal of care from their network. "We just have a tremendous number of people from all the churches we have been members of or where we have worked who would be here in a minute if we need them: to take care of Anthony, to cook our meals, to give us money, to clean the house, or whatever is needed—even people we met through the adoption, social workers. Many of them are lesbians. We could call Marcy, whom we haven't seen in two years, and she would be here. There is a network, though not a planned one, among gays and lesbians who are Christians. It is there for support and care."

A major source of care is found through Kaiser Permanente, their health maintenance organization. This has made expensive medical procedures affordable. "The Advice Nurse is great. She hugs me when I go in. My doctor came to Anthony's adoption party. We did have one bad experience. The doctor who took the initial blood test called me on the telephone with the results, rather than asking me to come to the office. A lesbian nurse heard about it and reported him to the Advocacy Group. The

Advocacy Group reprimanded him for this. He later apologized, but I changed doctors. The doctor I have now is Japanese-American. He admits that he doesn't know a lot about AIDS, but he finds out. He makes calls to specialists. He explains things to us and allows us to make decisions together. He told Anthony that he has a family who cares for him and wants to see him grow up. The doctor wanted Dan to have durable power of attorney written into the medical records. We have never had any problem with Dan being with me when I am in the hospital. When Dan walks into the hospital, the nurses say, 'Here comes your partner!' They let Anthony come in too. It is great that I don't have to fight the system medically!"

When Giff was visiting his mother in Memphis, Tennessee, he had to go into the hospital. The treatment was very different. Dan and Anthony were gone. The hospital staff would not deliver his mail from them. Nurses and the cleaning lady came in with gloves and masks. His room was marked, "Quarantined, Biohazard." Dan's participation was not allowed. His phone calls were not returned, and he was not put through to Giff's room. The nurses had to take some blood in Memphis and weren't trained to protect themselves. I said, 'Be careful of that blood. I am HIV-positive. I don't want you to stick yourself and get sick.' They were shocked that I would even mention it. They don't talk about it back there. There is a lot of other support from Kaiser as well, like handling out-of-plan treatment. The medicine is very expensive, and Kaiser has never refused to provide what we need. We have much to be grateful for."

Giff and Dan credit their faith as a major source of sustenance and care. Giff said, "Through my illness my faith has grown a great amount. I feel that I am ready when my time comes. It is nothing that I am scared of. I feel that my faith is a lot stronger after coming out of the closet, after being diagnosed with AIDS. I get scared. I have difficult times. But I don't think it is possible to be like I was when I first came out of the closet. I am older. I feel like my faith is very strong. I think it is dwarfed by my mother's. I don't think I know anyone who has a stronger faith than she has. She is an awfully, awfully strong woman. But I really do feel good about where I am, with all I have right here. And with my church. I go to church to sing in the choir and be with others, not to sit alone in the sanctuary and have an experience. But when I first got sick, I needed time to be alone, and I went to the sanctuary a lot of times for that, because of the quietness and peace that I felt there. I know that all this has to make me stronger in faith and a stronger Christian. It was very helpful to have the Bible study and realize that the depth of relationship is what is important, and to learn that the negative passages were taken out of context. It was very helpful to learn that you didn't have to be gay *or* Christian." Dan has always found meaning and strength in prayer, and continues to do so.

Dan and Giff were very grateful for their life together and pledged to each other that they would support and care for each other as family. Because only their mothers and a few others in their family of origin supported their life as a gay family, they had to create a new definition of family for themselves and find other sources of care for their nuclear nontraditional family structure. Dan summarized the sad, but realistic, experience of many lesbian and gay persons: "I realized after coming out the first few years that I had been hoping that the rest of my family would change their ideas and accept me, but they hadn't. I realized that my whole definition of family changed. I came to realize that they were not really family because they did not accept me. I realized that other people were my family because they were in my life. They offered support. I stopped wasting my time worrying about whether my aunts and uncles could be in my life. It was like, 'I can't worry about this anymore, but I have to build my life.' It took a long time to realize that my real family are those who are in my life who accept and understand."

The interview with Giff, Dan, and Anthony took place in their home in January 1994. Giff died in June of that same year. Dan and Anthony have relocated to a new home outside of Oakland and remain active in their congregation. In the next chapter, I will discuss some of the features of care that they received in Giff's last days and in the aftermath of his death.

Redefining the Family

One of the conditions for positive care is the affirmation of lesbian and gay orientation as a healthy variant of human sexuality. Full participation of lesbian and gay persons is the foundation for any other care and is itself a caring response. Included in this affirmation must be the active welcome of gay couples and families into a community that provides reliable support and uses their wisdom and experience for the enrichment of the larger life of the community. In one way or another, the partnerships and family units established by Katie and Cynthia; Teresa, Marcy, and Meredith; Doug and Bill; and Giff, Dan, and Anthony have been welcomed into communities of faith. And even more, they have been asked to make a contribution to it based on a positive appreciation of their same-sex experience. This affirmation has helped them to heal the wounds of past relationships and to find strength to oppose the condemnation existing against them in the church and culture. The affirmation they have received has also helped them to grow and to thrive in their relationships together and in their ministry to others.

To come to this place of strength and depth, much suffering has had to be endured and to some extent transformed. They awakened to the realization that their sexuality was irrevocably different from the majority and that very few in the majority culture could appreciate or even tolerate it. They faced the devastating painful truth that relationships they had supposed to be permanent must come to an end. They have found the courage to move ahead in spite of huge obstacles. They have had to let go of cherished hopes about their future and confront new and unfamiliar options with few guides or role models. They have had to redefine their intimate relationship to God and their core narratives of self. They have had to rethink what it means to belong to and create partnerships and families. Indeed, they have had to reconsider the whole concept of family and to refashion its interpretation in radical terms.

It seems that much of what our culture has inherited about family structure and purposes is being challenged today. We are looking for ways to maintain continuity with positive dimensions of our heritage, as well as to create new forms of families that respond to the dynamics of a complex postindustrial society. For some, lesbian and gay partnerships and families are in themselves indicative of the decadence of our society and culture. They oppose the legal right to marry or to establish some other statutory basis for securing full social legitimation, with all the rights, privileges, and responsibilities afforded permanent heterosexual couples and families. As I write, there is a national debate emerging based on a case before the Hawaii Supreme Court (*Baehr v. Miike*) considering the legality of same-sex marriages. Should same-sex marriages become legal in Hawaii, it appears that all other states would be obligated to recognize these marriages under the "full faith and freedom" clause of the U.S. Constitution. To avoid the onslaught of same-sex marriages, many states are currently considering legislation to make them illegal. The Defense of Marriage Act (DOMA) passed by Congress and signed into law by President Clinton in the fall of 1996 is an attempt to make it possible for states not to honor same-sex marriages from other states, but it does not prohibit states from legalizing same-sex marriages. Legal debates on these matters will no doubt continue in the years ahead.

At the same time, not all lesbian and gay persons desire to build their relationships on ideas of heterosexual norms. For them, it is inappropriate, even destructive, to define intimate partnership and committed family life along the lines of sex-role expectations and biological parenting. The organization of permanent relationship according to a hierarchy defined by gender and age is for many lesbian and gay persons (as well as for many straights) an oppressive holdover from the past that must be challenged and overcome if the conditions for justice and true love are to be realized. Whether it is inherently and uniformly oppressive for heterosexuals may be a debatable point, but it is clear that the traditional heterosexual organization of marriage and family simply misses the rich uniqueness of the relational capacities of lesbians and gays.

The persons I interviewed for this study made a choice to affirm their sexual identity as lesbian or gay. They chose not to live a lie about themselves or to force their sexuality and spirituality into a mold fashioned by alien norms. They found courage to create new relational rules and venture new family possibilities for themselves and, indirectly, for the larger culture. Giff recognized, once he was helped to look again at his religious tradition, that "what Christ wanted in relationships we had. The Bible was not against the kind of relationship that we have. What we have is what the Bible is for." Katie suggested that if lesbians broke the rules about sexual intimacy, then they might as well break all the other rules about status, age, parenting, and the heterosexist domination of relationality. She saw it as a gift to the culture to help all of us discover new relational possibilities. For her, in effect, the "margin" has become "center," and it is little wonder that the center is shaken and reactionary.

What is the new center, and how might it be regarded as a welcome opportunity rather than as a destabilizing threat? Katie summarized it when she said that "what matters to families is commitment, honesty, and love." Katie described her family as a "big table" with a place for everyone. They insisted on respect for difference and found a way to ensure that each individual's needs and aspirations would be honored. Giff said that the root of family life was understanding and acceptance, and if that could not be provided by the kinship family structure, then family should be redefined in terms of those who can do this.

In chapter 1, Christina Troxell found that her partnership was a one-flesh union that disclosed the inner meaning of the doctrine of the Trinity in Christian faith because it showed the character of love. She also believed that committed one-flesh unions disclosed the love of Christ and the church: "God's one-flesh union is holy, submissive, celebrative, giving. It is compassionate and respectful, esteeming another as higher than oneself. We see in our holy, celebrative, directed, purposeful, and fulfilling love a type of the relation that we have in God." In chapter 2 we have seen how the erotic connection of lesbian and gay persons opened them to a new spiritual apprehension of the love of God and neighbor, and enabled them to love rather than condemn themselves. In this chapter we entered the lives of many wonderful persons whose same-sex relationships are graced with fidelity, generosity, and faithful commitment to the highest Christian values and practice. In all these examples, we discover the potential of lesbian and gay partnership and family living to mediate or image what Christians have centrally affirmed about the nature and purposes of God in the world. Lesbian and gay families disclose important elements of the generativity of God in bringing forth new configurations of creative communion. They disclose the diversity of humanity and the intractable mystery of "otherness" in the human family. Without this intractable mystery of otherness, which characterizes both divine and human experience, the conditions for love and creativity are absent. Without "otherness," love is little more than fusion or narcissistic mirroring. There is no corrective on sameness, no basis for overcoming the idolatry of making ultimate the experience of the majority.

The partnerships and families described in this book invite all couples and families to consider new depths of relationship and organization. All are invited to consider the extent to which assumed gender structures, blood and kinship factors, and the place of children should be regarded as the *defining* elements in families. Perhaps they are best seen as important dimensions, each accountable to the norms of mutuality, fidelity, and love, rather than as divinely appointed requirements for all human beings. If God is imaged as a God of love and relational justice, as suggested by the heritage and the experience of those we have presented, then love and justice have priority among all other family values for both heterosexuals and homosexuals. If God is the one who participates in the coming forth of a diverse creation, then the diverse forms of relational and family living, accountable to the values of love and relational justice, disclose rather than distort the image of God. Like Katie's family, God's family sits at a "big table" in which all have a place. Or better, the big table at which each member of Katie and Cynthia's family has a place is the table set all along by God. It is the table of a richly diverse creation and a complex, multidimensional humanity. At this table, everyone is invited to discover and share in the diversity, respect, belonging, honesty, and committed loving that images the life of God, our host. As we will also see, it is a table to which we may bring our brokenness and find solace and healing.

5

THE DESOLATION
OF OUR HABITATIONS

Care in Loss and Crisis

The need for care is most compelling in times of crisis and loss. When the structures giving meaning and hope to our lives collapse or become unstable through internal and external threat, we reach out for stability and guidance. We look to caregivers and to God for healing and new life. We search deeply within for a reservoir from which to be replenished. Crises that are generated by loss become "dangerous opportunities" through which might be accrued either a spiritual advance or a spiritual demise.[1] The central task for caregivers is to assist those in crisis and loss to become more fully human and more fully aware of divine participation in life through the transformation of suffering into spiritual and communal strengths.

The interviews that I conducted for this study surprised me in many ways. One of the biggest surprises was the depth and range of losses suffered by lesbian and gay persons solely because of the sheer fact that they were same-sex oriented in a rejecting and punitive culture. For example, I sat with a group of men who were theologically trained for ministry but had to leave their church because of its policies. Their wounds were yet unhealed. I heard stories from closeted clergy about fear of discovery. They had feelings of guilt or shame at choosing to remain hidden as they pursued their calling. I heard the pain of lesbian and gay laypersons who thought that they had found an accepting congregation and minister, only to have the minister leave and be replaced by a homophobic individual. I witnessed the distress generated when the larger religious institution ejected from membership lesbian- and gay-friendly congregations. Some of the persons I interviewed found it difficult to maintain faith in a God they once loved and trusted because God's people were so unaware of their cruel hostility. The sense of God's abandonment and the subsequent loss of faith in an affirming God were excruciatingly difficult to bear (and very painful for me to hear in the interviews).

In addition to religious loss, I heard countless stories of relational loss.

Cherished family members became indifferent or rejecting once they learned of their relative's sexual orientation or when they learned that he or she was HIV-positive or had full-blown AIDS. Even gay-affirming family members sometimes lost the support and goodwill of other family members and of their congregations and communities. Because of the extremes to which lesbian and gay persons must go to find and build relationships, there was great fluidity in establishing and maintaining partnerships. Often, unresolved grief from former relationships was carried into new ones. This "old business" had high potential for destabilizing the new relationship and compounding pain and loss. And when intimate relationships ended, it was not uncommon to maintain ongoing contact because the lesbian and gay community is so small and self-protective. This ongoing contact in the long term was sometimes a resource for support and relational richness. But in the short term, it frequently undermined the well-being of the individuals themselves. Further, to be in frequent contact after a relationship ended put huge demands on their mutual friendship network. I came away from many of the interviews with the sense that relational brokenness and loss was burdensome and discouraging, and that it was an ongoing subtext even when it was not momentarily focal.

In the social and vocational arenas, lesbian and gay persons lost jobs or opportunities for promotion when they came out of the closet or when it was assumed that they were homosexual. They had to leave their rural and small-town communities and relocate in more welcoming, yet often culturally alien, urban environments. These dislocations were sometimes quite costly.

Nowhere was the sense of loss greater than when persons I interviewed discussed HIV and AIDS. Several persons I interviewed were HIV-positive, and a few had AIDS. At this writing, three persons have died of AIDS since our interview. Many were grieving the loss of lovers, partners, friends, and family members to AIDS. I visited AIDS support groups and attended AIDS healing services. To say that the crisis and loss generated by the HIV virus and AIDS is shattering is to woefully understate the situation. It is truly a "plague," as Bill Weaver's poetry discloses.[2] A lesbian minister of a large Metropolitan Community Church congregation told me that she had over five hundred funerals a year. These deaths were mostly AIDS related. This was enormously costly to her and to the congregation.

Compounding the grief of those suffering from all the dimensions of loss evoked by AIDS is the question of God's providence and care and the question of human compassion and solidarity. The age-old question, Why is God letting this happen? emerged frequently. Working toward an answer to this question more often than not meant, at least in part, a confrontation with the judgment by some that "AIDS is the punishment of God upon homosexuals for their immorality." All of these considerations challenged for lesbian and gay persons their capacity to believe that they live in a "good world" that "receives" and works toward the fulfillment of their humanity. These questions assaulted their belief in God's goodness and reliability, threatened their foundations for hope, and further strained their sense that the human community could be nourishing or healing. It was painful to listen to the anguish generated by the AIDS crisis. The loss of vitality and human potential brought into the lives of lesbian and gay individuals by the fear, anger, grief, and crisis of meaning through HIV and AIDS left me feeling sad and helpless as I listened to their life stories.

At the same time that I felt saddened and overwhelmed by the varieties and depth of loss, I felt even greater surprise to discover the courage and spiritual strengths that became apparent in the face of these crises. "In, with, and under" the radical evil that unjustly diminished and in some cases destroyed the lives of lovely people, there emerged or was found a gracious faithfulness and communal solidarity. In this chapter, we will explore some of the ways in which lesbian and gay persons have found forms of care that have enabled them to bear pervasive losses and to become sources of transforming care to others as well. We will throughout the chapter touch on the question of God's relationship to suffering, especially to undeserved suffering arising in the context of viral infection and human oppression.

BJ: A Veteran and a Homeless Woman

BJ Jackson was orphaned at an early age. She was reared in two foster homes, was never adopted, and remained a ward of the state until the age of seventeen. She remained single throughout her life. Because of economic circumstances she lost her home and lives out of her car. Licensed and registered as a nurse, and retired from the military, she has a career and a means of earning a living. But this fifty-year-old African and Native American lesbian woman has no established "place to lay her head." She has suffered grievous losses, and she has had to resolve numerous crises throughout her life. What has been the shape of positive care in her life? What does it look like now in the face of her homeless status?

The center of care of BJ has been in two sources. First, there have always been "certain people who have popped into my life at critical times. They help me over a hump and are gone." Second, her sense of providence and God's spiritual presence has seen her through. "I have a positive view of spirituality. I wouldn't have lived this long without help from outside, somewhere. I learned short helpful prayers from one of my foster mothers that Someone Out There is trying to steer me: 'Lord, have mercy; I don't know what I am doing. Help me.' I have had enough crises in my life that I have learned that there is someone out there to talk to."

BJ received a great deal of care from her foster mothers and from the grandmother of a Jewish family whose children she helped raise while in high school. "My foster mothers were meticulous in teaching me what I would need down the road. One taught me table prayers and that 'the truth will set you free.' My second foster mother was more accepting of people just the way they were. She was German and Irish, and her biggest contribution was her kindness. The Jewish grandmother and I became close over the years. She was very down to earth."

In the Air Force, people "turned up" to help BJ find what she needed to survive in Vietnam. One friend helped her understand her sexuality and be more comfortable around "alternative lifestyles. She taught me what to say and not to say, what to do and not to do." BJ met another woman on a three-day weekend leave. "We had an encounter on a blanket that helped me understand who I really was. We had to go to separate duty stations, but after that I began to look for situations. I finally had a serious relationship in my thirties."

Another example of people "popping up" when BJ needed them was when she spent one summer in Brooklyn. "The woman upstairs was a lady of the night. She was my saving grace. She taught me how to survive in the city. She just told me things, and I got to ask her a lot of questions that I couldn't ask anyone else. She knew everything. She had a little girl and supported herself and the child by working as a prostitute. She taught me how to live in New York City."

In her present church, an urban Metropolitan Community Church congregation, BJ finds that the senior minister's sermons are encouraging and uplifting. "I go to church regularly. Sometimes pearls of wisdom come from the senior minister's mouth. That is one reason I go to church. Pearls of wisdom also come from others. The associate minister and I are on the same wavelength, as he is more direct and 'to the point,' as opposed to just being a diplomat. The congregation is familiar. Another person of color (male) and I are working to bring more people of color to church. The church has not been real supportive. It needs to be revamped. There are pockets of support. There are some who don't have a clue what women are about."

BJ has found "spiritual heroes" in Maya Angelou and the late James Cleveland. She said that in spite of "pockets of support" in her present congregation, "what we call the church has been of no help to me, except for occasional social gatherings and for occasions to talk about political things. It was no place to go for support and care, though maybe I didn't know how to get in touch with helpful people in the church. I now realize a person can be so devastated, exhausted, and ill that one can't think what to do or whom to contact for assistance. My help has mostly come from strangers. It has been grace 'big time.' I met people who just seemed to know what I needed to know: Brits, Canadians, French, Vietnamese nationals. I resent it that the people I should be able to talk to never were there for me! It has always been a stranger who has been hospitable to me. I am sensitive to what the Bible says about being hospitable to strangers."

As an example of not receiving care from those closest to her, BJ recounts how the other children in her foster family have not been a source of support to her. In one case, when she lent one of them some money, her foster sister secretly gave it to a sister who had once tried to shoot her. When she has needed financial help herself, she was turned away by these foster brothers and sisters. Further, she generally found her acceptance as an African American from people in other countries to be more positive than her own compatriots, even though she was risking her life for her country in Vietnam combat/support situations.

At the time of the interview, BJ was "a working poor person. I raised three children and I owned a home for fourteen years. I got caught by a scam and I lost my home. I am not a vagrant. The law has not been helpful to me. The grace of God has been helpful to me. I have been beaten by cops. Some judges would not listen. I retired from the military after twenty years, but some records are lost. My story doesn't seem real to me."

BJ's main source of care at the present time comes from "a couple of friends and acquaintances. I draw on Project Angel Heart that assists homeless people. A student has offered her house when she is not using it. Always strangers help. People just pop up."

BJ said that care is most effective when people "judge not, lest they be judged by the same yardstick. People are too isolated, busy, caught up in their own things to include others. People are too exclusive. To care, people must remain open and remember that none of us have the same experiences in life. None of us deal with problems the same way. To help, people must learn to just listen! Not to make a judgment, just listen. No one was born to say, 'I want to kill my child,' or, 'I'll be gay so someone can beat me to death.' You will hurt yourself and others jumping to conclusions. There are those immature people who build themselves up by pulling other people down, but it really doesn't work."

Care, for BJ, has come over the years in a serendipitous manner through strangers, people who just "pop up," and through spiritual heroes. She felt cared about through listening without judging and validating her identity as a woman, an African American, and a lesbian. Care has also been conveyed through preaching, pastoral presence, and participation in the political and social occasions of the congregation. Currently,

BJ's experience as an African American has been used by her church in asking her to be a part of an outreach team to other persons of color. The church, in her view, has some distance yet to travel in dealing with sexism. Care has also been mediated through providing legal, financial, and housing services to her as a working poor person. She is presently stable and safe and is working toward rebuilding her life by saving enough to secure suitable living arrangements. During the interview she communicated sadness and bewilderment at the turns her life has taken; her story seemed unreal to her. At the same time, she conveyed an exquisite dignity and personal courage, and a determination to work for a better day for all of us. Her sense of God's grace was real, and her appreciation for those who "popped up" along the way was genuine. There was absolutely no doubting her resolve and her ability to survive, to overcome, and to reach out "to welcome the stranger."

Grieving Elizabeth

Barbra and Elizabeth were partners for seven years before they decided to end their relationship. They lived together in Oakland, California, and had an excellent support network. They went to the same church, which is a welcoming and affirming Baptist congregation, Lakeshore Avenue Baptist Church. Barbra says that she and Elizabeth "were very nurturing and caring. She supported and encouraged me when I was trying to go to school. She did not hassle me when I was busy in school. She was very loving and warm. I got a tremendous amount of love and support from her. She helped my family. She took care of me when I was sick. She held my hand when I was scared."

Around Barbra's fortieth birthday, she and Elizabeth decided to end their partnership and remain friends. The loss of the special partnership was significant for Barbra. Her grief, which was acute, was complicated by her concerned reaction to the Bay Area earthquake in the fall of 1989 and being forced to leave their home for eight months as a result of the quake's damage. Turning forty was not an easy transition either. She was in serious crisis and confronting a major loss. There were several sources of care for this crisis that bear mention. First, her therapist was a helpful ally. Second, her friends and family offered care. Third, her congregation and its healing service provided assistance.

Therapy was critical for Barbra to have a place to talk about her feelings. "My friends got sick of my talking about the earthquake! I could get support from the therapist. She was a good listener. She asked difficult questions to help me look at what I was feeling. She validated my feelings, especially the negative feelings that I and others felt that I shouldn't have. This helped me grieve Elizabeth and to discuss my anxiety regarding the earthquake. She was available midweek if I needed to call. She really validated my feelings of anxiety and panic. It was like I had a friend, though not a friend. She was not lesbian, but she understood. When Elizabeth and I were in couples' therapy, it was important to have a lesbian therapist who understood fusion issues for women. But here, this therapist helped me validate my feelings as an individual and grieve Elizabeth. It took about a year in therapy to be able to move on."

The second source of support was Barbra's friends and family. Barbra's parents had always been supportive and affirming of her sexual orientation and had participated with her in lobbying for full inclusion of lesbians and gays in the American Baptist Church. "My family offered incredible support; they helped my lover and me buy our first house. They tried to help me and my lovers as they did my sister's husband. They included me and my partners as family members; when we broke up, it hurt them too." Barbra defines family as larger than her kinship network, as do many lesbian and gay persons. "I have many extended families: people in church and people not in church. We have built a family of friends. Gene and Rick live upstairs. They are incredibly supportive. They are like family. It's like having two brothers upstairs. I have lived in one house or another with Rick for over fifteen years. We have shared households; it's one way to buy a house in California."

The Bay Area itself is a kind of extended family for Barbra in that it provides supportive resources and an ethos of acceptance and normality. "Living in the Bay Area is a blessing. When I talk to others living away from here, I am grateful. You can find a support group for anything you need. You don't have to worry about finding other gay people to talk to who understand what you are going through. The Metropolitan Community Church (MCC) provides a resource. The Baptist Church is a part of me, but there is a lot of warmth at the MCC. I wish everyone had the Bay Area! You can walk down the street holding hands with girlfriends and not get shot. This is a tolerant place where you can find others doing what you are doing. It's normal to be yourself here."

Another dimension of reliable community on which Barbra has drawn for healing is her congregation and persons within the larger community of faith. In her congregation she has found "a cohesive group of supportive lesbian and gay persons (though there are some tensions because not all in the congregation are comfortable with lesbians and gays). My boss and a group of people I have met through the Caucus have been supportive. In my home, family, and church, I know that I can grow. Sometimes it is hard to tell my gay friends why I am a Christian, because of what these communities do to them. Sometimes my faith in God is shaken. I know that we have free will, but I want a little more divine intervention! My friends and family in the church help me deal with this and talk about it."

One of the specific ways that her church has provided care for Barbra's grief is through its regular healing services. "We have healing services a couple of times a year. It is at the regular church service. People go up with prayer requests and get anointed. I always go up. It is wonderful. It has always happened when something big happened in my life. My Dad was really sick; we didn't know if he would make it. It was incredible to go up and have someone with you a few minutes to pray with you. You are only there a short while, but it's having that focus. It's having someone's arms around you. It's being cared for and being taken for healing. It is easier to go to the healing service to get what you need than it is to call up the minister and say that you have a problem that you want to talk about. It is a powerful experience of caring in a community. Doing it once, you want to go back. It is so wonderful!"

Finally, a significant factor in Barbra's healing her loss is Elizabeth herself. Elizabeth is still a friend and an ongoing part of Barbra's life. There is no emotional cutoff; there are no push-pull demands on one another. They have resolved their relationship so that it now can be a positive source of care, even though it has changed its dimensions in their lives. Barbra said, "Elizabeth is still family. She is one of the people I call when I need help or when I am upset. I call her when I need someone to bounce things off of or I am having a faith crisis." Thus, though their committed partnership has ended, their relationship continues to offer blessing and care and assists Barbra in her journey toward a richer and fuller humanity. Through positive caregiving by family, friends, therapists, and the liturgical and theological resources of the religious community, Barbra has been able to grow and thrive rather than wither and diminish in the face of the loss of her partnership with Elizabeth.

Grieving Bill

Kenneth Ulrich was in considerable pain when I interviewed him in New York City in October of 1993. Kenneth was thirty-five years of age and was grieving the loss of a five-and-a-half-year relationship with his partner, Bill. This was a difficult challenge for Kenneth. He had let himself be intimate and trusting in a relationship that failed to provide fulfillment to him. The missing piece was domestic partnership. Kenneth and Bill never lived together, a situation Bill was quite comfortable with but Kenneth found a source of much unhappiness.

Ending this relationship put enormous stress on Kenneth's relationship to himself, to God, to his friends, and to his family. It also provided an occasion for growth and healing in and through these relationships.

Kenneth's parents had accepted his gay orientation, and they knew about Bill; but they didn't want to know much about him or be very involved in their relationship. "When Bill and I separated, I wasn't going to tell my parents because they didn't seem to want to be involved. I told my sisters, who were very supportive. My youngest sister is forthright. She gave my parents a hard time. She said, 'Don't be so hard on Kenneth; he is going through a difficult time.' This led later to a lot of talking with my parents. My father said that he was concerned about me. I appreciated their effort to reach out to get over their discomfort and to be concerned about me."

Kenneth was a part of a friendship network. A minister friend in New York was particularly helpful with Kenneth's grief. "I can call up and babble on. She listens. She also gives feedback. She helps me learn about myself in the process. She raises questions that are helpful to look at, like, for example, 'Have you thought about what a passionate person you are?' She was right. I am focused and intense in relationships. She brought it up to help me understand why my grief is so deep. The more passion in the relationship, the more grief. This led to greater self-awareness."

Kenneth's resolution of his grief is tied in with his capacity to accept himself as a gay male loved by God. It has not always been easy for him to bring his faith in God and his sexuality together. The gay/lesbian group at the Riverside Church in New York City, Maranatha, has helped with this. Being able to march in the Gay and Lesbian Pride March in New York City for seven or eight years and the March on Washington in April 1993 provided a great deal of healing and affirmation. "Being with a large number of gays and lesbians is supportive. It has an inspiring and lifting of spirits quality. If you don't know what it is like to be isolated and alone, you can't know what it means to be together."

For Kenneth, healing involves "reclaiming the Sunday School experience I received growing up in the Methodist Church: you are a child of God; your relationship is made feasible through Christ. It is the grace of God that connects you. I realized that I was not separated from God because I was gay, but I was created this way by God as part of the natural order. I came to understand that like anyone, I can be thinned or thickened in my relationship to God by sin. Realizing all this has made me more comfortable in my own skin. It is feeling comfortable in my sexuality and connected to God—all the pieces of the puzzle coming together. Like a garden, it goes through phases and seasons, but ongoing tending is necessary. There are times of resting and times of beauty."

At times in his grief, Kenneth has not felt connected to God. "I am a good person. Why are bad things happening to me? It felt like God had stopped believing in me. Suddenly there are weeds in the garden. The soil has betrayed me. Bulbs don't germinate, and you feel betrayed by the soil. Intimacy is like a vine—many branches going into other things. Friends, God, family, and acquaintances are part of the intimacy vine. If there is a withering of the vine at one point, it affects the whole. The withering of the vine because of Bill has affected my other relationships, including God. So, flourishing expands intimacy in other ways, including God. I have experienced this as I have experienced the grieving process: I tell myself that I'll never be romantic again so that I am never hurt again. But I know that if I cut off my intimacy here, it will affect intimacy in other areas as well."

Kenneth is in the process of recovering from grief and has a reliable network of care to assist with this process. Like Barbra, he needs someone to talk to regularly who helps him share his feelings and to see himself and his resources more clearly. He finds healing when his life as a gay man is validated by the larger church and culture. His family is learning to be supportive and would probably benefit from pastoral assistance along these lines. Kenneth's relationship to God is challenged but growing as he struggles with the meaning of his loss. He recognizes that his spiritual maturity and capacity for relational wholeness and self-fulfillment lie in integrating, rather than closing off defensively, his erotic desires for intimate male partnership. His capacity to accept and integrate the range of his own feelings was part of the healing process, as well as an internalized theological conviction that he was loved by God and that his relationship to God, self, and others was a unified whole that could be "thinned or thickened" by sin. He was working hard to find a "thickening" in his healing and was hopeful that in time this would occur.

Losing a Leg and a Mother

Not all loss experienced by lesbian and gay persons results from matters of sexual orientation. Yet how one deals with crises and loss related to sexual orientation may be greatly influenced by the way these other crises and losses are resolved. Doug Lawton is an example of this.

Doug and John are in their forties. They have been together over seventeen years. Doug is a regional representative for the Rehabilitation Services Administration. He and John joined Morningside Presbyterian Church in Atlanta, Georgia. Each has had leadership roles in the church. "But," Doug said, "we joined as a couple, we are known as a couple, and everyone considers us a couple. From the little old ladies all the way down, we are very much a couple. But what is the crucial part for me for church membership is a sense of family. That to me is the idea and definition of congregation. And that is something that we have had strongly at Morningside."

Doug and John have relied on the pastor under whom they joined the church for relational counsel. They found it quite helpful. Doug especially appreciated this minister because she was a friend of John's sister, who is also a Presbyterian minister, and was sensitive and skilled in working with people. "In order for someone to talk to me about my relationship, either with my spouse, my significant other person, whatever, or my relationships either with my natural family or my chosen family, that person must have a knowledge of relationships as well. I guess it's just a sense of knowing that the counselor has a full understanding. Part of it you can sense fairly early on, I think, whether someone—a therapist, or counselor, or pastor—has a sense of empowered relationships and that his or her definition of relationships is relevant not only to a heterosexual or married relationship, but to a broader scope."

Part of the broader scope of relationships is Doug's sense of an inclusive church in which the gifts and needs of all members are recognized and responded to. He is very angry that the church as a whole does not welcome and use the contributions that lesbian and gay ministers could make to its life. Yet he does not want the church to be only a gay church. "If I wanted a gay church, I would have gone to a gay church. Like single parents, of which we have a lot, empty nesters, older folks who have lost spouses (and most of those are women), gays have special needs as well as spiritual needs. It's sort of affirming to me to be in a place where other people have similar needs. As much as I need them to understand what my issues are, it's important for me to know what their issues are and for me to be supportive of them. This is part of what it means to be in a community. I don't like separatism. No matter what—race, sexual orientation, whatever—I despise separatism. My understanding of the gospel is inclusivity. The larger part of Jesus' ministry was to the marginal lives. So that means that we all have to understand each other. If I go to a gay church, I can't do that."

This sophisticated vision of inclusive care and relational justice is unquestionably grounded in two experiences of care that Doug himself received earlier in his life. The first was a highly sensational shark attack when he was eight years old, in 1958. While Doug was swimming, a shark severely bit through to the bone on his leg. He was losing large amounts of blood and was several miles from medical care. "When I was attacked, my father pulled me up onto the beach and my uncle ran up onto the road. He just literally flagged a car down by basically standing in the road. In it was a couple and their daughter who was five. The driver was an orderly, and his wife was a registered nurse. She ran down onto the beach, and he drove across the street and called the hospital. He told the hospital to prepare a surgery room and get the doctors in. This was four o'clock on a Sunday afternoon. He asked them to send an ambulance.

"The nurse came down to the beach, saw how much blood I was losing, and said, 'Get him in the car, we can't wait.' That was the major decision that saved my life. Nobody in my family had panicked, but they were quite unsure what to do until someone said, 'We can't wait!' So they piled me into my uncle's white Lincoln, and we drove off. We met the ambulance halfway. It turned and escorted me in. That was the first thing.

"The second thing was that there just happened to be an orthopedic surgeon and pediatrician across the street doing paperwork, so they were there waiting for me. It also happened that the only surgery room at the hospital was clear. They were preparing for elective surgery, so they could take me first. The guy wrote me later and said that he was more than happy to give up his surgery time. There's a whole series of things.

"That's the only reason I am here. It was not any choice of mine. It was serendipitous. I don't mention this a whole lot. It's just one of those things that has been there, but it was also sort of burdensome to have to repeat that. I had well-meaning Christians tell me that 'God had a plan for you.' I haven't heard that a lot lately, but early on it was painful. So I've spent a lot of my life thinking, 'Okay, what am I supposed to do? Or, have I done it?'"

One of the consequences of the providential care he received after the shark attack is that Doug does not feel that he has to plan out every detail, but that he can jump into things with some basic confidence that they will work out. Another is the sense of importance of creating a community of people where the specific needs of each are acknowledged and responded to in a timely manner.

The second major influence on Doug's commitment to inclusive congregational care is the way his church responded to his mother's death when he was fourteen. His family had been active in the Methodist Church throughout his growing up, and they had a lot of friends who had been ministers. But the main impact of the church on Doug was its capacity to be "family in time of need." He did not carry away "great religious tenets from the pulpit. What I got instead was the fact that when I and my family were in need, the church family came together. That's probably the most significant part." The church demonstrated its care by "making sure that we were eating—making sure that all sorts of things were being taken care of. Losing my leg was one of those phenomena where people felt compelled to send money. Dad always talked about that. He was a very independent Yankee and had never accepted charity. He never had to accept it. There was no way that he could turn back money that was given anonymously. It helped us learn the difference between charity and pity. It happened again with my mother. There are times when you have needs and people are there for you. One of the outcomes of my mother's death was that my Dad and I were alone together because my brother was at college already. We had the recognition that we really didn't know each other. My father did make the effort that following year to redevelop a relationship. We got to know each other."

Today, Doug's father and stepmother are "Charismatic Fundamentalist Christians. As we say, Big 'C' Christians. So they pray for us *every* day. I've never understood my father's dilemma because he loves me, and he told me point blank that if John is part of my life, then John is part of my entire family. And his actions have carried that out. My father and my stepmother have given us presents jointly. They write to us jointly. They send John birthday and Christmas cards. So they've acted out their acceptance as well. I just don't know how he gets through that conflict of religious tenets being told to him and his love for us. We also have the support of John's family. Our siblings on both sides of the family have been just phenomenal. They have been wonderful. We have had it very lucky. We have had the support of our natural families. And to have it on both sides is even more astounding."

Though Doug wondered about the connection between his positive family life and the support and care he received from the church during personal and family crisis and loss, it seemed clear to me that a reciprocal relationship existed. Doug was very sensitive to the importance of providing a church family for lesbian and gay persons who had been rejected by their biological families. He was supportive of a group of lesbian and gay persons who were advocating for the Presbyterian Church to ordain lesbian and gay persons. Doug has said to the church, "So you are telling me that you can minister to me as a disabled person. It's safe to talk about issues of access, and speak directly to me about that, and talk to me about how inaccessible our church is physically. Now, that's safe to talk about from the pulpit, but it's not safe to talk about the inaccessibility of the church to me as a homosexual, when I feel a hundred times more marginalized as a homosexual man in that church than as a disabled man."

Doug is politically aware, but he does not spend the majority of his effort in direct advocacy. Rather, he and John spend considerable time and personal energy in caring for persons with AIDS. This ministry of care is a source of care for them, as well as for others. The reciprocity of care received and care given could hardly be more apparent than it is for Doug and John. Doug says, "I am in the disability field. A lot of the disabilities from the AIDS infection are not new. There are many social issues tied up here in the United States to the disease because it started in the gay communities. Then it went into minority people, so that the disease and disability are marginal. We're talking about the very edges of the margins here. The people who have come forward to say, 'I'm going to care for you people,' are really phenomenal. I get strength from what I see others doing.

"People have told me that what John and I have done for a lot of folks, others think is phenomenal. We think that it just had to be done. I know that other people feel that as well, but to me the joy and power is that the people who are giving of themselves because they want to don't see themselves as being superhuman beings. But you are allowed to see others that way. And that kind of gives you the strength to go on. I get it from others.

"I always think, because I had close friends, as well as some of the survivor guilt, you know, 'Why them and not me?' I feel like I have a certain need to respond. When I see people who have not had AIDS helping those who have AIDS, it's just seems right. Their faith system says that this is what to do. Then I get a real charge out of that. I really do."

Doug went on to say that there is another aspect. "I haven't even thought about this before, but it goes back to the fact that to me it's a repayment of debt. We love because we are loved. I try to explain that to other people. John and I have been called the Lawton and Rogers Home for Wayward Children because we've always had people there. A roommate just left who has been there for two years. Rent free. He didn't even get on his feet. And we've had others. We had a close friend of ours who had actually never roomed with us, but when he finally got so sick that he couldn't live by himself, he came in. And he died. People say, 'You all are amazing!' And I respond, 'No, people took me in when I needed it. People took care of me and my family when we needed it.' That's just what you do!"

Through these rich experiences of giving and receiving care throughout his life, Doug has arrived at some core spiritual and theological convictions. "What I find in the gospel and in the teaching of Jesus is that when Jesus says 'God is love' that means that God is in the relationship. And I get it that God is in each of us. I think I believe that it's that oneness that we have with ourselves and nature and all that sort of thing. We are all connected. That's what I see as God. That's what I thought Jesus taught, that God is love. That means that I have to put up with you, and I have to respect you, and all those sorts of ideas. I have to care for you as well as care for others. Separation from God is letting all that other shit get in the way. Therefore, relationships, family, chosen family—that's where we function best. Obviously, John feels this way too."

To conclude, Doug and John disclose that care received in the face of acute loss generates the capacity to include a fuller array of human need and to discover and mediate the power of divine love in human community and family. Those who mediate this care, like the woman pastor who helped them, demonstrate a sensitivity and skill in relationship dynamics. Communities of faith must reach out in concrete acts of support and welcome. And all must trust the providential serendipity of God, who brings resources for our care when we are least capable of helping ourselves.

Confronting AIDS

Throughout this book and in this chapter we have touched on the massive way in which AIDS is plaguing the human community, especially gay men. I want to return to Giff Douglas's narrative in chapter 4. When I interviewed Giff, Dan, and Anthony in January of 1994, they had a strong network of care helping them with Giff's diagnosis of AIDS. Dan was Giff's primary caregiver, and Anthony, their ten-year-old son, participated in offering support and assistance with some of the medical treatments. Giff and Dan's mothers took part in his care, and there was a strong medical response from his doctors, nurses, and the entire Kaiser health plan in which he participated. Their friends, congregation, and pastor offered support and concrete acts of care such as housework, child care, food preparation, and occasional gifts of money. There was a comprehensive network of care available, and the faith Giff and Dan had in God was strong and sure. Giff felt that he was ready when his time came.

Giff died the following June. Dan provided a detailed account of Giff's last days and the care that he and Anthony received during Giff's last days and after his death. "During Giff's last weeks and following his death, I have truly experienced the real meaning of Christian compassion and care.

"Looking back, we now see that Giff extended his life in order for us to enjoy the Caribbean cruise with our moms and Anthony. Following the trip, Giff began to deteriorate both physically and mentally. Only a couple of weeks after the vacation, Giff expressed his desire to not fight anymore. He was very weak then, he had begun to experience blindness, and I believe that he knew that the quality of his life was never going to improve. He was ready to go.

"We had prepared for him to die at home, using the wonderful services of the Kaiser Hospice Program to provide us with home medical care, counseling, and emergency treatment. I had to call upon them many times to help Giff, but of course I needed more than the nurses and counselors could give.

"Friends from our churches, colleagues at both our workplaces, and family once again were there for Anthony and me. In addition to Giff's brother and mother flying out to be with us, we also had the help of our closest friends, James and Franklin.

"Schedules were developed for a host of people to assist us. Someone was always available for our every need—sitting with Giff, grocery shopping, baby-sitting, transportation, laundry, and so forth. Because of these marvelous people, I was able to continue to work and Anthony's schedule, including Little League, went uninterrupted. Even the Little League parents surrounded us with much love and support.

"Because of an infection that could not be controlled at home, Giff went into the hospital and died there on June 16, 1994. Even though I had prepared Anthony for his papa's death at home, I was relieved when Giff died in the hospital, surrounded by his mom, my mom, two of his pastors, and three other very close Christian friends. Anthony arrived shortly after Giff's death and did not hesitate to give Papa a hug and tell him goodbye.

"Giff's room was truly filled with spirit. There was a tremendous sense of relief for him and a calmness that I cannot explain. That 'peace that passes all understanding' was evident. With joined hands around Giff, we sang several of his favorite hymns, remembered wonderful stories, and praised God for the tremendous life that Giff brought to us.

"We found it very interesting that after we left his room, a doctor who was not familiar with the case remarked, 'It usually isn't this way.' She said so much. It is unusual for a gay man with AIDS to die surrounded by his mother and mother-in-law, his partner and their son, his pastors and his friends. It is unusual for Christians to be singing hymns, praying, and telling stories around this gay man who had just died of AIDS. It is unusual for there to be such calmness.

"Anthony and I miss Giff tremendously, but without a doubt we know that he is with us. We certainly feel his presence all the time, and both Anthony and I have grown more spirit-filled because of it.

"Throughout our trying to decide what to do with our lives after Giff's death, we always knew that Giff's spirit was helping us make good decisions and keeping us at peace. It was a big decision to sell the house that was filled with so many wonderful memories, but when the time was right we knew it. When I asked Anthony if he would miss the old place and be sorry to leave so many reminders of Papa, he responded, 'It doesn't matter where we live. We will take Papa with us.' And he was certainly right. Since we have been in our new house, we have felt Giff's presence, and we know that we are still a family."

Another example of the need for care in the face of AIDS was shared by Donaciano Martínez. Donaciano is a human rights activist with an international perspective; he is based in Denver, Colorado. He is a gentle, soft-spoken Latino in his late forties. Donaciano (whose name comes from *donación,* which means donation), is a leader in La Gente Unida, a Latino gay and lesbian advocacy group in Colorado.

Donaciano realized that he was depressed and withdrawing from life. He didn't want to go to work, and he did not want to be around children. On asking himself why he was acting this way, he realized he was in deep grief after the death of a friend of fifteen years. He sought counseling for his grief.

Donaciano's friend had been diagnosed three years earlier as HIV-positive. They were not lovers or partners but were both active in Latino movements and in gay and lesbian organizations. "When he became ill, we shifted gears from being friends to parent-child. I always called him 'Hito,' which in Spanish means 'my dear little son.' It is a very endearing term. Everywhere you go in the Southwest, you hear

Mexican parents say, 'Come here, my Hito' or 'Come here, my Hita.' He always told me that I reminded him so much of his mother. He was very close to his mother. She had died about ten years ago. In the last year his dad came back into the picture and was a good source of nurturance for him.

"The night before he died, I went in to check on him and give him his medication. And change his diaper. And give him his Teddy Bear. He became like a child. He needed a lot of that good stuff: a lot of hugging, a lot of affection, lots of caring. When he went blind as a result of the disease—cytomegalovirus retinitis, a typical blindness that comes with AIDS—he was devastated. He was a very avid reader. He always read books and magazines and newspapers. All of sudden he couldn't do that anymore. I was the person to whom he turned to read to him. He said it was gentle and soothing and healing for him for me to read to him.

"That night I went in to give him his medication and his Teddy Bear, and to say, 'It's time to go night-night,' like I always did. He would always say, 'OK, it's time to go night-night.' I would hug him, and kiss him, and cover him up. That night he turned his head to me and said, 'This is my last night to go night-night.' By that time his little head was so small because he had lost so much weight. He told me that I should be sure to come back early in the morning. I told him okay. I came early and found that his body functions were shutting down. I could tell he was going. Later that day he died.

"He died June 26, 1994, the day they were celebrating the twenty-fifth anniversary of the Stonewall riots. Some friends of mine were in New York for the parade, and when I told them he had died, they asked when. I told them, and they said, 'My God, that was the moment in the parade when they stopped the parade for thousands of people to have a moment of silence for all those in this country who had died of AIDS, or acts of violence against them as gays and lesbians, or committed suicide.'

"I felt this tremendous relief for about three weeks after he died. I felt relief that his suffering was over. At his funeral I read this beautiful thing he had written about his mother—what a wonderful thing it was growing up with her. He said that he was a Mama's boy, that she had treated him like a prince. When I got through reading it, I started talking in Spanish about the love and care between a parent and a child. And I began talking about how his suffering was now over. I said, 'You are now resting in peace. May you go with God, and may you go with your mother.' I felt I was turning him over to his mother. Everyone who was there who knew Spanish was just torn apart by what I was saying. Interestingly enough, those who did not understand Spanish knew what I was saying. They knew that I was saying something very caring and very loving. A friend of his father was there. He said to Hito's father that he had been against

117

lesbians and gays, but from the funeral he could see how much love there was and that it changed his attitude."

After several weeks, Donaciano's symptoms of grief and depression surfaced, and he found a Latina therapist. She was not lesbian, but she was comfortable with his gay orientation. He wanted a female therapist. However, for him to have confidence in her, it was important that she be skilled in working with grief and depression, that she understand his culture, keep confidences, and be supportive of his sexuality. Because she has met these criteria, Donaciano reported that she was helping him, though it was hard going. When asked for specifics about what she did that was helpful, he said, "She is more like a sounding board. She is not familiar with all the parties, so she helps me be more objective. She provides pointers, but doesn't give answers. She lets me work it out myself. She doesn't get into causes from childhood. It is a safe space. I know it is confidential. In searching around for a therapist, I was told by some lesbian feminists not to get a lesbian feminist therapist because they don't keep confidences. Some gay men told me that gay therapists don't either. She is Latina and understands my culture. She has helped me look at so much. She gets me to express *feelings*. It was important that she asked me how I felt about her not being a lesbian."

During the course of therapy, Donaciano discovered that he was grieving more than the loss of Hito. He was also grieving his mother's death, the death of many family members, and the loss of other gay friends through AIDS. It is not uncommon for distress in one arena to be the means of healing and spiritual advance in another. Putting these losses together has been difficult and yet has led to greater self-awareness and healing.

Through his therapy, Donaciano became more aware of the critical role that his mother had played in his life and is more grateful for that role. "When I came out at age fifteen, she was right there with me. She had always supported me. She was very poor. She was a waitress in a rough Mexican bar. When she divorced my father, the church and her family blamed her. She always grew up in poverty. Besides being poor, she was a woman, a Chicana, and later, a lesbian. From her I learned to think and ask questions. When I was a little boy, I saw the Russian Ballet, and I wanted to learn ballet. She saved her tips so I could. I finally stopped going to lessons because of social pressures from Latino boys and men. It wasn't something a boy was supposed to do. But I liked it very much."

Donaciano believed that he failed his mother in some ways. As he grew older, he became aware that she was probably lesbian. "When I came out at age fifteen, my mother, who didn't speak English well and who was a strong Catholic, was right there with me. However, many years later she was beginning to relate to women in the final years of her life. I had a hard time accepting that about her life. That was a time in my life when I was actively involved in gay liberation, back in the late sixties. I was involved in antiwar, antipoverty, antiracism, and pro-gay activities, but when it became known to me that my mother was relating to this particular Chicana lesbian, I pretended that they were just friends. I wouldn't acknowledge that it was any more than that. Time went on; as months went by, it became more obvious that they were having a very intimate, close relationship. When my mother died, this woman showed up at the funeral. She was at the back of the church. She was a real butch-type lesbian. She was what we call in our culture a 'pachuca,' which is a real rough, street-type person from the forties and fifties. I remember that she stood at the back of the church, and all the immediate family was at the front. Technically she should have been right at the front, because she was part of my mother's immediate family for her final years. But I really had a hard time with that. I really did. To this day, I could not bring this to the attention of my seven brothers and sisters. I know what their attitudes toward gays and lesbians are, and for them to hear a story about her being a lesbian in her final years would bring the heavens down and the world would come to a standstill!"

Donaciano is resolving his losses and accepts that he may never fully understand why he had so much difficulty affirming his mother's lesbianism. He is grateful for her life and has shared a great deal about her influence on him. He identified with her as an "outcast" and was using this position to seek justice for the downtrodden and the oppressed. Although he found institutional religion to be a huge impediment to lesbians and gays and to his Latino culture, he also was living the values of love, care, and justice that he learned from the church through his mother. "There was a period of guilt, or a feeling that I was wrong. I thought, 'Maybe they are right, maybe I shouldn't have this lifestyle.' Then I began to look at my mother and her being an outcast in the eyes of the church for being divorced. I knew that she wasn't a bad person. I knew that she lived her life in a very caring, very loving way—the way that Christians were supposed to live. Then, I thought that I am not a bad person. I am very loving. I am not hurting anybody. I am not lying. I am not stealing. I am not violating anything. I am not violating anybody. I got over the negative. I realized that I was going to be an outcast, but that didn't mean I was bad.

"Growing up Catholic, a lot of the official teachings are to love, and to care, and not to judge. That was the message I got—not to judge. A lot of those basic tenets hooked in me. I was also very impressed when I was involved in the civil rights struggles in the sixties that a lot of people involved were Catholic priests and nuns. A lot of them were real draws to me to be involved against the war, against poverty, and for civil rights. That played a role in my decision to be involved in protest movements in this country. I do have a lot of love, and I don't think it is okay to be judging people. Even though I had a lot of unresolved issues about the role of the church in relation to Mexican culture and to homosexuality, I also found some things in my religious background that make me want to be a community activist. I think if Jesus Christ were here today, he would be in the vanguard of some of those things that have been happening in the last thirty years. I live my life with compassion, especially for those suffering and oppressed. For the downtrodden I seek social justice. A lot of this springs from how I was brought up. I emphasize compassion and flexibility and an open mind. Love and care are very important."

Donaciano's narrative illustrates the degree to which grief is the price one pays for loving another from the heart and dedicating, or "donating," one's being to the welfare of the other. When there is love, there is pain at the absence of the other, as we see in his inability to relate to children after the death of Hito, "his dear little child." And when there is love, there is remorse for failing to be adequate in caring and understanding the needs of the beloved more fully, as in the case of his mother's lesbianism later in life. Yet, through the love and support of the community, therapy, friendship, and his own intellectual capacities and spiritual maturity, Donaciano is finding healing to transform his grief into greater personal strength. He is recommitted to the love that he has known and shared with his mother, Hito, and others, and extending it through care and justice more fully to the downtrodden and outcast. Through grief and loss, the character of love in his life has been revealed more clearly and affirmed more thoroughly. In spite of serious loss, the "dangerous opportunity" afforded him by the crisis of Hito's death has led to a spiritual advance rather than demise.

Common Features of Caregiving: HIV-Positive Individuals and Persons with AIDS

In addition to Giff, Dan, Anthony, and Donaciano, I interviewed many who were dealing with HIV and AIDS or who were helping others to do so. Without detailing their narratives, I would like to highlight some of the main positive features and sources of care reported by some or all of these persons. First, it was critical that caregivers were able to listen to honest feelings toward the disease, no matter how unpleasant or "unsaintly" those feelings appeared to be. Over and over, HIV-positive individuals and persons with AIDS said, "It is important that I am listened to and understood." The feelings could range from rage against God and the universe to self-blame for not being more fully aware of the dangers of sexual activity. They often included pain at abandonment by family members and insensitivity by others. Sometimes they were connected with the anguish of physical discomfort and the frustration of the unavailability of affordable and effective treatment. It was not uncommon for people to express fear at what would happen to their bodies as the disease progressed. Some were scared about dying and needed to have someone to be comfortable enough with them to discuss death and dying in realistic rather than euphemistic terms.

It is important for caregivers to be honest about their own feelings too. The pressures of supporting the dying are enormous, and the loss of friends is costly over time, as Donaciano helps us understand. Self-care and relational care are critical for the caregiver. I noticed in my interviews and observations of an AIDS support group how emotionally real those without the illness were. They expressed their love and concern openly, and they did not hide their pain. One leader of a group, on learning that a member with AIDS had taken a major turn for the worse, began to cry and said, "I hate this disease! I can't take it anymore. It is tearing me up. I didn't think it would go this fast, and I don't like seeing you this way. I love you and think it is so unfair that this is happening to you and to so many others." The group ministered to her too and later found the resources to call long-distance to an absent member in Puerto Rico and inquire about how that friend could send a box of Christmas presents and tree decorations! It was quite a moving experience of pain and compassion commingling for all of us to share.

The feelings expressed by HIV-positive individuals and persons with AIDS were not always negative. They included fond memories of good times and the warmth of family and friends. Gratitude for care was a central feeling. The depth and beauty of life sometimes took on new meaning. As one pastor graphically said, "The AIDS crisis has helped us see that life is precious and that we don't have time for the bullshit!" For many, there was a genuine resolve to "live with HIV and AIDS" and not to die until they had to. I heard several persons say something to this effect: "After I got over the initial shock and felt that I had nothing to live for, I realized that HIV or AIDS was a sentence to life rather that to death. I had to make my days count because I did not know when the end would come."

A second source of help were the AIDS healing services and other liturgical responses. When pastors included in the Prayer of the Church or the Pastoral Prayer concern and compassion for those who are HIV-positive and living with AIDS, a great gift was being given. It was spiritually comforting to hear sermons and attend classes in the church's educational program about faith in the face of unwarranted suffering. Of particular value liturgically and communally were the AIDS healing services offered by a number of congregations. As I indicated earlier in the chapter, these are times for the community to gather and recognize the acute needs of its members. These services allow individuals to be prayed over and to receive the comfort of the pastor and of the whole community in a particular, specialized way. At one of these services I attended during my research, an AIDS quilt was present with pictures of loved ones who had died of AIDS, along with mementos and brief writings about their lives. The compassion and solidarity evoked by this service and the AIDS quilt were unlike any I had experienced among people I had not previously known. There was a sense of a spiritual community among those present; they seemed to be linked with those who had gone before.

Third, it is important that there be ongoing pastoral presence throughout the disease, particularly at the end. In chapter 8 I will return to this point when I discuss Andy's death. Here it is important to say that his priest, Rev. E. Claiborne Jones of the Episcopal Church of the Epiphany, was in the room when Andy and his partner John, along with Andy's family members, knew that the end was imminent. This was extremely significant to Andy and John, and the reverend's leadership afterward in the memorial service allowed Andy's death in the privacy of the hospital to be connected to the larger life of the grieving and celebrating congregation. In this way, the courage and grace of Andy's dying became, through the presence of the pastoral leader, a resource for the blessing and communal solidarity of the congregation as a whole. Even though the congregation as a whole and some of Andy's family members at the time did not know that Andy had AIDS, their support in the time of loss played a significantly positive role for his partner John and their extended kinship network.[3]

Finally, caregiving must draw on the gifts of those who are HIV-positive or who are living with AIDS. These persons have much to teach others by way of confronting catastrophe, of relying on others, and of finding an exquisite grace for living. Cliff and Paul came to a class on human sexuality and shared how Cliff's AIDS had deepened their relationship with one another, with God, and with their church. The effect of this sharing was to assist the class to talk more deeply about life and death, the meaning of love, and the purposes of life. We sensed the power of God's grace in their love for one another and in Paul's commitment to care for Cliff. Paul said, "I believe with full conviction that God has brought Cliff and me together. A lot of transformation has taken place in me. I have to serve others now. I don't feel like my life is my own. There is more to me than my desires. I understand more of what Jesus is, what Christianity is. The only real purpose of life is being of service. In our love for each other and in our network of care is the way the living Christ works. They are 'heart family.' We are all pastoral caregivers to one another." Cliff said,

"With Paul our relationship is pure. I don't feel dirty anymore. Before, I did. Paul showed me that love was not just a fifteen-minute sex act. He showed me it was going to church, sitting down to dinner, talking, making the bed, arguing things out."

Cliff and Paul enriched us by sharing the spiritual strengths of their relationship. In turn, they reported that it was a gift to them for people to hear their stories and be affected positively by them: "Speaking our stories to groups is a way of caring. People hear our stories and engage us, and accept us and care for us. It means a lot to us." Since these words were spoken, Cliff has died. Though the pain of his death is keenly felt by Paul and those who knew and loved him, his spiritual legacy was rich in the lives of many whom he touched through his AIDS-driven ministry. Paul says, "Cliff has witnessed to me 'the way of the cross' in the way that he met his suffering with tremendous courage and spirit. The witness of Cliff's life and death is ongoing and continues to evolve and to deepen my understanding of the authentic Christian life—the life that Christ calls me to in the depth of my own heart. Through Cliff's life I have glimpsed the ongoing work of Christ's salvation. For me, Cliff's legacy is a blessing of inspiration; it is the challenge of the call to a life of grace."

Conclusion

There can be no romanticizing or idealizing the evils arising from loss in human life, especially when loss arises from undeserved suffering and unjust social oppression. Although all human beings, as a condition of finitude and sin, suffer losses, it is clear from these narratives that there are those among us who suffer disproportionately because of their social situation. Race, class, gender, and sexual orientation require a critical awareness of the relationship between justice and care in the healing process. In all cases, effective care was grounded in the memory and knowledge of a loving communal foundation and mediated by those who in some way stood against injustice in the larger social order. For care to be real, it had to be blended with love, justice, proper information, and timely skill. When these conditions were met, the crisis of loss eventuated in healing and spiritual gain. In most cases, a sense of God's undergirding grace emerged. In all cases, we saw a recommitment and enhanced ability to work toward a fuller humanity in terms of acceptance rather than condemnation, and participation rather than isolation and rejection. Egregious and pervasive losses have not defeated the capacity to hope and love, and to work toward the transformation of the conditions leading to unwarranted suffering. We turn now to an exploration of the fuller dimensions of comprehensive care that are suggested in the narratives that we have encountered so far.

6

AFFIRMATION, ADVOCACY, AND OPPOSITION

Dimensions of Comprehensive Communal Care

Pastoral theology is the academic discipline that constructs general features of caregiving on an analysis of what occurs in the specific practice of the ministry of care. In this chapter, I will seek to answer the question, What are the features of a comprehensive communal approach to the practice of care for gay and lesbian persons? I will link the insights derived from positive care for lesbian and gay persons to the care for straight persons as well. In the final two chapters, I will more systematically engage the relationship of positive care to theological construction. The specific question to be raised in those chapters is, How might the realization of fuller humanity through caregiving with lesbian and gay persons help us to see more clearly what it means for all humans to be in the image of God?

Many features of care were discussed in connection with the narratives presented earlier in the book. We also considered a preliminary framework by which to illuminate the manner in which attempts at assistance became positive acts of care. We identified care to include active welcome and normalized participation of lesbian and gay persons in the life of an accepting and reliable community. Care included strategic utilization of their "gifts and graces" for the benefit of the life of the community. Care involved structured or intentional organization in response to the specific educational, relational, and existential needs of lesbians and gays. Finally, care extended beyond private and relational considerations to public advocacy by individuals and communities seeking to ensure just participation in the larger social order.

Building on this preliminary framework, a fuller understanding of the dimensions of positive care can now be advanced. The criterion for developing a comprehensive understanding of care, it must be remembered, is the "witness" of those receiving care, coupled with an interpretive description of what is reported as positive. The framework that follows, therefore, is formed from the testimony of those I interviewed and does not purport to address the full range of care needed or received by all lesbian and gay persons. Neither does it reflect the full range of the secular literature on the care and therapy of lesbian and gay persons. Yet, based on conversation with lesbian and gay persons and a fairly wide reading in lesbian and gay literature, I do believe that this comprehensive framework is relevant beyond the experience of those I interviewed.

In the discussion that follows, it will be critical for the reader to understand that care is not a linear matter, based on a few techniques and practices. Care is an ecology of interacting features operating simultaneously at a variety of levels. If human beings, including lesbian and gay individuals, are ultimately a part of a relational web, then care must fundamentally be interpreted as a series of interactions that secure a livable place within the web that the recipient of the web is also spinning. Therefore, if care is to be effective—leading to healing and spiritual advances in relation to self, God, neighbor, and the social, natural, and communal orders—it must be considered as an engagement with the totality of another's life in the world. The discussion that follows seeks to identify and investigate that totality, as well as suggest some strategies for promoting its fulfillment.

A Normalizing Ethos

To be cared about, one must feel that he or she is normal and has a valued part to play in the world and in the social order. One does not have to hide the truth about oneself, but is eagerly encouraged to participate as an equal in the life of the whole. For lesbians and gays, care includes the creation of a social milieu where "we can walk down the street holding hands and not have to worry about getting beat up." A normalizing ethos is found in churches that preach and live, as Christina Troxell said in chapter 1, that "there is no condemnation in Christ." A community that normalizes lesbian and gay experience is a community in which strangers become familiar, where differences enrich rather than separate. They are inclusive communities that draw on the resources of each to the benefit of all.

To create a community of care that normalizes lesbian and gay orientation and behavior in all dimensions of its activities requires, first, that there be an active welcome. "The church must write in big letters on the bulletin board that gays and lesbians are welcome here." There must be no attempt to convert lesbian and gay persons to heterosexuality or to interpret their sexuality as inferior or flawed. A normalizing ethos insists on recognizing same-sex orientation as a healthy variant in human sexuality and organizes caregiving to help all sexual variants, including heterosexual variants, to remain healthy and fulfilling in their actual expression.

Second, to demonstrate care that normalizes lesbian and gay experience means to use the wisdom and gifts derived from that experience for the benefit of the whole community. It was of transforming significance for Bill Weaver and Doug Johnson to be asked to be on a panel on types of families in the congregation. Sharing their forty-year partnership not only educated members of the congregation, but it made them feel that they were a significant part of the community. It confirmed and extended their faith in the God they had trusted and believed in, and gave them a renewed sense of hope. The act of care by which their experience was used and thereby normalized functioned to heal remnants of earlier estrangement from the church. It empowered their capacity to be involved in other activities of their diocese to normalize lesbian and gay contributions to the church. (A fuller description of Bill and Doug is found in chapter 4.)

Another example of normalizing lesbian and gay experience is the use of their gifts for ministry to the sick and dying. The lesbian and gay community rightly takes great pride in the way it has mobilized itself to confront the AIDS epidemic. Not only have lesbian and gay persons found ways to educate themselves about safer sex; they are helping the culture as a whole develop safer sex practices. Not only have lesbian and gay persons had to face unwarranted disease and early death; they are helping the culture face its denial of death and to discover spiritual strengths and resources for fuller living in the face of early demise. When religious communities are able to draw on these resources, not only are they themselves enriched by the spiritual gifts of lesbian and gay persons; gay and lesbian persons themselves are cared about and made to feel welcome as a normal part of the life of the community. Cliff, a person with AIDS, remarked to a group after he and his partner Paul had told them what they had learned from the disease: "Speaking our stories to groups is a way of caring. People hear our stories and engage us, and accept us and care for us. It means a lot to us." (See chapter 5.)

Using the experience of lesbian and gay persons is a radical act of care because so much of that experience has been hidden due to the hostility from straight people and from the dominant heterosexist ethos. To care, therefore, is to make public that which has been hidden, to value and celebrate that which has been denigrated. It is to normalize what has improperly been regarded as abnormal and flawed.

Third, a normalizing ethos is created, allowing hidden and denigrated experience to become a valued dimension of the life of the community through liturgical recognition of issues pertaining to lesbian and gay persons. Liturgy probably plays the greatest role in conveying to members of a community its operative norms. It does so in a preconscious and kinesthetic manner, as well as through a combination of symbolic, mythological, and discursive sharing of information, perspectives, and values. Through singing, praying, reading Scripture, preaching, and participation in the sacraments, the norms of the tradition and Scripture are pervasively communicated. One person I interviewed told of how the hymns of his fundamentalist church sustained him in the face of antigay haranguing from the pulpit and in the educational program of his congregation: "I never listened very well, but I loved to sing hymns, and the hymns did not teach what they said from the pulpit! I found acceptance and hope in them."

Doug and Bill found great comfort knowing that their relationship was normalized liturgically. Their fortieth anniversary was celebrated in the Prayers of the People during the service following their anniversary. It meant a great deal to them that they were invited as a couple to present the bread and the wine to the Lord's Table during preparation for a congregational communion service. Connie found enormous comfort and support when she was asked as a laywoman to preach a sermon to the congregation on why Christians should oppose legislation in Colorado that, if enacted, would deprive lesbian and gay persons of their civil rights. Barbra and many others found consolation and renewed strength to face illness and grief through their participation in regular healing services in the congregation (chapter 5). Many people I interviewed shared how important it was that they could attend church with their partner and families and not have to hide their relationship. To be able to hold hands in the service if they chose and to be publicly identified as a normal part of the congregation were sources of significant care and affirmation.

Barry and Ken found wonderful joy in the sermon at their union service that linked Jesus' presence to the sensual intimacy shared by two people who physically touch each other in love (chapter 3). When preaching links lesbian and gay love to the highest forms of relationality affirmed by the Bible, the foundation is laid for overcoming rejection and self-hate. Lesbian and gay persons are instead able to regard themselves in terms of those great role models and mature spiritual presences in Scripture. Giff reported that through Bible study he became aware that he in fact had the kind of relationships that God wants for people in Christ. Consequently, he was able to feel that he was normal and valued rather than judged and condemned (chapter 4). David's unconscious identification with "baby Moses" served for him as the basis to move from self-hatred to a sense of radical acceptance by God. This spiritual apprehension of one of the most normative figures in Scripture worked to help him to believe that he was normal in God's eyes as a gay man and that he could link his sexuality to life rather than to death (chapter 2).

Finally, lesbian and gay experience is normalized by the ethos of a community when that community has a positive view of diversity and a capacity to handle conflict constructively. In the last chapter, Doug Lawton summarized the importance of a diverse and inclusive community as a source of positive care for lesbian and gay persons, as well as for all members of the church: "It's sort of affirming to me to be in a place where other people have similar needs. As much as I need them to understand what my issues are, it's important for me to know what their issues are and for me to be supportive of them. This is part of what it means to be in a community. I don't like separatism. No matter what—race, sexual orientation, whatever—I despise separatism. My understanding of the gospel is inclusivity. The larger part of Jesus' ministry was to the marginal lives. So, that means that we all have to understand each other. If I go to a gay church, I can't do that" (chapter 5).

The experience of Temple Emanuel in Denver, Colorado, illustrates the necessity of a congregation to have a capacity to engage conflicting values about lesbian and gay life, and to fashion an organized commitment actively to welcome lesbian and gay persons at all levels of congregational life (chapter 2). To be sure, there were sharp differences of opinion held by members of the community, but these were expressed openly in a process by which all could be heard and decisions made and implemented by the board as a whole. Conflicting opinion was not allowed to run rampantly and unaccountably throughout the congregation, but it was contained and worked through by those responsible for establishing the norms that would inform the larger ethos of the congregation.

During my interviews, a number of people told me how important their congregations were precisely because they had established an ethos that normalized and positively valued lesbian and gay persons as valuable contributors and participants. Sometimes, lesbian and gay persons found the Metropolitan Community Church as the most normalizing context for their personal and spiritual development. They did not have to justify their sexuality and spirituality in this setting. As in the case of Katie Bowen (chapters 3 and 4), it helped them heal the wounds from earlier church affiliations that did not normalize same-sex experience. More often, those I interviewed reported that they welcomed more diverse congregational settings so that they could feel that they were a part of a full range of human experience from which they could be enriched and to which they could contribute. In whatever context, however, it seemed clear that the most fundamental foundation of care was for religious communities to offer a reliable presence that actively welcomed lesbian and gay persons. These communities normalized same-sex orientation as a positive dimension of all aspects of their life together.

A Liberative Hermeneutic and Prophetic Action

If care is characterized by the normalization of the same-sex orientation of lesbian and gay persons, then care also requires opposition to viewpoints and practices that denigrate their sexuality and its fulfillment. Positive care assumes and is based on a liberative hermeneutic. A liberative hermeneutic assists all of us to recognize the full dimensions of heterosexist oppression and homophobic attitudes in our lives, and to join the process of becoming emancipated from them. For lesbians, a liberative hermeneutic assists in the emancipation from sexist norms, even as these are sometimes perpetrated by gay as well as straight men. For persons of color, a liberative hermeneutic assists in the emancipation from racist norms that are still perpetrated by the dominant white culture and even sometimes by other lesbian and gay persons. Prophetic action is the individual and collective strategic effort to change the social order to be more relationally just toward all its members.

One of the biggest sources of injury to lesbian and gay persons was the injustice perpetrated by the culture and the church. Based on ignorance, stereotyping, fear, and hatred, along with a selective use of the Bible and tradition, it has been possible for the culture and the church to oppress and persecute same-sex oriented persons. In some circles, physical violence against homosexuals is increasing and seen as a social good. Had Amendment 2 adopted by the voters in Colorado not been overturned by the U.S. Supreme Court, lesbian and gay persons would have been deprived of legal and judicial protection against discrimination. It would have been illegal for local bodies to legislate in their behalf. Lesbian and gay persons who are seeking to build a full and public relational life are deprived of ordination in most religious communities. Neither do they have legal protection for their committed relationships in civil society.

All of these deprivations are perpetrated by a heterosexual majority. Certainly, as a group, homosexual persons would not support the ideologies and practices that debase and marginalize them. If lesbian and gay persons, rather than heterosexuals, controlled the levers of ecclesiastical and civil power, the rules governing our lives would in fact be considerably different. (This fact no doubt contributes to homophobic panic about what will happen to society if lesbians and gays were to make the rules.) Although it is highly doubtful that there would be laws and policies against being heterosexual in orientation and practice, one could be sure that laws and policies against homosexual orientation and practice would quickly vanish.

Teresa Neal, whose interview is reported in chapter 4, said, "If more people were fighting to change the church, it would make me feel more cared about." Teresa links care to social change. Most persons that I interviewed reported that for them care is more than personal tolerance or interpersonal intimacy. It extends to concerted public efforts to address the core issues giving rise to the need for care in the first place. It has an enormously healing effect when persons in the church and society clearly say, "This treatment of gays and lesbians is wrong!" A number of people I interviewed were themselves activists in the public arena to change unjust policies and laws. This liberative and prophetic activity was healing for them. Those who joined their effort were important sources of care. For them, there can be no genuine care without genuine actions on behalf of justice.

Throughout the interview process, the Stonewall Revolution in Greenwich Village in New York City on June 28, 1969, was frequently mentioned as the beginning of the gay rights movement. There was an enormous sense of pride connected with this. Those who were willing to risk their safety by protesting the injustice of heterosexist and homophobic oppression empowered the capacity for thousands and thousands of lesbians and gays to think of themselves in positive rather than negative terms. The Stonewall Revolution symbolized for many whom I interviewed that "coming out of the closet" was a group phenomenon, and not just individual emancipation. In turn, Stonewall gave rise to a collective consciousness that induced courage and power in individuals. This collective consciousness assisted individuals to feel that they were not alone and inferior, but that they were a part of an emerging social movement that would never again be defined and disadvantaged by an unjust dominant society. Stonewall combines a liberative hermeneutic and prophetic action that stand against injustice and undergird efforts toward a more just and inclusive social order. Some of the ongoing sources of care derived from Stonewall are annual gay pride parades and the March on Washington in April of 1993. In the previous chapter, I discussed how much it was a source of care to Donaciano to realize that the moment of Hito's death coincided with thousands of people in the Gay Pride Parade in New York City pausing for a moment of silence in memory of those who had died from AIDS and who had suffered abuse from others because they were gay or lesbian. Others told me that their participation in these larger events helped them overcome isolation, fear, and a sense that they were flawed or marginalized. (See chapter 8 for a poignant description of the effect of the March on Washington on Michael and Paul.)

Lesbian and gay persons appreciated the care that was conveyed to them when straight persons involved themselves in gay pride parades. Not only were such events opportunities to educate straight people more fully about the diversity of persons and lifestyles within the lesbian and gay community, they also offered some protection and solidarity against the "picketing detractors" along the way. When church bulletins announced these events and when congregations organized delegations to participate within them, a liberative hermeneutic and prophetic action were expressed. This was experienced as care that normalized lesbian and gay sexuality and opposed that which denigrated it.

Michael and Bob, whom I interviewed in Atlanta, expanded a liberative hermeneutic and prophetic action to include ecological considerations. Bob grew up as a Lutheran but left the church after realizing that he could not find support for uniting his sexuality and spirituality in the Lutheran context. Bob was "incensed with Luther's acute anti-Semitism. I was crushed, hurt, and livid. That was the final nail in the coffin." Currently he finds spiritual nurture in "the Native American way of thinking. It is healthier in terms of linking personal wholeness with the spiritual wholeness of the earth. Some readings I have done in Native American literature suggest that shamans were gay, combining male and female characteristics in a unique way. No other culture puts a gay person in such a prominent place."

Michael grew up as a Methodist. He went through a painful divorce while he was in seminary preparing for ordination. The rejection that he felt as a divorcing gay man coming out of the closet was so acute that he became suicidal. "The pastor I talked to introduced a way of thinking that led me to seriously consider suicide. It was the opposite of care." As a result of this hurt, he has attended church only two times since coming out. After a lengthy spiritual and intellectual odyssey, Michael too has drawn on Native American spirituality for healing and for linking gay liberation to ecological responsibility.

Both Bob and Michael come from broken homes, and before they became a couple they were in abusive relationships with other people. In their relationship, however, they have found healing, honesty, and mutuality. Bob says, "Michael raises issues about religion in a way that makes you have to think. I like this. So many people in the churches just want to be told what to think and be led by the nose. That's not the way I am." Michael elaborates: "We have found in each other the kind of mutuality and empathy by which to talk about serious things. Our therapists told us that we were working out things so well through our relationship that we really didn't need individual therapy any longer. We were providing good listening and that kind of thing to each other."

Bob and Michael are both HIV-positive. They draw comfort and support from one another. They have a healthy lifestyle and are taking AZT. Their health has remained stable for several years. They have been active in the care of persons with AIDS, and they are part of a network that provides food and veterinarian service for the pets of persons with AIDS when the pet owners are too sick to care for their animals. They help animals find adoptive homes when necessary. "Because we love animals, we do this; we want to be caregivers."

Knowing that they are HIV-positive and enduring the loss of close friends through AIDS have led them to consider the ultimate context of their lives. They have come to the realization that their lives are part of a larger ecology and "that working in the yard leaves something behind after we go. When we bought the house, we wanted to make a home and see things grow. We have a greenhouse out in the back. It is hard for us to cut anything down because it is taking life. When we bought the house, people asked us why we took a thirty-year mortgage when we are HIV-positive. We asked, 'Why not? We need a place to live. We are planning on living. We don't see HIV as a death sentence.'"[1]

Michael and Bob think of themselves as "homemakers." They are creating a home that is not based on stereotypical gender roles and hierarchical patterns characteristic of heterosexual norms. Indeed, they recognize that these are the kinds of broken homes in which they were reared and that some of their closest relatives still try to maintain. Some of their siblings are living in abusive situations now, and because Bob and Michael are gay they are excluded from participation in the lives of their nieces and nephews. Michael states, "Our relationship is healthier than theirs, but it is regarded as sinful and negative. We haven't seen a heterosexual relationship yet that we would like to imitate!"

But even more than creating a relational home with each other, Bob and Michael are discovering and creating a home on the earth that includes both social justice and ecological partnership. Drawing on a variety of writings, they have recognized that this world is all that we have and that its proper care is a source of liberation, health, and healing from an oppressive "heteropatriarchal" and ecologically toxic culture. "Our commitment is to this life, to this earth. I am not eager to leave," says Michael. He expands these insights from the interview in a book titled *Beyond Our Ghettos: Gay Theology in Ecological Perspective*[2]:

> The demands of relational justice and responsibility in gay theology also imply the demand of *ecological* justice and responsibility: as gay men and lesbians, our deep existential understanding of exclusion and disvaluation, our liberational efforts, and our erotically empowered and loving relational embrace must be extended to all other oppressed persons (vs. sexism, racism, classism, etc.), to all persons generally (including, albeit difficult, loving those who oppress), and most certainly to all the earth as our equally valued and valuable copartner against all the forces of oppression, devaluation, exclusion,

and exploitation that are arrayed against us. We cannot champion—in our theology or in our lives—the liberation of ourselves alone.

Central to the idea of a liberative hermeneutic and prophetic action is
the conviction that life is a living web of interdependent entities requiring both diversity and harmony for survival and fulfillment. Patterns of
domination and subordination are relationally unjust and must be challenged. Exclusion and marginalization must be replaced by inclusion and
shared influence at the center of decisions about values and norms. Com-
petition and control must give way to cooperation and mutuality for justice to become relationally embodied through our human and natural
ecosystems. Bob and Michael are inspiring examples of two gay men who
have stepped out to bring these liberative perspectives into concrete
form. Their commitments to care for each other and their backyard mi-
crosphere are prophetic acts by which all of us might be guided to open
our windows to view expanded horizons of liberative and relationally just
care.

One way to expand the horizons of liberative and relationally just care
is to extend civil and ecclesiastical recognition of lesbian and gay unions.
Couples like Michael and Bob, Katie and Cynthia, Giff and Dan, Teresa
and Marcy, and Christina and her partner more than fulfill the qualities
of loving commitment, social responsibility, and religious vocation honored among Christian heterosexuals. Doug and Bill are wonderful contributors to their congregation and diocese. Yet it is not possible for them
to have the full legal and religious status afforded other couples in our culture and church. Because homosexual, or same-sex, marriage is not allowed by any state, these and the nearly 150,000 other couples like them
"lack many benefits the law confers upon their married counterparts."[3]
Lesbian and gay couples lack adoption rights, divorce court rights, and
hospital visitation rights. They lack access to hospital insurance, Social
Security, and green cards for immigrant partners. They cannot make
claims to their partner's assets, and they cannot bring suit against someone injuring their partner in an accident. There is no exemption from inheritance and gift taxes. They cannot collect money from a deceased partner's private pensions or receive money from workers' compensation and
Veteran Affairs.[4]

At the writing of this book, a major court case in Hawaii is challenging these injustices. In 1993 the case of *Baehr v. Lewin* argued that it
was discriminatory to allow marriage to be available only to heterosexual couples. The Hawaii Supreme Court supported this argument and
sent the case back to a lower court to show why it is in the compelling
interest of the state to bar same-sex marriage, whether couples comprising

the same-sex relationship are straight or gay. If Hawaii extends legal status to same-sex marriage, all the other states will likely be required either to reciprocate or to pass laws to ensure that marriage is restricted to heterosexual couples. (See page 98 for other legal dimensions of this case.)

These political and legal efforts to extend the rights of lesbians and gays to include the legal protection of their committed unions derive from a liberative ethic and embody prophetic action in the civil sphere. They can be seen as positive acts of care that link the political and the personal in transforming ways. Bishop Desmond Tutu, Anglican Archbishop of Capetown, South Africa, and winner of the Nobel Prize for Peace, has turned his attention to liberative and prophetic efforts in behalf of gay and lesbian unions and full participation in the church and social order. Tutu has been active in South Africa to ensure that the new constitution protects lesbians and gays from discrimination, and he has forcefully opposed the active campaign of President Robert Mugabe of Zimbabwe against the rights and welfare of lesbians and gays.[5] Tutu wrote a letter to Bishop Rosemarie Köhn, a gay-affirming bishop in the Norwegian Lutheran Church, offering "support for various groups who are campaigning for gays and lesbians to be treated on an equal basis with all baptized persons." Although lesbian and gay couples have the same rights as heterosexuals in Norwegian civil society, the Lutheran Church has not extended full acceptance to them. Tutu links discrimination against gays and lesbians to apartheid: "It is my prayer and hope that in the same way the Church in Norway stood by us in our struggle against oppression, so it will continue to champion the cause of justice on the part of those who are marginalized by society or discriminated against simply for being gay or lesbian." Bishop Köhn shares this liberative and prophetic agenda, against considerable opposition. She and others are mobilizing efforts to change attitudes and practices toward lesbian and gay persons in the church. She believes that "it is important that homosexuals are accepted as responsible, caring, loving people, and are not to be judged by their sexual orientation. . . . Their behavior should be supported by the church."

An Extended Network

A third characteristic of care is the presence of an extended formal and informal network. When I began my research, I expected that psychotherapy would be a mainstay of care for lesbians and gays. To be sure, it plays a significant role. However, therapy was episodic and circumstantial and only part of a fuller picture. One of the leading questions of the study was, Where have you found positive care as a person, and what effect has that had on your sexuality as well as other dimensions of your life, including your religious outlook? Part of the answer to the question of the source of care is from an extended network of persons, organizations, and other resources.

1. *The extended family, or kinship, network is a major source of care when it is able to genuinely work toward full affirmation of the sexual orientation of its gay or lesbian members.* The coming-out process is a huge challenge for gay or lesbian persons, and it is no less so for their families and loved ones. Families themselves need to be ministered to if they are going to be able to meet the challenge of caring for their lesbian and gay members. In my research, I found many examples of family strength and courage that became a resource for care and healing of its gay members. Sometimes a sibling or extended family member helped a parent to overcome his or her rejection of the homosexual child. On other occasions, parents educated other members of the family in order to reduce stigma and exclusion and to maintain family togetherness. In chapter 4, I provided several examples of how new forms of family were created by lesbian and gay persons or how existing family configurations were expanded to include new patterns of sexual commitments.

One of the more positive examples of family care was reported by an interviewee about his father's struggle to move from rejection to care. Raymond is now fifty-six years of age, and his father has been dead for about twenty-five years. From even earliest childhood Raymond was aware of his preference for his same gender, but not until puberty and high school did he begin to realize that this preference was also sexually oriented. Not even then fully aware that he was gay, admitting only to being different, this was enough to be construed as a sign from God that he should enter the monastery. Raymond continued, "I had no aspirations for the priesthood, but the cloistered life certainly was a place where I might hide my affliction. Over the years, my visits to my aunt's bar, a gay bar, and my associations with openly gay men and women brought some concern to my father. He approached me one evening with questions that I was not fully prepared to answer myself. 'How can this be?' 'Why did you choose this lifestyle?' 'What have we done wrong to make you this way?' 'Would you like some help to get better?' 'What would the priests at the monastery say about this change in you?' My father asked if we could go to the monastery and speak with my adviser. Although I was certain this would lead to excommunication, I agreed to take my father with me to see the priest.

"We met in the priest's office and began with cordial chitchat. Finally, my father could no longer tolerate my attempts at prolonging the inevitable discussion. So he took a few minutes and explained to the priest how over the past several years he saw me leave my Protestant upbringing and convert to Catholicism; he saw my hopes of entering the

135

monastic life and then, finally, sharing my life with these 'funny' people. He knew that surely the priest would tell me to stop these 'funny' things and I would get on with my life, either in the monastery or as a 'real' man.

"Neither my father nor I was prepared for the priest's very brief reply. I certainly was not prepared for my father's reaction to the advice. Simply the priest asked, 'Why be so concerned over this? It is his life, and perhaps he is not at fault. He was born this way. He cannot change. So, love him in spite of it. Just accept it.'

"My father paled and buried his face in his hands. We knew he was weeping—though only briefly, for real men did not cry in front of others. He raised his head and said softly to the priest, 'Thank you, Father. You've been a lot of help.' After that, my father thought that this last child of his eleven children was not the perfect child he always wanted. But, flaw or no flaw, my father was determined that ours would be the 'perfect' relationship. We became closer with each day, and as the years passed, he mentioned my 'flaw' only to point out to me the dangers that were outside waiting for me. He knew that there were people who just didn't like 'that kind of people,' and surely they would find pleasure in hurting me.

"Now I am aging, and I have a very serious illness, but I continue to live my life as my father would have advised. I do not curse the illness, but I accept it. And the fact that this serious illness that will one day take my life is not AIDS or another 'gay' disease is kind of a tribute to my father. Apparently, as my father advised, I was careful enough to avoid those people or situations that might hurt me. I don't have to shout out loud to the world that I am gay, nor will I hide in a closet. I accept my gayness. God only knows I've enjoyed it; there really were some great times that only a gay man from my age group could understand. But for me, the good old days are gone. I've done my best. I've been true to myself. Above all, I have been true to my father's image of me—a little different, but not so different that I was any harder to love, once you had accepted the difference."

Another example of family care was when John, a forty-year-old Latino gay man, discovered that he was HIV-positive. He became very depressed. He decided to end his life. He called a younger female niece on the telephone and told her that he was very depressed and saw no hope. He hung up the phone and took a kitchen knife upstairs to the bathroom to draw a bath and take his life. Before he could complete the act, his niece and sister rushed in and confronted him. They called the ambulance and police and convinced him that he needed help. John was taken to the hospital where he was later stabilized. He was able to find a purpose for living through the care he received from the medical team, his niece, and a priest who attended him in the hospital. Afterward he reflected: "I don't know how my niece knew to come. I did not tell her what I was going to do. But somehow she made a three-mile trip across town with her mother in time to save my life. I now see myself as having something to live for, and I want to be a role model to others. I have been painting again, and people at work say that I am much more positive in my treatment of them." John attributes these changes to the way members of his family responded to his crisis, to the ongoing influence of the priest, and to his participation in a support group for HIV-positive persons that the priest leads. Through these events, John feels that God has come back into his life in a spiritually vital way.

2. *Friends provide positive care and ongoing stimulation and sustenance for lesbian and gay persons.* Friendship is an informal nonkinship relationship that provides many resources to lesbian and gay persons. We have seen many cases in this study where friends were regarded as "true family" because the kinship network was not supportive or understanding. Friends are usually available and long-suffering, and they find a way to be honest without rejecting. As I indicated in chapter 4, in the gay community there is often a continuation of friendship after people are lovers or partners. Relationships are more fluid, and this fluidity is usually a source of care. Friends provide advice, material assistance, and often a shared view of the world. They are the basis for stability and perspective when families, lovers, and the larger structures of church and society are unable to provide a context of acceptance and understanding. In chapter 1, William Carroll's story was told. One of the significant sources of care for William was the friendship relationships he had developed over the years. He and I had become friends, so when his crisis of coming out emerged, he could count on my assistance both as a friend and former professor. He had several friends in his small town in which to confide his struggles. When it became time to relocate, he called on a long-standing friend in a large urban environment to help him find employment, housing, a church, and access to a larger network of lesbian and gay persons who could "help him learn to be gay."

Sometimes the presence and importance of friendship is overlooked. It may be necessary for caregivers specifically to ask about the nature of the friendship network in order to bring it to mind and make it operative. In some cases, it may be necessary to help persons build or repair friendships. But it is clear that healthy friendships are significant sources of care and need to be recognized and developed. For example, one person I interviewed said that he was especially glad for a special friend who helped him through the transition from a heterosexual marriage and family to a long-term committed relationship to his gay partner. Don said of this friend, "Because of him, I met Tom, so we call him our 'Fairy Godfather.' He was a real mentor about what I had gotten myself into. He had also been married and had two sons, so he helped with a lot of things I needed to know."

3. *Gay-friendly therapists, chaplains, and pastoral counselors provide focused assistance in crisis and expertise for resolving long-term difficulties.* By far, the majority of people I interviewed benefited from therapeutic assistance at one or more points in their lives. In many cases, pastors or chaplains referred them to therapists, and sometimes, though less often, pastoral counselors were those providing the therapeutic services.

When helpful, pastors and chaplains were reported as "good listeners," "understanding," and "accepting." These characteristics are central to effective pastoral care for any person, but they carry special weight for lesbian and gay persons because of the heavy burden of rejection and denigration that daily confronts them. Further, pastors and chaplains were effective caregivers when they provided gay-positive religious interpretations and had access to a viable lesbian or gay subculture. It was quite helpful for pastors to be able to refer to excellent therapists, point to useful literature, and help lesbians and gays identify organizations and other social contexts suitable to their needs.

Therapists were most helpful when they understood the dynamics of coming out and the complexities of relationships in the lesbian and gay context. Therapists were also required to be adept at helping with matters of death and dying, grief and loss. It was useful for therapists to have some basic family therapy training in order to help lesbian and gay persons to respond best to their families of origin as well as to the families they were creating. In all these cases, for therapists to be helpful they had to be gay friendly, if not lesbian or gay themselves, and fully accepting of same-sex orientation as a healthy variant of human sexuality. It did not appear to me that the orientation of the therapist was necessarily an issue in itself. For some I interviewed, it was essential that they work with an out-of-the-closet lesbian or gay therapist, at least at certain times and for certain concerns. For others, such as Donaciano in the previous chapter, it was more important that the therapist be from one's own culture and have expertise in the problem under consideration than that the therapist also be lesbian or gay.

The principal guideline emerging from my interviews is that it is critical to identify what one needs in a therapist before actually contracting for therapeutic help from a specific therapist. Exploring a range of issues such as age, gender, orientation, specific expertise, reputation, and overall approach is critical to assisting lesbian or gay persons—as well as all others—find the most appropriate therapy. Ideological and doctrinaire considerations may play an important part for some, but they should not override other considerations. It is a debatable matter whether one best comes out of the closet with an already out-of-the-closet therapist or with someone who withholds his or her own story in order to empower a person authentically to chart his or her own course. From my interviews, it has worked both ways, and in some cases straight therapists have played a critically important role in helping lesbians or gays come out. But for sure, among those I interviewed, no therapist was found to be helpful who covertly or overtly attempted to convert persons to another sexual orientation or to cure individuals of their lesbian or gay sexuality.

4. *Educational and support groups devoted to special concerns for lesbian and gay persons are essential for positive and effective care.* There is no doubt from my interviews that one of the single greatest resources for care is the utilization of a variety of organizations and groups that provide information, support, advocacy, and outlets for lesbian and gay concerns. The list could become quite long. Parents and Friends of Lesbians and Gays (PFLAG) is one of the best-known sources of support and education. Many religious denominations have gay and lesbian advocacy and support groups. There are numerous resources for support of HIV-positive persons and persons with AIDS. Some people drew on gay Alcoholics Anonymous groups, others on sexual addiction groups. Others found support in a "Gay Fathers" or "Gay Mothers" group. As Barbra reported in the previous chapter, "You can find a support group for anything you need [in the Bay Area]. You don't have to worry about finding other gay people to talk to who understand what you are going through." This is true in all the parts of the country where I interviewed.

One of the benefits of affiliating with these educational support groups is the literature and other informational resources they make available. Many persons found books to be invaluable. Gay and lesbian bookstores offer a variety of services as well as access to the best literature. Churches that include gay-affirming literature in their libraries go a long way toward welcoming and normalizing the experience of lesbian and gay persons in their midst. Many people expressed appreciation that pastors and chaplains put them in touch with gay-affirming literature and taught them that there is more than one way to approach homosexuality in the church.

5. *Social services targeted at the special needs of lesbian and gay persons provide care in critical situations.* One of the most significant achievements of the gay community is the way it has become visible and politically active in response to the AIDS epidemic. It has identified social neglect of this disease and mobilized public awareness and public funding for its prevention and cure. Many lesbian and gay persons are well placed in circles where important decisions are made affecting the welfare of lesbians and gays. As I indicated in chapter 4, Giff and Dan were able to fend off a legal challenge to their adoption of Anthony in part because the caseworkers were lesbian. Doug Lawton, a gay man, has an important administrative post in the Civil Rights office of the United States government. Many doctors and medical researchers are lesbian or gay.

The lesbian and gay community has become increasingly politically savvy and is exercising and extending the legal rights of lesbian and gay citizens.

It was a great source of care to Giff and Dan that their health maintenance organization did not discriminate against them as a gay couple or because Giff had AIDS. I interviewed several persons in Denver who drew on services from the Denver Nursing Project, a publicly funded program connected with the Colorado Health Sciences Center. This project was designed to respond to the needs of HIV-positive persons and persons with AIDS, and their families, with the expressed purpose of attending to spiritual needs along with the other dimensions of HIV and AIDS. It was through the Denver Nursing Project that Paul Furr and Cliff Strunk came into this study (chapter 5).

It was important to the care of lesbian and gay persons to have legal services available, in addition to medical services. Legal help was needed for matters of adoption, dissolution of relationships and sharing of property, durable power of attorney for medical decisions, and assistance in formulating documents pertaining to domestic partnerships. Several couples I interviewed were considering artificial insemination, for which medical, legal, and other social services were essential. All of these social services were found to be important resources for care and a normal part of the extended caregiving network that compensated for the rejecting and unavailable services elsewhere in our society. Pastoral caregivers who can guide persons to these sources of support and care will provide invaluable assistance in time of need.

6. *Finally, immersion in a lesbian and gay subculture is a source of care that assists lesbian and gay persons to receive nurture, survive heterosexual domination, and find a basis for both opposing and contributing to the mainstream culture.* Because the heterosexist norms in our culture are so pervasive and because they distort and deny the legitimacy and diversity of lesbian and gay experience, gay and lesbian persons are creating a unique and diverse subculture. Although it is currently not possible to characterize this subculture without stereotypical thinking and denying its multiple, and sometimes conflicting, expressions, it was apparent from my interviews that there are pockets of gay- or lesbian-defined influence that provide significant care for its members. In chapter 3, Don described the powerful role played by gay clubs in the lives of African-American gays. He described secret "codes" by which gay men could signal their affiliation and by which they could communicate within the alien heterosexual community. Gay or lesbian writers, pastors, realtors, therapists, teachers, lawyers, social workers, doctors, politicians, and the like all constitute an underground network that sustains and protects lesbian and gay persons in significant ways. In every community there are lesbian and gay gathering places: bookstores, churches, bars, restaurants, and theaters. There are activist organizations whose leader-

ship is lesbian and gay. Clinics and community service organizations focused on the needs of lesbian and gay persons provide more than special services. They provide a cultural context in which same-sex oriented persons are normal and their way of life is predominant rather than subordinant and under attack. These environments are critical for helping lesbian and gay persons to "learn what it means to be lesbian and gay" and for building solidarity, self-esteem, and a sense of hopeful well-being.

There is some debate among lesbian and gay persons about whether there is such a thing as a lesbian or gay culture alongside the heterosexual culture. There is also debate about who should enter and define it, if it exists. I am not able to discuss or adjudicate this debate, but it is clear from my interviews that lesbian and gay persons found it almost universally necessary to have solidarity with other lesbian and gay persons in settings where they could be fully themselves and relatively protected from intrusive heterosexual norms. It was pointed out on several occasions that if heterosexual persons wanted to provide care to lesbian and gay persons they could do so by staying away from those settings so that closeted lesbian and gay persons frequenting them would not be exposed or "outed." It was also important for heterosexual persons to enter, on invitation, settings where lesbian and gay lifestyles were dominant, to read lesbian and gay literature, and to affiliate with groups such as PFLAG. Such openness went a long way to convey friendship and acceptance. It is a profound expression of care to respect someone else's cultural experience by being willing to enter it as an appreciative learner.

For those readers who lack any firsthand experience with lesbian and gay culture, perhaps the safest place to begin is to attend a gay pride parade or to rent some videos in which lesbian and gay life is given appreciative attention. If your community has a congregation affiliated with the Metropolitan Community Church, attending worship and educational services would be an excellent way to enter a significant slice of the lesbian and gay world.

For lesbian and gay persons, there are significant opportunities to enter and expand their relationships to other gays and lesbians through the Internet. Children of lesbian or gay persons can share ideas and experiences through Kidsofgays. This is a safe, private, virtual meetingplace for children of gays, lesbians, bisexuals, and transgendered people of all ages. Subscribers contact the moderator before joining, and all messages are e-mailed continuously to private mailboxes.[6] Rachel Hallstein said that "initially COLAGE (Children of Lesbians and Gays Everywhere) was a means to eliminate the isolation I have felt as a child of a gay father. I now know that I'm not alone and have a place to tell my story, vent frustrations, or just establish ties with those who also come from alternative families. Now, I have a place where I can be politically active in areas that affect kids like myself, and I am volunteering time to co-lead a teen group, and so forth. Plus, I have found new friends! I don't think that the importance of an 'extended network' is unique to children of lesbian and gay parents. I think it's the absence of recognition by society on the whole that families like ours even exist, or the acceptance that those that do exist are positive and loving environments for children, that makes our need for a network or for those who are sympathetic to our situations so important."

Courageous Rabbinic and Pastoral Leadership

It has long been said that one of the greatest sources of pain and suffering in the world is when good people do nothing. I can also say on the basis of my study that one of the greatest sources of care is when ordinary pastors take strategic initiatives to welcome lesbians and gays and to assist the congregation in becoming a welcoming place. William Carroll and Christina Troxell in chapter 1 found pastoral acceptance and authoritative theological interpretation of their orientation in positive terms to be critical to their care. In chapter 2, I detailed how Rabbi Foster's courageous and innovative leadership helped the Temple board to become open to the potential of hiring a lesbian or gay rabbi. In chapter 3, we saw how their priest helped Ken and Barry link their holy union and sexuality to Christ's sacramental presence. A pastor-teacher assisted Don to affirm his sexuality and to hear God's acceptance in a new way (chapter 3). Allen was affirmed and led to effective pastoral counseling by his accepting and sensitive pastor (chapter 3). Teresa, Marcy, and Meredith, described in chapter 4, have found solace and care in their female pastor, who has set the tone for the congregation to be inclusive and welcoming. Dan, Giff, and Anthony's pastor has done the same, even though the congregation's lesbian- and gay-affirming stance has subsequently led to its expulsion from the American Baptist Churches of the West.[7] (See chapter 4.) Doug Lawton and John Rogers discovered essential pastoral-care resources from their pastor to help them resolve relational tensions. They grieved her loss when she moved to another congregation (chapter 5). Many people I interviewed extolled the sensitive and visionary leadership of E. Claiborne Jones at the Episcopal Church of the Epiphany in Atlanta, Georgia, for her role in assisting the congregation to become more welcoming and inclusive (chapters 5 and 8).

Space does not permit a full discussion of the qualities of effective pastoral leadership, but it seems to me that several characteristics stand out. Caring and courageous pastors are available to and genuinely appreciative of all members of their congregations, without getting trapped in the particular agendas or ideological stances of their members. Effective pastors have clearly defined viewpoints but are not strident or self-righteous. They demonstrate the capacity to deal with conflict comfortably and to design processes to handle differences of opinion constructively. Competent pastors do not avoid difficult issues on the one hand or allow them to polarize congregations on the other. They use their leadership to inspire congregations to new understandings and patterns of relating. They are homiletically effective, relationally skilled, lay involving, spiritually attuned, and liturgically sophisticated.

None of the religious leaders I heard about or interviewed were "single issue" people. They had a balanced ministry centered in education, preaching, worship, and outreach. Pastoral care served these ends rather than defining the purpose of ministry. That is, pastoral care of special needs was a part of the larger mission of the congregation and not the sole definition of ministry and mission. All gay-affirming pastors whom I heard about or with whom I talked in the interviews, including those affiliated with the Metropolitan Community Church, wanted to increase the diversity and pluralism of the congregation with respect to race, class, gender, sexual orientation, and age.

Part of the courage required of pastors was the courage to be present in the face of loss and suffering. Claiborne Jones was in the room when Andy died. This meant a great deal to Andy's partner, John, and to their families. It meant a great deal to the congregation, as far as I can tell from the feedback that I received (see chapters 5 and 8). One pastor I interviewed had been involved in hundreds of funerals of those dying from AIDS. Her capacity for care was highly regarded by the community, though it was quite costly to her in many respects. Offering healing services in the regular life of the congregation and publicly welcoming HIV-positive persons and persons with AIDS are examples of courageous care.

For lesbian and gay persons to be cared about in the context of religious congregations, it is necessary for them to identify credible pastors and rabbis who are taking risks to confront the heterosexism of their communities and the larger society. Because the pulpit and liturgy are the normalizing centers of the ethos of the religious community, it is important that pastors and rabbis convey the message that lesbians and gays are welcome, that they are valued, and that the religious tradition is wrong to say otherwise. One of the best examples of a courageous, gay-affirming welcome that I encountered in my research was at a worship service I attended in San Francisco. At City of Refuge United Church of Christ, a multicultural urban ministry led by African-American female ministers, I heard a sermon from a female lay minister that linked the book of Job to the doctrine of justification by faith. The minister said: "There were many who blamed Job for his diseases. They were wrong! There are many who would blame gays and lesbians for the bad things that happen to them. They are wrong! There are many who say that AIDS is God's plague upon homo-sexuals. They are wrong! It's not your fault that you got AIDS. It is a dis-ease. God loves you. God does not want you to be sick. God wants you to be whole. God accepts you as you are. You are justified by faith. You don't have to be straight to have God's love. You don't have to be HIV-negative or AIDS-free! God loves you as you are! You are God's child because Christ died for you! When people blame you for bad things, they are wrong! Don't believe what they tell you. Stand up to them like Job did!"[8]

Sometimes pastoral leadership puts the minister in conflict with pow-erful elements within the congregation, as well as with the religious hier-archy in which the congregation resides. Sometimes the religious hierar-chy comes into internal conflict on these matters, as in April 1996 when fifteen Methodist bishops issued a statement of conscience and broke the silence against the church's belief that homosexuality is not compatible with Christian teaching. Such conflict is never easy, and no one can de-cide for another how to position oneself in relation to controversial and costly issues. But courageous leaders, whether operating publicly or pri-vately, are persons who make a choice to act. They decide how and when to make their care known and their voices heard. Even when care is ex-ercised in small steps and hidden ways, it takes courage and it helps.

A Context of Ultimacy

To conclude, it seems that the most effective caregiving for lesbian and gay persons discloses and expands the features of care for all persons. When it is experienced as positive, caring helps the receiver to affirm his or her life as meaningfully connected to the ultimate context of reality. Through listening, liturgy, education, preaching, worship, and outreach, those seeking care are actively welcomed by the community of care in the totality of their lives, including the sexual and relational. The link be-tween their spiritual lives and their sexuality is strengthened, and both are attuned to God as their source and goal. They no longer have to face the impossible choice between God and their sexuality, but see each as necessary for the other to be vital. Relational justice replaces the injus-tice of exclusion, indifference, and denigration. Eros is understood in sacramental rather than secular terms. Individuals are turned from isola-tion to communion, from self-condemnation to self-affirmation, and from despair to hope through the ministry of care. They gain a world, a self, a community, and a God worth having. In short, they are becoming fully human in the image of God. In the chapters ahead, we will explore in some detail how positive care with lesbian and gay persons, mediated in a context of ultimacy, helps us more clearly to discern how all persons might embody a fuller humanity in the image of God.

7

CONSTRUCTING THE
IMAGO DEI

The narratives of care that we have considered indicate that lesbian and gay persons participate in richly textured relational networks. We have encountered persons moving from denial and shame about their basic humanity to self-acceptance and intimacy. We have seen how the intensity of erotic love in relationships of mutual sharing and commitment have healed deep wounds and opened hearts in gratitude to God for such a wonderful gift of life. Through journeys of compassion and solidarity in the face of grief and loss, we have seen the power of hope and pride turn persons from isolation to community. Prophetic confrontation has emerged from solidarity with persons with AIDS and in the development of subcultures of gay arts, literature, dress, and sexual mores.

In advocating for lesbian and gay rights, a sense of God's liberating power has crept into the consciousness of many lesbian and gay persons. Reconciliation has replaced estrangement with God. A sense of God's gracious participation in life has emerged through involvement in novel forms of partnerships and families that in turn have contributed to fuller personal experiences and to richer communities. Spiritual strengths have emerged in lesbian and gay persons as they have transmuted their suffering into the capacity to survive, gain perspective, and share their vision of a transformed humanity with others. It is clear from an encounter with these stories of care that a rich and full humanity is present among lesbian and gay persons and those individuals and social structures that nurture them.

When I put this positive experience with lesbian and gay persons against predominantly negative religious interpretations in the church and culture, a profound incoherence became apparent. How could people who experienced their gay sexuality as inherently empowering and spiritually enlivening be regarded by others as so evil and unnatural? It became clear to me that the prohibitions in some of the biblical passages often cited as condemnatory of lesbian and gay persons were addressed to concerns other than the personally fulfilling and constructive quality of life experienced by most of those I interviewed. Indeed, the gentle beauty, transformed suffering, and vital faith in God professed by many of these lesbian and gay persons seemed to resonate with the highest religious calling. Rather than being dissolute, selfish, and evil people, I discovered many persons whose lives were most fully worthy of emulation and respect.

Thus a challenge emerged to explore how this quality of full humanity could be interpreted theologically. The core theological question is, If caregiving can contribute to such positive outcomes for those receiving as well as giving it, how is it that the tradition is so negative about qualities in lesbian and gay persons that it affirms in heterosexuals? Why is the humanity of lesbian and gay persons reduced to their sexuality in a way that is not the case for heterosexuals? Is there not a more positive way of regarding the lives of these persons, which certainly seem to be God-inspired and God-directed? Is there anything in the Christian theological tradition that might help us rethink the status of lesbian and gay persons' lives when these lives express such exemplary qualities of virtue, compassion, and relationality?

As I lived with these questions, I began to realize that to be fully human in the concrete relational fabric of life is to fulfill the destiny of humans created in the image of God. According to the doctrine of creation, human beings are created in the image of God for fellowship with God and neighbor, and for stewardship of the natural world of which we are an integral part. So, if we are reconciled to God, sharing life with our neighbor in responsible and loving partnerships, and contributing to a sustainable environment beyond our own immediate interests, then we are living as the Christian tradition teaches that God wants us to live. When this quality of life occurs, the image of God is reflected, and God is present in a particularly gracious manner. Could it be, I wondered, that what has been disclosed in the outcomes of caregiving among lesbians and gays provides a window by which we can better understand what it means for all humans to be created in the image of God and to reflect that image in our sexually mediated relationships?

I returned to the Christian tradition, then, with two clear and compelling questions: Are there legitimate grounds for understanding the Christian concept of *imago Dei* (image of God) as relating positively to the full humanity experienced by lesbian and gay persons? And, can the experience of caregiving with lesbians and gay persons correct negative theological judgments about lesbian and gay life, and provide fuller illumination of what Christians affirm about being fully human beings created in the image of God?

Constructing Theology

Before proceeding to consideration of these questions, two key issues must be raised. First, why is the concept of the *imago Dei* selected, from among many possibilities, as the central construct for theological discussion of lesbian and gay experience? Second, what do I mean by theology and theological interpretation, and how am I going about them?

In Christian theological reflection, knowledge of God and knowledge of humanity are correlative. Knowledge of God discloses what it means to be authentically human. Knowledge of human beings, as disclosed through a variety of interpretive lenses, is foundational for saying something significant about the nature and activity of God. The doctrinal symbol of the *imago Dei* is the major term used to designate this correlation. The concept *imago Dei* links theological anthropology to the doctrine of God and is the basis for delineating what is authentic human behavior and the moral codes by which to guide personal and social behaviors. The concept *imago Dei* is also one of the clearest symbols used in Christianity to convey Christian teaching about what it means to be fully human. It is both a statement about humanity's high status before God and a description of the positive outcome of human living.[1] To embody the *imago Dei* is to reflect God's intention for humanity; it is to be whole, or in the process of becoming whole, rather than to be fundamentally flawed.

My analysis of the narratives of care, however, demonstrates that lesbian and gay persons must overcome religiously inspired internalized cultural messages which say that they are inherently flawed and less than human. A great deal of Christian teaching has judged them according to their sexual orientation, and their sexual orientation alone, as individuals who distort what it means to be human as God intended in creation and redemption. In this view, they are persons in whom the *imago Dei* is not reflected, and who are under divine judgment accordingly. To be lesbian or gay is to be flawed at the core of their humanity, with only two ways of being restored to the image of God: conversion to heterosexuality or abstinence (expressed in denial, sublimation, or celibacy).

Thus one key theological issue is whether lesbian and gay orientation is in fact inherently flawed and whether *imago Dei* requires heterosexual embodiment for persons to be capable of full humanity as intended by God. If the *imago Dei* is equated with heterosexual orientation and its associated gender hierarchy and procreational activities, then, by definition, lesbian and gay persons are a particular class of sinful or inferior human beings who inherently do not reflect the *imago Dei.*

But the narratives of care we have explored do not disclose evil human beings. They disclose a variety of richly endowed persons who reflect spiritual depth and moral sensitivity. If the *imago Dei* reflects God's being as loving, how do we assess the capacity for love, care of neighbor and earth, and commitment to God and human justice on the part of lesbian and gay persons? Does their orientation discount or render invalid these virtuous achievements that arise precisely from their capacity to overcome their estrangement from their embodiment as lesbian and gay persons?

The theological argument that follows will claim that the embodied sexual orientation of lesbian and gay persons, like that of heterosexuals, equips them with the inherent capacity to become fully human in the *imago Dei,* and that it is a distortion of the authenticity of their lives and of God's intentions for humanity when they are judged as sinful or flawed simply because of their sexual orientation. To care for lesbian and gay persons, then, seems to lead to a revision of the doctrine of the *imago Dei* so that it validates their embodied sexuality and spiritual achievements as correlative with the nature and purposes of God.

In addition to clarifying why the doctrine of the *imago Dei* is central to developing a theological foundation for positive care with lesbian and gay persons, it is necessary also to state how I view the theological task, including what I regard as authoritative in religious interpretation. There is no simple or unchallenged position on questions of theological method and religious authority. It is most unfortunate that frequently matters of theological method and authority are not explicated from the beginning on matters relating to human sexuality, and perhaps most especially on issues of sexual orientation.

I stand in the line of Protestant thinking that understands theological interpretation to be a constructive and creative activity, arising out of ultimate questions facing individuals and communities in concrete historical periods. By constructive, I mean that we fashion new understandings based on the interplay of resources from the past and insights from the present. These new understandings then become the basis for contemporary thought and action, nurturing selves and communities as they seek to be faithful in fulfilling their call to be Christian servants in their local settings.

Christian theology understood this way is a precarious and vulnerable activity, filled with ambiguities and tensions. Interpretations provided by one theologian or by theologians representing particular communities may not be compelling. In fact, they may be offensive and wrong to theologians working in other particular communities. All paths or theological understandings do not lead to the same place. They are not all compatible. They have different personal and social consequences. Decisions are required; the way persons live their Christian discipleship is embodied in the theological choices made by individuals and communities.

The approach that I am following takes past formulations and self-understandings very seriously. Indeed, there can be no coherent or meaningful theological discourse without engaging the tradition in which questions of ultimacy are being currently raised. But it does not take past understandings as prescriptive for either the present or the future. To accept past formulations as prescriptive authorities for today is to misunderstand their emergence as itself a humanly creative and constructive task in response to the challenges of the environment in which they arose. It also ascribes a priority to the past and the experiences of others over contemporary resources and thereby minimizes our call to affirm fully our own experience and to take responsibility for it. Further, it misunderstands the creative nature of tradition, which is living and developing precisely through the kind of engagement I am affirming.[2] Overreliance on the past limits our experience of God, self, world, and neighbor by confining our range of experience to a restricted knowledge base. And finally, it overlooks or diminishes the necessity of making judgments among fluid and contradictory prescriptions from our past. Even if one says that the authority of our theological interpretations arises from a repristinated past, there remains the difficult human constructive task of determining what from the past will be secured and what will be released. For example, we cannot affirm democracy in the modern world without opposing some of the Pauline injunctions to "obey the Emperor," and we cannot work against slavery and racism without deconstructing some of the central tenets of our biblical and historical prescriptions.

The interpretive convictions I bring to the deliberations in this book, therefore, affirm the need to respect and be informed by the past, but to do so from the perspective and requirements of the present. I believe that this is essentially what our forebears did in constructing the traditions that we inherit, and that it is the most morally accountable way of letting our histories be redemptive even while we acknowledge that they have been destructive in too many ways.

To return to the concept of *imago Dei* in the light of the question of its relevance for lesbian and gay experience, I want to provide a detailed examination of the dominant theological argument for judging homosexuality as "incompatible with Christian teaching." Then I will explore how the experience of lesbian and gay persons in the context of care may help us challenge the dominant position and provide the basis for rethinking the doctrine of the *imago Dei* in relation to lesbian and gay experience.

A subtheme of this discussion will be the way in which the doctrine of the image of God has been related to the experience of women and men. I find a general parallel in the argument between the status of women and lesbian and gay persons and the *imago Dei*. The history of the development of the doctrine of the *imago Dei* moves from the exclusion of women, or from a hierarchical ordering of the relationship between men and women, to inclusion and egalitarian status. I will be looking for ways in which this move might be parallel for lesbians and gays, and the foundations in the tradition that now make it possible to move beyond earlier forms of exclusion, subordination, and condemnation of these persons.

Because all Christian theology is human construction, the task of the remainder of this chapter is to examine how heterosexist domination of homosexuals has been constructed by humans and not necessarily given by God. This chapter will identify diverse Christian opinion about what it means to be human in the image of God. The final chapter will explore how contemporary caregiving of lesbian and gay persons, when connected to other resources in the Christian tradition, enables us to construct a view of the image of God that affirms same-sex orientation and behavior.

Imago Dei
and Heterosexuality

Paul A. Mickey, a Methodist minister and a former faculty member at Duke Divinity School in Durham, North Carolina, has written a book that appears to represent the current prevailing position of American Protestantism toward lesbian and gay persons. Under the title *Of Sacred Worth,* Mickey develops the argument that "heterosexuality is the paradigm for the family of God." Mickey begins with two questions pertinent to this discussion: "Does the Bible in fact give guidance on homosexuality? Does God create men and women only to be straight?"[3] He states at the outset that biblical passages do not constitute the sole basis for answering this question; tradition and social sciences play a role as well. However, as his viewpoint unfolds, it becomes evident that his normative position is clearly determined by his interpretation of the Bible, which he believes reveals the authoritative intentions of God. We will return to the question of his theological method below.

Mickey argues that according to Genesis 1 and 2, humans are the "highest order of creation," created to have dominion and stewardship over creation. This means that we are to be loving, not exploitive. We must express our power, including our sexuality, in responsible ways. Mickey affirms that humans are "similar to God, being more complex and creative than all other creatures. We have great freedom in and high expectations for enjoying and using wisely God's gift of life." God-like responsibility includes receiving, enjoying, and managing our sexuality. Mickey believes that our sexuality is created by God, and that God's incarnation in Jesus Christ "calls us to wholeness and unity of body and spirit . . . away from the alienation or rejection of sexuality and toward being a Christian." Sexuality is more than acting on our desires, but it "implies a relationship. God is glorified as we come to experience our sexuality in relation to others and to God." Further, God is sexual, in Mickey's view, for "God participates in creation" and is the "author and finisher of our faith and sexuality."[4]

Mickey goes on to say that "we are called to a multidimensional expression of love and our sexuality." He ties this to 1 Corinthians 13 and argues that there is a hierarchical relationship between the "dimensions of love: sexual desire (*epithymia*), *eros*, mutuality (*philia*), and *agape*." All of these comprise love and are necessary dimensions "of our creation as sexual beings," but agape is the highest: "The high call of *agape* love is to transform *epithymia* into sexual wholeness, as opposed to alienation and abuse. Therefore God is actively transforming all four dimensions of human love and sexuality toward salvation and *agape* through Christ in our lives."[5]

At this point in the discussion, Mickey links humans created as sexual beings, comprised of the interconnection of four dimensions of love, to the image of God: "As human beings we are sexual beings and created in God's image. God, in some respects, includes *eros* love in his love for us. If God is love, and not all love is *agape* love, then God also participates in love that is other than *agape* love, namely *eros* and *philia,* and an aspect of *epithymia*." He recognizes that to be in the image of God is not limited to the possession of sexuality, but also to responsibility for how we live the totality of our lives. He argues against "the free, careless, abusive, and exploitive expression of sexuality." Rather, the norm is "where sex between human beings is used to express warmth, affection, nurture, and tenderness designed to help the other achieve self-esteem and self-respect (*philia* love)."[6]

Up to this point, Mickey does not say anything about gender or orientation in his argument. Though he would disagree, so far, it appears on the basis of this line of thought that gay and straight persons (and bisexuals) could reflect the image of God in their sexuality. That is, inasmuch as their sexuality, like God's, is made up of the four dimensions of love and is not used exploitatively, it mirrors what it means to be in the image of God. Further, when any person's sexuality is characterized by responsible "warmth, affection, nurture, and tenderness designed to help the other achieve self-esteem and self-respect (*philia* love)," it may be considered as fulfilling God's intentions for sexuality. The capacity to let all the dimensions of love have full sway in a life ordered by the characteristics of relationship delineated in 1 Corinthians 13 is available to all, apart from gender or orientation. Sexuality is a means of responsible fellowship and partnership, which reflects God's intention as the Creator and Incarnate Lord. Libidinal dimensions of sexuality are included as part of the image of God and are not in themselves denigrated or excluded.

God's will is that humans not be alienated from or discount our sexual embodiment, but see it as part of the goodness of our creation in the *imago Dei*. On all these counts, gender or sexual orientation would not seem to be an issue, because these characteristics, reflecting God's intentions, are possible in principle for all persons.

However, in the remainder of the book, Mickey proceeds to build his argument that heterosexuality alone is the paradigm for the Bible's understanding of relationality, including what it means to be created in the image of God. For him, the characteristics of sexuality and responsible relationship presented above are, by God's intention, limited to the committed, heterosexual marriage. We may discern four bases for his argument.

First, he argues that intimacy is the key purpose of sexuality, but homosexuals are not capable of the intimacy intended by God for human beings. His argument here is not as clear as at other points, for on the one hand he defines intimacy in very general terms that seem possible for all human beings, while on the other hand he identifies it with procreation, which is only possible for heterosexuals. In his more inclusive vein, Mickey states that intimacy is "more than overt sexual behavior," but "has its focus on the quality of one's relationship with body, feelings, sense of self, and interpersonal relationships, including those with God, the church, Jesus, and the Holy Spirit." For Mickey, the key function of sex is neither what he calls "recreational (relational) sex" nor procreation. Instead, the key function of sexuality is "to move us toward higher levels of intimacy with one another and with God." This higher level is the "goal of the Christian life" and requires that we "place our sexuality in the larger context of mutuality, intimacy (spiritual, emotional, and sexual) that draws us toward greater wholeness and does not relegate sexual behavior to strictly physical acts."[7]

Though it is not Mickey's intention, it could be implied from his discussion that the norms of mutuality and intimacy take precedence over the gender or orientation of the partners, because procreation and recreation, by Mickey's account, do not in themselves serve the highest purposes of sexual intimacy. Accordingly, it would appear that both homosexual and heterosexual persons would be capable of the highest forms of intimacy, because these by definition are tied to embodied life, but not necessarily to the particularities of gender, sexual orientation, or procreative outcomes.

Yet, in spite of these "inclusive glimpses," Mickey's main argument privileges heterosexuality. He contends that because one of the purposes of sexually mediated intimacy is openness to procreation, homosexuals are incapable of fulfilling God's intentions here, but use sex only recreationally. Even heterosexuals who limit their sexual activity to recreational or intimacy needs and are not open to procreational sex "engage in the same kind of sin" as do homosexuals whose "sexual enjoyment preferences" are out of the sexual revolution that emphasizes "fun, feeling good, and feeling close to someone."[8]

At best, there is ambiguity in Mickey's assessment of the nature of intimacy and its relation to the purpose of sexuality. At worst, there is a stereotypical distortion of the actual nature of sexual experience among lesbian and gay persons, and incoherence and contradiction in his theological argument. His normative position, with all its ambiguity, is probably most evident in his interpretation of Paul: Intimacy is so important that "it moves beyond one's status as male, female, married, unmarried, single, or single again," yet it "does not deny the sex act nor does it erase one's awareness of the sexuality of being male or female." Both are integrated "into a higher order of relationship and sensitivity."[9] Intimacy, then, is based on a heterosexual norm, which it both affirms and somehow transcends. Homosexuals are excluded from this norm, even though by other definitions they may fulfill or at least approximate it in a manner similar to that of heterosexuals.

The second basis for Mickey's negative assessment of homosexuality is his view of what it means to be created by God as gendered sexual beings. For Mickey, according to Genesis 1–3, God created human beings as heterosexuals for heterosexual sexuality.[10] Humans are created by God as male and female, and in creation God established males and females as spiritual and social equals.[11] Mickey realizes that a sexist patriarchy has emerged that negates this equality and that Christians are morally obligated to work toward overcoming it. For Mickey, this equality is most fully disclosed in the New Testament, especially in the relationship that Jesus established with women as revealed in the Gospels.[12] "In Christ we are equals and need to begin to exercise the freedom we have in the gospel to become peers with one another as male and female."[13]

Mickey asserts that it is not possible to consider that God created two types of sexual orientation. Homosexuals are really heterosexuals who engage in homosexual "longings, fantasies, and acts."[14] Thus, in this respect both homosexuals and heterosexuals are created in the image of God, as heterosexuals; but only those who live out a heterosexual intimacy (in all its complicated dimensions as noted above) are living as intended by God.[15] Homosexuals who choose their orientation or who may be genetically predisposed to it are living against their nature and are at variance with God's created intention.[16] Whether their onset is by choice, learning, genetic predisposition, or trauma, homosexual thoughts and feelings are recognized as "symptoms of sin," and, as such, they are changeable.[17]

Thus, for Mickey, although gay and straight persons are in the image of God by virtue of their real or potential underlying heterosexuality, they deviate from living in God's image when they do not embody and transcend heterosexual intimacy as prescribed by his reading of Genesis and St. Paul. In short, "the companionship, mutuality, and camaraderie that God proposes for human beings cannot be supplied by any means other than the man-woman or male-female relation."[18]

The third and fourth bases for Mickey's proheterosexual position are what he takes to be the heterosexual paradigm assumed by the Bible and specific biblical passages prohibiting or condemning homosexual activities. I will be briefer on these, because these considerations are better known and are not as relevant for considering the question of the *imago Dei* as are Mickey's discussions so far. Reviewing biblical presentations of the Adam and Eve story, family life, friendship, and the like, Mickey concludes that the biblical "metaphors used to draw attention to the nurturing power of God and the Holy Spirit within the life of the church employ heterosexual language." He documents rather clearly that "wherever sexual intimacy is discussed or analogies or metaphors are employed the paradigms and safeguards assume heterosexuality as normative" in the biblical materials.[19]

Finally, Mickey discusses what he terms the "traditional" and "revisionist" interpretations of the several passages in the Hebrew Bible and New Testament where homosexual activities are addressed. Although he is quite measured in presenting both sides of the argument, Mickey finally concludes that homosexual activities, especially as viewed through Paul's eyes, "represent rebellion against God the Creator and the creation," though these sins should not be isolated from the larger context of universal human sinfulness and the need for God's grace in Jesus Christ.[20]

In reaching his conclusions, Mickey does not permit Christian tradition beyond the Bible or the concrete experiences of lesbian and gay persons to inform or modify what he believes to be the Bible's unequivocal teaching on homosexuality. He states that teaching on this matter is determined purely by theology. For him, theology is the application of biblical teachings to contemporary experience. Psychology, psychiatry, praxis, and sociology, where they disagree with the theology of the Bible, have no contributive voice.[21] For example, his reference to "the biblical bottom line"[22] as a basis for deciding against the ordination of homosexuals demonstrates how he privileges the Bible as the exclusive source of ultimate moral authority for our day and time. Accordingly, he comes to what he believes to be absolutely clear answers to his organizing questions about whether the Bible gives guidance on homosexuality and whether God creates men and women to be heterosexual. For him, the Bible teaches that God created males and females to be straight and that to be lesbian or gay is against God's intentions for humanity.

Given his interpretation of Scripture and given the sources he uses for answering the question of the religious status of homosexuality, it would be impossible for Mickey to think that the experiences of lesbian and gay people can contribute to an expanded interpretation of what it means for human beings to be created in the image of God. Neither would he find it possible to claim that the doctrine of the image of God could be interpreted in a manner that would legitimate lesbian- and gay-oriented sexuality. For him, to be created in the image of God is to be created in a way that includes openness to an equal heterosexual partnership, characterized by love, intimacy, mutuality, openness to procreation, and the affirmation of responsible bodily life. Although some of his formulations about love, intimacy, sexuality, and the highest purposes of sexuality may in principle relate to lesbian and gay experience, ultimately for him they do not. For Mickey, there is no doubt that the creation accounts are thoroughly heterosexual and that the underlying structure of experience by which human fulfillment might occur is heterosexual.

Finally, the explicit prohibitions and condemnations of homosexual activities found in the Bible convince Mickey that there would be no basis for affirming that lesbian and gay people can be considered to be created in the image of God as lesbian and gay. They are flawed and sinful beings, incapable of full humanity in the image of God unless their underlying but unrecognized heterosexuality is actualized. Thus it would be impossible for Mickey and those who take this constructive approach in theology to think that lesbian and gay experience could be positively related to the concept of the *imago Dei*. Neither could the doctrine of the *imago Dei* positively be extended to include lesbian and gay experience, nor could lesbian and gay experience be drawn on in such a manner as to expand our interpretation of this doctrine.

Imago Dei: *Interpretive Options*

I believe that the contemporary conventional approach represented by Mickey and others is inadequate on several grounds. First, it assumes that the materials from the tradition are given, rather than creatively constructed by the best (and worst) judgments of human individuals and communities over time. Second, it assumes that its interpretations of the biblical texts are unassailable and accurately represent the self-understanding of the original writers. Third, it assumes that the church has always held the position they represent, rather than offering diverse interpretations of the same materials they so confidently draw on. Fourth, it assumes that the contemporary experiences of real persons cannot challenge, correct, and expand inherited traditions. Finally, it tends to "proof text" specific biblical passages for its authority, rather than placing the discussion within a larger theological horizon or context of meaning within the Bible and beyond.

In this section, I will demonstrate that Mickey's construction is not the only way to interpret the biblical heritage he draws on. I will show that certain of his arguments are in fact later constructions that, like most theological interpretations, go beyond the original texts. Yet I want to affirm his opposition to the patriarchal exclusion of women from the *imago Dei* and apply much of his own argument on that issue to challenge heterosexist subordination of lesbian and gay persons. Finally, I want to demonstrate that ultimately to be in the image of God is not to possess some type of "essential endowment," such as heterosexuality, rationality, or masculinity. Rather, the *imago Dei* is characterized by love, intimacy, mystery, otherness, mutuality, and relational justice in communion with nature, humanity, and God.

To open the possibility of a lesbian and gay reading of the *imago Dei,* it is important to acknowledge that the Scriptures themselves, as well as any interpretation of them, are human cultural creations. They reflect the unfolding self-understanding of individuals and communities of faith faced with challenges of ultimacy. Mickey's interpretation, therefore, is only one cultural creation among other possibilities. Historically there have been a variety of ways of linking *imago Dei* to full humanity other than through heterosexuality. Mickey's is a plausible but not compelling rendering of Scripture and tradition. That is, in the light of other readings of the same materials and by drawing on resources that he neglects, I want to suggest that Mickey's view is a particular cultural creation, just as the scriptural materials he uses are unique cultural creations, and that more promising interpretations can be developed that confirm, oppose, and move beyond some of the conclusions that Mickey finds so convincing.

Specifically, I will examine four plausible alternative interpretations of the *imago Dei.* In the next chapter I will relate these critically to Mickey's position and draw on them for the formulation of yet another constructive option.

1. Imago Dei *is an asexual disembodied status that stands in conflict with embodied gender or sexual orientations of any kind.* Is Mickey correct in linking the early creation accounts in Genesis to heterosexuality? There is evidence that the creation accounts do not connect the *imago Dei* to heterosexuality or to embodied relational life at all. For example, according to one of my New Testament colleagues, Dennis MacDonald, an examination of the concept of the *imago Dei* reveals that it was interpreted in Hellenistic Judaism and early Christian Gnosticism to refer to an incorporeal sexless existence. Bodily life, including relationship and procreation, were considered as the fall from the *imago Dei* rather than

as its fulfillment. Further, the concept of *imago Dei* did not refer to an original gender equality, but to a gender hierarchy in which men, or the male androgyne, were in the image of God in a manner qualitatively superior to women. To be fulfilled in the image of God, therefore, involved asceticism, or a flight from bodily life, including marriage and procreation, to the original spiritual essence of the male androgyne.[23]

MacDonald characterizes this Hellenistic Jewish and Gnostic Christian "order of creation" as it operated in the church at Corinth, as follows: "(1) God; (2) the pneumatic, sexually unified *Urmensch,* who by dint of the image of God, enjoyed hegemony over the spirit world; (3) the psychic, sexually divided human made out of clay according to Genesis 2:7, no longer in God's image and therefore not sovereign over angels; and (4) Eve, whose fall women mourn by wearing veils."[24] There was no basis in this early Christian view of the *imago Dei* for the social equality ascribed by Mickey to men and women in the image of God. Neither does it support Mickey's positive appraisal of heterosexually embodied intimacy or his glorification of procreation. Many Hellenist Jews and early Christians would have read these texts far differently than does Mickey.

2. *To be in the* imago Dei *is to be embodied as male and female, but a social hierarchy between males and females is maintained.* Against the dominant Hellenistic tradition received by Judaism and early Christianity, Paul added his own constructive appraisal and modification. In Paul, we can see the tradition grow. He contended that the Corinthian women neither had to become like men nor had to deny their embodiment and procreative capacities to be considered in the image of God. With Mickey, Paul affirmed embodied life as a positive dimension of God's creation and connected it to the image of God. However, although Paul regarded women as full members of the body of Christ, in the Corinthian correspondence he maintains their social and ecclesial subordination to men. So, although there is an affirmation of embodiment and procreation, there is no social equality connected with Paul's reinterpretation of the concept of *imago Dei* in 1 Corinthians. Because Paul appears in his letter to Corinth to be so committed to interpreting the *imago Dei* in terms of heterosexual male superiority and heterosexual female subordination, it is difficult to see how Mickey and others can so readily claim him as normative for their views of gender equality. This is a retroactive reading of Paul, made possible by experience and reflection occurring hundreds of years after Paul's writings.

3. *To be in the* imago Dei *is to be characterized by sexless spiritual virtues held equally by males and females, while maintaining male-dominated social inequality.* A third constellation of interpretations of the *imago Dei* grew out of another line of Paul's thinking and continued through Augustine. This foundational period evoked the dominant

cultural construct for understanding the relationship of *imago Dei* to sexuality until the modern period. Kari Elisabeth Borreson traces this development.[25] The traditional Christian anthropology emerging from this period seeks to reconcile a polar tension in its doctrines of creation and redemption. According to creation, to be in the image of God is to be a male; women are subordinated to men and can be regarded only derivatively to be in the image of God. The doctrine of redemption in Christ, however, says that "human equivalence in the sense of women's parity with men is realized through Christ."[26] Paul and the early church fathers confronted this asymmetry; they struggled to include women fully in the *imago Dei* while maintaining their subordinated role to men.

We have seen already how Paul attempted to deal with this tension in his engagement with the Corinthians. In Galatians, Paul tries to find a basis for gender equality that differs from his approach at Corinth. In the Galatian correspondence, he lays the foundation for the social unification of those who have been united spiritually through baptism into Christ.[27] In Galatians 3:27–28, the Christian community is "the new creation in which alienated social groups—Jews/Greeks, slaves/free, men/women— were united." MacDonald argues that this new interpretation is a creative advance on the part of Paul, who crafted his own version of an inherited oral tradition of including the outsider at the center of the salvation story. MacDonald believes that Paul's creative theological construction evolved from "two fundamental convictions": (1) that the body must be affirmed and (2) the new creation must "raze the wall protecting the privileged . . . and excluding the disadvantaged." Although the tension between women's equality in Galatians and their inequality in Corinthians is not fully resolved in Paul, "by including sexual equality in the pairs of opposites to be united in Christ he has inspired in subsequent Christian tradition innumerable quests for egalitarian communities. Paul's own failure to develop the implications of his vision in Galatians 3:26–28 has not deterred his spiritual offspring from doing so."[28]

Thus, in Paul we see a person who has received a tradition and radically modified it on at least two different occasions. Although he does not fully move to today's consciousness, he provides a foundation for making a more radical theological leap to include the sexual outsider at the heart of his view of the image of God. The church has found it infinitely more difficult to make this inclusive move in relation to lesbians and gays than to women, as difficult as the latter move has been. However, it seems warranted to claim Paul as our spiritual ancestor in relation to each.

In spite of Paul's unfolding attempts to de-spiritualize *imago Dei*, affirm embodiment, and challenge inherited gender hierarchies, Clement of Alexandria and Augustine fashioned the "classical stratagem" for resolving the incoherence between spiritual equality and social hierarchy.[29]

According to Borreson, this stratagem "defines *imago Dei* as an incorporeal and consequently sexless quality, linked to human capacity of virtue and intellect."[30] Thus both women and men embody God-likeness, or *imago Dei,* by virtue of their creation with a rational soul, or a mind like God. This genderless, asexual human capacity establishes male and female, indeed, all humans, as reflecting the *imago Dei,* apart from their sexuality.

However, when gender is considered, Augustine affirms that women are created corporeally inferior to men and only fully reflect the image of God in marriage. Further, the male capacity for autonomy and greater rationality, as opposed to the more dependent and emotional female, marks males as more God-like. Although all humans share the *imago Dei* spiritually, apart from gender, when gender is regarded in social terms, it is clear that God created women to be subordinate to males. Thus "it follows that human female beings are theomorphic *in spite* of their bodily sex, whereas men's spiritual *imago Dei* corresponds to their exemplary maleness." And even in the qualities of the "superior element of the human soul," which males and females hold in common, the female version is less advanced and inherently inferior to the male's.[31]

From this discussion it is evident that Augustine, like Paul and others before and after him, both continued and modified the tradition he inherited. Although he is the first church father to disagree with Paul's argument in Corinthians that females are in the image of God only derivatively from males, he also, along with Paul's counsel to the Corinthians, upheld the social hierarchy characteristic of his times. For Augustine, "man's domination over woman is part of the natural order, justified by female inferiority; man's domination over another man is caused by iniquity." Thus, in spite of Mickey's claim that the *imago Dei* pointed to gender equality, Borreson demonstrates that the classical Christian viewpoint is characterized by an "incoherence between embodied humanity and bodiless *imago Dei.*" The "fundamental conflict between divinity and femaleness remains unaltered, since women's salvational God-likeness is backdated to the order of creation despite their deviance from exemplary male humanity."[32] Such a view contrasts sharply with contemporary emphases on democracy, gender equality, inclusivity, and the affirmation of embodiment as central to human fulfillment.

4. *The* imago Dei *in Genesis refers to egalitarian partnership and fellowship, not to sexuality or procreation.* Another basis for questioning Mickey's conviction that the Genesis creation accounts establish heterosexuality as the norm of creation in the image of God is provided by Phyllis Bird, an Old Testament scholar. Through careful exegesis of the text of Genesis 1:26–28, Bird concludes that the construct "image of God" refers to the human capacity to be like God by "identification

and correspondence," whereas the command to "be fruitful and multiply" and have dominion over the world establishes humans as continuous with the natural order. It does not characterize the divine image. She further argues that it would not be possible in early Israel to posit God as a sexual procreative being, as Mickey so easily does. These texts offer "no ground for assuming sexual distinction as a characteristic of *adam,* but appears rather to exclude it. . . . The idea that God might possess any form of sexuality, or any differentiation analogous to it, would have been for *P* [*priestly source*] an utterly foreign and repugnant notion. . . . *Unlike* God, but *like* the other creatures, *adam* is characterized by sexual differentiation."[33]

According to Bird, the meaning of humans corresponding to the image of God is left open to interpretation, but it is clear to her that God established humans to have a special responsibility to the earth and to "companionship, the sharing of work, mutual attraction and commitment in a bond superseding all other human bonds and attractions."[34] Although procreation is an important part of human responsibility, the reproductive task is for the purpose of "sustainability" of the natural order, not to specify the meaning of *imago Dei.* Thus, for the church and for thinkers like Paul Mickey to ascribe the concept of the *imago Dei* to a gender-equal heterosexuality is to misread the original textual evidence, if you follow and accept Bird's argument. Though the text affirms embodied gender equality, heterosexuality is not the mark of the *imago Dei.* Rather, reproduction is seen as part of our continuation with the natural order, whereas the link to the *imago Dei* appears to be reflected in the human capacity for various forms of partnership.

Bird specifically argues that the *imago Dei* refers to the species as a whole and is not confined to gender differentiation.[35] The early creation account disallows hierarchical thinking "within species, either of gender or function; all of its statements pertain to the species as a whole. Thus it may serve as a foundation text for a feminist egalitarian anthropology, since it recognizes no hierarchy of gender in the created order."[36] Following Bird's interpretation, Mickey and others are correct to find a basis in the Genesis account for gender equality. However, to ascribe the doctrine of the image of God to a procreative heterosexual status is to misread the original textual evidence. On textual and exegetical grounds, it is possible to conclude, against Mickey, that heterosexuality ties us to our place in creation, but it does not limit or specify the dimensions of our likeness to God. Our likeness to God and our full humanity derive from the nature of our partnerships and bonds to one another, God, and the earth. It would seem that Bird's interpretations stand in strong support of Mickey's more inclusive interpretation of intimacy and against his tying intimacy exclusively to heterosexuality.

Viewed this way, it appears that the Genesis account of creation may, at least in principle, be drawn on to link lesbian and gay experience to the *imago Dei.* Its lack of sexually based hierarchies within the species, its disconnection from procreation, and its emphasis on relational partnership and commitment, as marks of the image of God, may stand in support of affirming lesbian and gay sexuality as expressive of God's intentions for egalitarian intimacy and partnership. We will build on these concepts in the next chapter.

To conclude, on the basis of this sampling it is evident that the relationship of the doctrine of the *imago Dei* to human sexuality, and especially to gender equality and heterosexual marriage, is diverse and contradictory in the Christian tradition. Several interpretive constellations contended with one another, and each emerged over time in the light of a variety of cultural, ideological, social, and experiential factors. The tradition by and large did not see the concept of *imago Dei* as related to gender-equal heterosexual marriage, but to a nonsexual spiritual status that, nevertheless, for the most part supported male-dominated gender hierarchies. Procreation was not universally affirmed as a mark of the image of God, and some interpretations considered bodily processes to be incompatible with the image of God.

There seem to be five main interpretive constellations of the relationship of *imago Dei* to human sexuality, especially with regard to gender and sexual orientation. A contemporary constellation, represented by Mickey and many Christian churches, ties the *imago Dei* to heterosexual gender equality and its procreative mandate. Second, early Christians and Hellenist Jews under the influence of Philo disconnected the concept *imago Dei* from embodied sexuality and gender differentiation altogether, and identified it with a God-like, noncorporeal original masculine perfection. Third, against this inheritance, Paul seemed to have two interpretations. In the Corinthian correspondence, he linked the *imago Dei* to spiritual equality but social inequality between males and females. In Galatians, however, he seemed to suggest a spiritual gender equality in the *imago Dei* that might be the basis for a transformed egalitarian social order. The fourth constellation is the "classical stratagem" identified with Augustine. This constellation identified the *imago Dei* with the power of the rational soul, available to all, but more developed in males than females. Females were social subordinates to males and reflected the image of God only by virtue of their relationship to men through marriage. The fifth constellation, identified in the creation accounts by Phyllis Bird, links the *imago Dei* to embodied egalitarian human partnership and intimacy, but not to procreation or to sexually derived hierarchies within the human species. Although the creation accounts seem to underscore the importance of gender differentiation, and heterosexuality can be assumed to be the dominant social expectation, there is also room to affirm more inclusive readings and to take the text in new directions. Thus, whatever the texts might or might not assume about homosexual orientation, it seems plausible that heterosexual partnership cannot automatically be identified with what it means to be in the image of God.

Conclusion

The diversity of interpretation of the concept of the *imago Dei* reveals the creative, contradictory, and ongoing constructive activity of Christian self-understanding. Lesbian and gay experience as it has disclosed itself in my research cannot be linked directly to any of the options we have examined concerning what it means to be fully human in the image of God.

Until now, our work has been deconstructive, inasmuch as it challenges influential notions that the concept of the *imago Dei* unambiguously links heterosexual marriage and procreation to what it means to be fully human. The tradition is more multivalent than that and is open to novel interpretive constructions. With these rich resources in mind, we are now able to explore how the experience of receiving and giving care with lesbian and gay persons may help us revisit and expand the question of what it means to be fully human in the image of God. Does the reconfiguration of sexuality and spirituality of lesbian and gay persons into a healing and creative unity give us clues about what fully human embodied life can become in positive terms? Does the grace that is conveyed by lesbians and gays (and all others as well) through "the sacrament of eros" disclose something of the "will to communion," in which we are being created in God's holy image? Can we link the lesbian and gay capacity for creative partnerships, novel expressions of family living, and relational justice to the original injunction that, because we are in the image of God, humans should participate in creating, caring for, and renewing the social and natural orders as representatives and partners with God? The next chapter seeks to answer these questions affirmatively.

8

DISCLOSING THE
IMAGE OF GOD

Consequences for Care

The primary theological question addressed in this chapter is, What, if anything, in the experience of care reported on by lesbian and gay persons, can be used to interpret what it might mean for all persons to become fully human in the image of God? If, following Mickey and some of the others that we have discussed in the previous chapter, we conclude that the *imago Dei* is equated with or requires heterosexuality, then it logically follows that lesbian and gay persons are inherently flawed and alienated from the *imago Dei*. However, we have also seen that parts of the tradition do not necessarily equate heterosexuality with the *imago Dei* and that in principle other interpretations of the relationship of *imago Dei* to sexuality are indeed possible. In this chapter we will explore some contemporary theological resources that build on certain aspects of the past and, when linked to the positive outcomes of care, help us think about the *imago Dei* in new ways.

From Experience to Tradition

When we begin our theological construction with the concrete experience of care among lesbian and gay persons, we recognize that our sexuality is a source of spiritual richness and theological knowledge. First, it is a means of engagement with ultimacy; through sexuality we sense that our lives are graced, morally accountable, and have the capacity for intimate communion with self, other, and God. Second, it enables us to see that there is much in the theological tradition that blinds us to the positive dimensions of lesbian and gay experience. Worse, it discloses that there is much in the theological tradition that is destructive to the humanity of lesbians and gays, and to many heterosexuals who might otherwise find a basis for loving rather than hating them. However, in the third place, the experience of our sexuality in the concrete context of care helps critique, clarify, and expand the theological heritage in which care occurs. When lesbians and gays find their lives reconciled to God and liberated from heterosexist oppression to participate in creative, loving communion, in part through the medium of their sexual orientation, we are invited to look at the tradition with new eyes.

Through this process of care and reflection, we are able to remind ourselves that the tradition is itself a human constructive activity that has taken many unexpected turns in the light of new experience over time. Our foundational texts change, as do their meanings, as a result of palpable contemporary immediacies, additional knowledge, and transformative encounters with God's grace in and through our sexuality, as well as through other arenas of living.

Therefore, to construct new interpretations of what it means to be fully human in the *imago Dei* means to rely on but also to move beyond foundational texts and classical formulations. As we saw in the previous chapter, Christian theological interpretation has always drawn on but gone beyond its originating texts and canons. Authoritative traditional texts take on dimensions beyond their original intentions. They cannot and should not control every aspect of future interpretation, because they themselves are situationally derived and therefore always partial perspectives. In the face of new circumstances and questions, they acquire novel, unexpected, and sometimes unintended dimensions. Phyllis Bird, whose interpretation of the *imago Dei* in Genesis we examined in the previous chapter, astutely observes that "the canon of scripture in which this word [text] is preserved and transmitted qualifies it by setting it in a larger literary and theological context, which brings it into conversation, and conflict, with other texts."[1]

Thus the experience of care and its transformative outcomes among lesbians and gays lead us again to the theological recognition that the Christian tradition is a living, vital, and responsive tradition; it is not self-interpreting and predetermined. Interpretation requires reasoned choices among conflicting values and options within the theological heritage. The tradition itself is conflicted and arose from contending options at the time many of these options became authoritative canon. Thus we inherit a multivalent tradition, and our own theological contributions will not be compelling to all. Such is the nature of the theological enterprise.

An examination of the nature and outcome of care in the lives of lesbians and gays, reflected on pastorally and theologically, therefore, in principle helps us to make choices among conflicting options and to advance our theological tradition to new levels of understanding. From these new levels of theological understanding and the practices from which they are derived, it is possible to promote the healing, sustaining, guiding, and liberating process for lesbians and gays, as well as for others.

From Endowment
to Relationship

It became apparent throughout my research that the central concern in care among lesbian and gay persons had to do with the nature, quality, and evaluation of same-sex relationality. In the coming-out process, in particular, the central ongoing question is, What does it mean for my relationship to myself, to my partners, to society, to my relationship with God and the church that I am same-sex rather than heterosexually oriented? For many I talked with, this relational theme was connected to a dialectical struggle between love and hate. Lesbian and gay persons had been taught to hate what they loved and to hate themselves for sexually loving people of their own gender. A core challenge of care was the need for help in moving from self-hatred to self-acceptance and self-love. When care assisted lesbians and gays to increase love and diminish hate, it led to increased vitality and focused vocation. When lesbian and gay persons affirmed rather than rejected their sexual orientation and lived it lovingly and honestly with others, there was mediated to them a sense of God's gracious and empowering presence. They found God's love, rather than condemnation, and often this changed relationship to God eventuated in a changed relationship to self, neighbor, and world. And for those lesbian and gay persons who had not internalized "homohatred and homophobia," care was still necessary to deal with the external expressions of these negative influences in society, culture, and church.

The hallmark of this changed relationality at the core of care is expressed by both William Carroll and Christina Troxell in chapter 1. William said, after he had shared with me his struggle with his sexual orientation, that he was able for the first time to look in the mirror and affirm something positive in relation to himself and to God: "Was that a homosexual person I was looking at? I saw a face and form I had hated and despised since teen years. I saw a person who had little or no self-esteem. Then I saw someone else. I saw a person who was deserving of love and not contempt. I had misunderstood myself. I owed myself an apology. I deserved better treatment. . . . For the first time in my life I really cared about that person in the mirror. Was this a gift of God's grace? Was the big 'sin' in my life that I had been so estranged from myself, not willing to be who I really was?"

Christina, likewise, moved from a sense of condemnation to affirmation through the many forms of care that she had received over the years. After trying to suppress her lesbianism and becoming more and more estranged from God, herself, her son, and the rest of the world, she discovered God's affirmation through prayer and the active welcome acceptance of a lesbian pastor friend. This changed her relationship to herself and others in a radically positive way. She realized that the quality, not the orientation, of one's relationships is the most important factor: both straight and gay people need to have healthy relationships "and forget the stereotyping. If God is not judging, then neither can we. I don't believe God judges homosexuality any differently than heterosexuality. . . . I believe that homosexual relationships can reflect God's will for relationships just like others. I work on the quality and meaning of relationships, not their orientation." She went on to say that same-sex intimacy, like heterosexual intimacy, reflects the quality of God's love in the Trinity and in the church: "I think that sexual coming together is like the coming together of the Father, Son, and Holy Spirit. It is private and very spiritual. The permanent monogamous marriage that we live out in our lives is like the relationship between God the Father and Christ and the church. We learn about our relation to God through the example of the church. Permanent, monogamous, one-flesh union is a type of how Christ lives in the church. Our one-flesh experience points to God's relation to the church. God's one-flesh union is holy, submissive, celebrative, giving. It is compassionate and respectful, esteeming another as higher than oneself. We see in our holy, celebrative, directed, purposeful, and fulfilling love a type of the relation that we have in God."

William and Christina, through the care that they received, came to the point where their sexuality is a means to a full and whole life, which "mirrors" or images something positive rather than something negative. Christina links her transformed relationality to the quality of God's "holy, submissive, celebrative, giving" love. If relationships reflect, image, or mirror God's "holy, celebrative, directed, purposeful, and fulfilling love," then we have a clue about what it means for human relationships to fulfill the intentions of God for human beings. To be in the image of God as fully human, therefore, is disclosed as a quality of relationship available to all and not limited to special endowments available only to a selected class of people. The quality of that relationship is love. Love is central to care, to sexuality, to healing, and to disclosing the image of God in human experience.

In chapter 7, we explored several approaches to the image of God. Most, if not all of them, thought that the image of God was to be characterized by a special endowment. Those having the endowment were more in line with God's intentions for humanity; those with less were inferior or a special class of sinners. We saw how Paul Mickey thought that heterosexuality was the special endowment marking the image of God. Hellenistic Judaism and Christianity thought that the *imago Dei* was characterized by an incorporeal spirituality that was in conflict with embodied sexuality. Augustine thought that masculine rationality and social inequality between women and men reflected the image of God in humans. When construed as a special "essential" endowment available only to heterosexuals or men, it is not possible to consider that lesbian and heterosexual women and gays are created in the image of God without violating the integrity of their sexual identity. However, if the *imago Dei* is a quality of relationship available to all in and through diverse forms of gender and orientation, then it is possible to affirm that lesbian and gay sexuality may actually mirror the *imago Dei* in a manner appropriate to their uniqueness, in common with humans oriented differently from them.

To be sure, in order to answer the question of what specifies the *imago Dei* in a Christian manner, the church has usually employed the strategy of identifying something essentially and uniquely human that sets humans off from other temporal creatures. John Douglas Hall, in his very illuminating historical study of the *imago Dei,* concludes that as a result of this "essentialist" strategy, a number of human excellences have been identified (at various points in history and in different cultures) as the concrete expression of the *imago Dei*.[2] The most consistent elements have been volition and rationality, but other traits also have been drawn on. In particular, "moral sense, spiritual being, speech, upright stature and bearing, the capacity for self-transcendence—even the fact that human beings cook their food—can be named in such a quest [to identify the *imago Dei* in human beings]."[3]

However, Hall points out that there has been a subordinated strand of reflection in Christianity that sees the *imago Dei* as a quality of relationship instead of an essential human trait or characteristic. Rather than reflecting particular "endowments" that by divine creation mark the natural or essential uniqueness of human beings in the *imago Dei*, the *imago Dei* is defined by a capacity for a quality of relationship that mirrors the relational characteristics of God. Specific endowments are secondarily means to relational ends; they are not the marks or determinants in themselves of what it means to be in the *imago Dei*. In this strand of the tradition, "to be *imago Dei* does not mean to have something but to be something: to image God."[4] Based on this subordinated line of thought in the Christian tradition, we can begin to see connections between the high form of loving communion in the lives of lesbian and gay persons and what it means to mirror God's way of being in the world.

Building on a biblical ontology, as interpreted or "intuited" through the Reformers, Hall contends that God has made us in and for relationships. Any identification of the *imago Dei* must be relationally interpreted if it is to adequately carry the central concerns of the Christian faith. Because God's being is a "being-with" characterized by love, we image God by loving. "We move toward real humanity, not when we have achieved all manner of personal successes of brain, will, or body, but when through the media of brain, will, and body we have entered as unreservedly as possible into communion with 'the other.'"[5]

To be in the *imago Dei* means to be fully ourselves—rather than living according to something externally imposed—in relationships characterized by God-like involvement in all the dimensions of our relational web: with God, our ground and source, with our fellow humans, and with the natural order. Full, authentic humanity in the *imago Dei* means to be with, for, and together in communion with all of these dimensions of our relatedness. Distorted, fallen, or alienated existence is to place ourselves against, above, or below these partners in relationship.[6]

For Hall, these three dimensions are interconnected and inform one another. The quality of our love for God ought to be reflected in the quality of our love for our neighbor and for nature. Hall says, "We must learn to attribute to our relationships with other human beings and with the nonhuman universe such spiritual attitudes as the sense of their awesome otherness, wonder, mystery, hiddenness, fascination, inner depth, and meaning—in short, their transcendence."[7] None of the dimensions of relatedness are really fulfilled until all are included.

Hall's purpose is to reconstruct the doctrine of the *imago Dei* so that it can be a positive resource for overcoming the domination of nature by humans. He believes that the early hierarchical and essentialist interpretations have contributed to the destruction of the ecological and social fabric of humanity. He is convinced that interpreting the *imago Dei* through a relational viewpoint helps us to make room in our universe for a caring and suffering God and for reworking our relationship to both the created and social order.[8] The same God who is the God of the earth is the God who discloses Godself as "being with" the world, and particularly the needy neighbor. This is the God who, "whether acknowledged or simply lived, is the source of our courage to go outside ourselves and to seek the other." It is this God who "is the source of our wisdom, whatever wisdom we have, in working out our responsibility for and solidarity with other created beings."[9]

To image our relationships in the likeness of God means to treat every person from the standpoint of service, not servant, according to Hall.[10] Against oppressive dominating tendencies, God's image is reflected in "mutuality, solidarity, participation in the life of the other." Rather than becoming lost in the "self" of the other, love that reflects God's image "insists on the inviolability, mystery, transcendence of the other." Love allows for true diversity and variety: It "presupposes that the other is truly other, is not simply an extension of my being, and thus never 'mine.'" Hall eloquently asserts that this new way of imaging God has radical consequences for creating new communities of "justice, mercy, truth, and peace" that reflect the God who is with us and for us. Our world's inherited hierarchies and "fixed typologies are under strict judgment in our midst:

And though their forms are not easily vanquished, the substance has gone out of them: men can begin in this community of faith, to recognize the full humanity of women; the dominant races can begin to treat members of subjected peoples as equals; the economically secure can begin to acknowledge the claim on them of the poor and wretched of the earth; adults can begin to appreciate children and youth, and vice versa.[11]

If the *imago Dei* is understood in relational terms, characterized by loving mutuality and respect for the diverse otherness of all members of God's creation, including fellow humans, then it seems that those who love in this nonhierarchical manner are becoming fully human. Hall does not extend his analysis explicitly to the quality of love disclosed in the lives of lesbian and gay persons; that is our task. However, he provides the way for us to link the transformation of relationships in lesbian and gay experience to a constructive relational understanding of the *imago Dei*. It is to that challenge that we now turn.

From Hierarchy to Partnership

Our examination of lesbian and gay care has made us sensitive to many of the ways that homosexual persons have been denigrated and oppressed by Christianity and most cultural contexts in which they live. A central issue in care involves overcoming internalized negative messages about being lesbian or gay and contending with social forces, including theological constructions of the *imago Dei*, that pervasively insist that lesbian and gay people are inferior and evil.

The messages that render homosexual orientation negative and inferior to heterosexual orientation ultimately derive from hierarchical thinking. Such thinking implies that to be in the image of God is to be superior to those who are not equally recognized as sharing the *imago Dei* or who are not considered to reflect its essential characteristics as fully as do others. Thus, during the long historical period when rationality was interpreted as the essential endowment marking the *imago Dei* in humans, because women were thought to be less rational than males it was assumed that they embodied the *imago Dei* to a lesser degree than males. Consequently, their roles and social status were subordinated hierarchically to males. Hall demonstrates that because humans thought that we were superior to nature because we alone were in the image of God, nature has been exploited and defiled. Today, the church links heterosexuality to the *imago Dei* and subordinates homosexuality accordingly.

Caregiving with lesbian and gay persons challenges this assumption of hierarchy in the *imago Dei.* As indicated in the many cases of care that we have examined and in Hall's affirmation about the nature of divine love, when mutuality and solidarity replace domination and subordination, lesbian and gay persons are empowered to overcome alienation in their relationships to God, self, and neighbor. Moving from hierarchy to partnership is critical to transformative caregiving among all human beings, and especially with lesbian and gay persons.

As a centrally relational category, the concept of the *imago Dei* imposes ethical norms on the caregiver. Rather than assuming a hierarchy of "essential endowments," the *imago Dei,* understood relationally, requires the removal of all unjust social hierarchies. As we discovered in chapter 7, Paul radically equalized and brought into spiritual unity groups that had failed to recognize the full humanity and equality of one another: Jews and Greeks, slave and free, male and female. It seems that in principle there is nothing to prevent Paul from saying, "lesbian, gay, and straight," as well. If all are one in Christ and this unity is finally taken to have social consequences, it seems incoherent that those using Paul to oppose sexism, slavery, and ethnocentrism would easily find it possible to hold on to Paul to maintain the unjust social inequality between heterosexuals and homosexuals.

If the concept of the *imago Dei* is linked to considerations of what it means to be fully human, then no longer can it Christianly be linked to unjust social hierarchies. These hierarchies work against what it means to be fully human; therefore they work against what the *imago Dei* can positively mean in our time for lesbian and gay persons or for any others. If it is to mean anything positive as a basis for caregiving, the doctrine of the *imago Dei* must be interpreted in such a manner that it is equally available to all humans and that it does not unjustly separate humans from one another (and from the natural order).

From Condemnation to Communion

In Christ, the stranger is welcomed and made familiar. It was transformative for Christina Troxell in chapter 1 to come to the internal conviction that "in Jesus Christ there is no condemnation." To be in the image of God is to overcome alienation in the center of one's being, to recognize a partnership with God and one another, and to celebrate our deepest affinities in solidarity and communion.

The affirmation found in this reading of the gospel of Jesus Christ is the core around which our views of God's relation to lesbians and gays and our ecclesial practices of care must revolve. It was this version of the gospel, when communicated relationally and incorporated spiritually, that contributed to transformed relationality in the lives of those I interviewed. This form of the gospel was efficacious in setting lesbian and gay persons free from bondage to oppression, creating just communities and rich relationships, and turning God and neighbor from aliens to companions.

Rather than bringing about a direct restoration to a static past, God's actions imaged in Christ are a radical setting forth into an undetermined future. In chapter 2, David discovered this radical setting forth into an unknown future when he found strength to accept God's acceptance of his homosexual orientation: "Once you have been expelled from the big heterosexual bubble, you are just out there, and God only knows how things will come out." David finds now that his sexuality serves healing and life rather than sickness and death. Conventional social configurations are challenged and destabilized. That which was rejected and estranged is brought close; acceptance rather than enmity is God's implacable commitment to humanity. From this changed status of reality, loving human communion and solidarity are possible; indeed, they are our destiny and vocation. Through God's unending engagement with the world in loving communion, individuals and communities are lured by the possibility of realizing the image of God's love in their concrete embodied existence. Just as Jesus Christ, through transformative love of God and neighbor, disclosed the image of God, so might those who live in love and openness to God in our day disclose the *imago Dei*.

The welcoming, destabilizing, and transforming love disclosed in the gospel reflects or images God's way of being and intention for humanity. It requires a movement from oppression to relational justice and from exploitation of the earth and its inhabitants to creative, sustainable partnerships. The ultimate norm of evaluating the Christian tradition is its ethical consequences and the quality of life it makes possible for the world and all its diverse elements. The tradition is always under critique when it fails the criteria of love of God, neighbor, self, and nonhuman nature. Rosemary Radford Ruether, a feminist theologian, from whose work I have long benefited, specifically links "a just and truthful anthropology" to human constructions about the image of God: "Does God support the realization of our full humanity or not? If the God of the Christian tradition does not support it, then this God is not our God." Ruether expands this conviction:

> [Feminist theology] understands God as the creator, sustainer, and renewer of the just relationality that can promote our redemptive fullness of being.
>
> All our images of God are metaphors and projections from our human standpoint of an ultimate ground of being and new being that is beyond all such images. The question is not

whether there are some images that are not human projections, but rather what human projections promote just and loving relationality, and which projections promote injustice and diminished humanness. Our images of the God-self relation may be more than, but cannot be less than, that which promotes goodness in human relations.[12]

In the light of these reflections on the participatory and transformative character of God's relationship to the world, to be fully and authentically human in the image of God is to be embodied communally within a web of just, diverse, and creative relationships characterized by honest and loving communion. Katie Bowen said, in chapter 2, "there is room for everyone here. It's a big table." Understood in this manner, all human beings are capable of reflecting the *imago Dei* when their concrete everyday lives and relationships are truthful, loving, creative, just, and diverse. There is no "double standard" for gay and straight, male and female, Jew or Greek; all are capable of mirroring the *imago Dei* and are being beckoned in countless ways by the God of life to do so. One's particular gender or sexual orientation, racial and social location, and personal qualities of mind, body, and spirit are drawn into fulfilling the *imago Dei* by the character of human life they make possible. In themselves they do not make up the *imago Dei* in human beings. The *imago Dei* is fulfilled not in what we have by way of social, cultural, or personal endowment; it is what we reflect concerning care, love, and justice that characterizes what our communities believe to be true about God's way of being in and with and for humanity. If the key to God's being is love, then the key to the fulfillment of the human being created in God's image also must be love, understood as the "will to communion."[13]

Marks of the *Imago Dei*

What, in more specific terms, is disclosed about the relational character of the image of God through reflection on positive caregiving with lesbian and gay persons? It is possible to suggest several "marks," or characteristics, of lived experience that give fuller expression of the meaning of *imago Dei* for our time.

1. *To be in the* imago Dei *is to regard our humanity and the humanity of every other human being as sacred, or "of unconditional worth."* Our humanity is sacred in its totality, including its sexuality, no matter what its orientation. It is not sacred because some of its members have achieved a superior social location or are endowed with certain "essential" traits not available to others. Rather, it is sacred by its capacity to

reflect the quality of God's loving relation to the universe and each entity within it. We are being created and coming to fulfillment within a network of relationships out of which we emerge and to which we are accountable. These structures of reality are not "secular" or religiously neutral. They are not structures that must be made sacred or holy through some religious or spiritual "addition." They are sacred because they stand in relation to God and one another for the purposes of creativity, enrichment, fellowship, and fulfillment. God's creative love for the world is the foundation for our valuing and affirming the diversity of entities that comprise our social and natural universe. As a part of a composite of beneficence, all reality is of sacred worth and reflects the image of God's positive relational engagement with the universe.

As sacred, in the image of a sacred God, humans are characterized by "otherness," or mystery and transcendence. Each is unique in the way life is configured, and that uniqueness is something to prize rather than denigrate. In Hall's terms, love that reflects God's image "insists on the inviolability, mystery, transcendence of the other." Lesbian and gay persons can remain "strangers" and yet be familiar to straight people; the *imago Dei* recognizes that to be sacred is to have an impenetrable, mysterious, and even elusive component at the heart of our being. The tendency to overexplain, to control by naming or knowing, or to impose familiarity on strangeness may distort the *imago Dei* and work against its affirmation of sacredness.

Another dimension of sacredness is the capacity to endure and to realize valuable purposes. It is to embody power and directionality. Self and others are held accountable; there is no escaping negative consequences of behaviors and attitudes that violate the sacred by seeking to deface or eradicate it. God promises never to "fail or forsake" humanity. God's power assures God's durability. God's love assures God's beneficence in the face of evil. When reflected in human experience, to fulfill the image of God is to embody the sacred trust of ensuring the integrity and future of fellow creatures and to stand against anything that desecrates or fractures their viability.

2. *To be in the* imago Dei *is to have the capacity for contextual creativity, or the capacity to configure our relational networks in a novel and life-enhancing manner.* (For a fuller discussion of "contextual creativity," see Larry Kent Graham, *Care of Persons, Care of Worlds: A Psychosystems Approach to Pastoral Care and Counseling* [Nashville: Abingdon Press, 1992], 63.) Contextual creativity is not a natural human endowment as much as a consequence of embodied relational engagement. To be in the *imago Dei* is to participate, like God, in the creation of new worlds of experience and in naming these worlds truthfully. Naming makes visible; it discloses truths of enormous proportion, and it

creates the reality that is named. Hiding and falsehood distort God's image. Closets deny vitality; they choke creativity. New worlds of value and visibility are evoked through naming. When all humans are able to name their experience fully, to create new forms of care and love based on their experience, and to disclose these forms truthfully in the face of the forces of devaluation and falsehood, they move toward realizing the *imago Dei.*

Giff, Dan, and Anthony, discussed in chapter 4, and their extended network in the Bay Area were able to bring forth a new family configuration that graced and enriched each member. This family in turn was made possible by and enhanced the larger cultural, religious, and social milieu in which it arose. Katie Bowen, in chapter 3, suggested that one of the gifts of the lesbian and gay community to the world may be the creative discovery that family is based on love, trust, and commitment, and that it does not have to be limited to kinship, gender roles, and procreative outcomes. This novelty reflects the contextual creativity of God, who "brings forth a new thing."

The power of truthfulness about sexuality as a source of greater knowing about the world was expressed well by Gary in chapter 3: "I couldn't know my feelings about anything until I felt my gay feelings." If we hide our unique sexuality, our capacity to know and name the world truthfully is impaired, and our capacity to reflect God's image is diminished. Creativity is negated and love curtailed. Alienation dominates, oppression prevails, and life withers. By contrast, care that seeks to nourish the *imago Dei* looks for, affirms, and expands opportunities for contextual creativity based on truthfulness and imagination.

3. *To be in the* imago Dei *is to have enjoyment and delight in the pleasures of erotically embodied existence and the extension of care, gratitude, and responsibility to those with whom we share these pleasures.* We can enjoy and delight in the sensuous vitality of our embodied life because it is a gift of God and a means for a deepened, wonder-filled apprehension of both God and the world. In chapter 3 we explored in some depth the range of erotic experience disclosed through the interviews. The quiet comfort that comes from touch and delight in another's presence and the intensity of sexually mediated intimacy reveal the extent to which eros is a dimension of care and one means of sensing our intimacy or communion with God. Many persons indicated that they did not feel that they really understood the intensity and tenderness of God's love until they could be truthful about and expressive of their own sexuality. Probably no one said it better than Katie Bowen when she enthused, "Until I fell in love with a woman, I never knew why wars had been fought over love, poetry written, and the Taj Mahal built! I had known pleasure before this, but never intimacy. Never coming home. . . . My coming out was more a coming home to God: 'You made me this way, you love me

this way, I am lovable, and I will find love in my life.' I used to pray very simplistically, like a kid praying for a ten-speed bike. I once prayed, 'Lord, let me be with a woman before I die. Just once, let me taste heaven on earth before I die, and I'll do anything.' I was bargaining. 'Just give me one special moment!' Instead, I found a relationship that is truly what I wanted. So even in those moments, God's abundant love was evident. All I wanted was a one-night stand, and I got a land flowing with milk and honey! So, God was very much at the heart of this, giving me the courage to go ahead."

Enjoyment and delight include, but go beyond, simple tolerance or acceptance. It is based on intimate knowledge and validation of the deepest truths about the uniqueness of the relational partner (whether this is friend, lover, fellow human, or nonhuman universe), as well as respect for their mysterious otherness that is never fully known or engaged. Jesus' conversation with his disciples in John 15 may symbolize the enjoyment of disclosure and the maintenance of mystery characteristic of the *imago Dei*. He calls his disciples friends; he discloses his life with God; and he brings them into a greater communion with one another through his embodied participation with them. In chapter 1, Christina Troxell discovered that the love, grace, intentionality, and freedom of God were known or made real to her in the "one-flesh union" that she shared monogamously with her female life partner. Embodied erotic partnerships, when characterized by love, mutuality, and commitment to the ongoing welfare of the other, image in concrete terms God's way with all of the universe.

4. *To be in the* imago Dei *is to have relational justice.* Relational justice is an emerging norm in a variety of advocacy theologies and is becoming more central in pastoral care and theology.[14] Relational justice underscores the need for "right relationship" to self, other, and world. It is opposed to social arrangements characterized by domination of one individual or group over another. Against the destructiveness of domination, relational justice promotes the values of egalitarian mutuality and ecological sustainability. Relational justice leads to shalom and celebration of the harmonious relationships established between God and humans, among humans, and between all entities of the ecosystem. Inasmuch as lesbian and gay persons have the capacity to participate in and contribute to relational justice, they reflect the image of God and are to be considered as fully human on theological grounds. Where human care opposes unjust structures of oppression and domination, it seeks to embody the image of God in concrete terms in the social order.

We have seen how difficult it has been for the church to construct understandings of the *imago Dei* that are relationally just; indeed, one could look at the development of this doctrine as an unfolding struggle to overcome unjust spiritual and social hierarchies throughout its history.

Systems of domination and subordination, we now know, are oppressive and work against the full humanity of all who are locked into these systems, both as perpetrator and victim. Heterosexism is an example of unjust relationality because it subordinates the legitimate needs and aspirations of one group to the unaccountable control and denigration by another. Internalized homophobia is the subjective appropriation of unjust relationality and functions to alienate persons from the *imago Dei.*

To reflect in human terms the love that God bears for the world requires a form of just relatedness that ensures the ongoing welfare of the relational partner. Such an ethical norm lays claim on all human relationships. For lesbian and gay persons in particular to thrive and fully flourish in the *imago Dei,* relational justice must be embodied in mutual respect, protection of the health and integrity of all partners, and overcoming internalized heterosexism and homophobia. Heterosexuals must also exhibit mutual respect and protection of all partners and must turn from attitudes and practices that subordinate and denigrate lesbian and gay experience in the name of God. Institutionalized heterosexism and internalized homophobia reflect neither the love of God nor the love of neighbor consistent with God's love. Therefore, if our creative and loving communion with others is to fulfill ethical norms central to Christian moral values, it must embody relational justice. Donaciano Martínez, whose life is discussed in chapter 5, shows how difficult and ambiguous relational justice can be; moreover, there is ongoing pain when it is unrealized in intimate relationships. As a gay Latino human rights activist, he is committed to gay and lesbian liberation as well as freedom from racism, classism, and other domination systems. At the same time, he is painfully aware that his inability to accept his mother's late-life lesbianism was unjust and ungrateful, rooted in his own fears of being rejected by her. Accordingly, he endures a painful tension between "justice realized" and "justice denied" as he works toward personal healing and social transformation.

5. *To be in the* imago Dei *is to have respect for diversity and multiplicity within the context of a dynamic wholeness.* To be related in deep and complex ways, characterized by just and reciprocal mutuality, requires that there be an enormous diversity and multiplicity in the universe. Love is not possible without diversity and difference; love is the force that keeps difference from becoming a source of evil; love reconciles the estranged. God's relationship to the universe is one of love, which means that God in partnership with humans and nature creates, protects, sustains, and works toward the fulfillment of every entity. God is big enough to let each entity be itself, rather than something else. So must we be, if we are to reflect God's love. God's being is richly comprised of the complex loving interplay with diverse forms of life. God's integrity is maintained, even as God's reality is expanded, through this multiplicity

of transactions. God participates in the emergence of diversity and novelty, while providing conditions for coherence, cooperation, and beneficence within the totality of the universe. To be in the *imago Dei,* therefore, is to ferociously protect and tenderly cherish the uniqueness of each entity in the world, while seeking the conditions of justice in which each might be fulfilled.

I was particularly helped by the works of gay liberation theologian J. Michael Clark and feminist theologian Sallie McFague to recognize that embodied life in the universe is both diverse and interconnected. Clark wisely links efforts at protecting and liberating the "biodiverse" universe from exploitation to the protection and liberation of lesbian and gay persons. He regards lesbian and gay orientation as part of the rich biodiversity of the universe. Efforts on behalf of one ought to contribute to the fulfillment of the other. Clark eloquently offers a realistic, yet hopeful, description of this link:

> Change is occurring. Just like gay men and lesbians, people everywhere are beginning to realize and to claim their own intrinsic value and to celebrate their own difference and the larger diversity that their difference enriches. As the disempowered peoples of the earth come to appreciate the intrinsic value and diversity of the human community, *those* values will be superimposed upon nature, supplanting the patriarchal values superimposed upon nature until now. Healing, caring, and nurturing will increasingly supplant exploiting and disposing of nature. These processes may have only begun, but they are nonetheless already reshaping both ecology and theology in liberational and restorative ways.[15]

Sallie McFague's recent work supports and extends the perspective that the unfolding of the "common creation story" of the universe discloses that all reality is ultimately comprised of common materials, interacting creatively in the unfolding of diverse life forms. We are unique, yet partnered, in a universe that can be considered as "the body of God." Respect, care, and love for the embodied diversity of this world is the only means available for connecting with God in a creative, redemptive, and fulfilling manner. In McFague's words:

> Embodied knowing and doing rest not upon the one ideal body (the white, fit and able, male, human body) that would absorb all its parts and all differences into itself for its own well-being. Rather, embodied knowing and doing should rest, for all intents and purposes, upon the infinite number of bodies in all their differences that constitute the universe. . . .

> One of the motifs of our analysis of the model of the world
> as God's body from the perspective of the common creation
> story is that all bodies are united in a web of interrelatedness
> and interconnectedness. This motif has been radicalized by
> the Christic paradigm that reaches out to include especially
> the vulnerable, outcast, needy bodies. . . .
>
> Moreover, if God is embodied, then bodies become special,
> and whatever degrades, oppresses, or destroys bodies affronts
> God. "Sins against the body," actions that deprive, abuse, mu-
> tilate, rape, or murder bodies become heinous. . . . The view of
> the body gives us a new way of seeing salvation and sin: as hon-
> oring and fulfilling or degrading and destroying the body.[16]

To conclude, following Hall and others, to be in the image of God is ultimately about the qualities of loving communion that come into being in
the universe. Love is a complex and rich term. It has many dimensions.
When reflective of the *imago Dei,* love is, as Mickey suggests, embodied,
sensual, mutual, unifying, and wholistic. (Though unlike Mickey, I do not
think that the image of God requires heterosexuality for it to be considered
moral and fulfilling.) The image of God is reflected where the diversity of
each entity is honored and its otherness respected and creatively cared
about. The *imago Dei* is characterized by creative and just relationality
in a context of accountability and mutual concern. However, because we
live in a world distorted by evil and sin through a panoply of unjust structures that promote their interests as God's will, realizing the *imago Dei* is
always incomplete, ambiguous, and precarious. No individual or social
group can claim superiority here; the best we can look for is sensitivity to
new configurations, courage to let them emerge, respect for those who
move with and against us, and the resilience to recover from misguided
images of what finally makes us fully human.

Imago Dei
and Pastoral Care

Building on the relational view of the *imago Dei* developed above and
the insights emerging from the reports of lesbian and gay persons, a very
particular picture of caregiving emerges. This caregiving is characterized
by three interlocking features. First, to care positively for persons is to actively welcome and accept their uniqueness in its totality, including an
explicit affirmation of the worthiness of their sexual orientation. Second,
positive care embodies communal solidarity characterized by liturgical
recognition, theological affirmation, and social inclusion in the formal
and informal structures operating within the religious and larger envi-

ronment. Third, positive care includes concrete ecclesial prophetic and pastoral engagement in the challenge all of us have to overcome internalized oppression and to develop healthy relationships in a transformed social and ecclesial milieu. Some of these factors are discussed more concretely in chapter 6. In the remainder of this chapter, however, concrete acts of care are linked more explicitly to the concept of the *imago Dei*.

Replacing Rejection
with Welcoming Acceptance

The first pillar in the framework of care is welcoming acceptance and validation as a total person, including full affirmation of one's sexual orientation as a gift from God. Christina experienced this when she discovered that in Christ there is no condemnation and through her participation in a community of faith that actively welcomes all persons. These modes of care have provided a sense of ultimate value and affirmation to her life and have been a wellspring of self-love and ministry to others.

Christina's witness parallels the experience of nearly every lesbian or gay person I interviewed who said that when they found positive care in the context of the church there was an honest welcome and positive valuation of their orientation by persons of faith. One person put it most graphically: "If you want gay and lesbian people in your church, you must write in large letters on the bulletin board: 'You Are Welcome Here!'" Passive toleration or lame inclusion is not the same as active welcoming that communicates the healing and caring message that lesbians and gays have unconditional worth as lesbians and gays, and that the church and society genuinely want to be in a mutually beneficial relationship. To be in the image of God is to be no longer strangers, but to welcome one another in our otherness and mystery. It means to embrace the opportunity to create new forms of community in the midst of genuine difference.

In concrete terms, active welcoming and wholehearted affirmation involve an empathic connection to the struggles and particular gifts of lesbian and gay persons. It was remarkable to experience the spiritual and emotional power of the empathic link that was established between Jack and the sexuality class, as discussed at the beginning of chapter 2. This coming together into mutual spiritual partnership was essential for Jack to overcome his alienated relationship to his sexuality, indeed to his whole personality. It also brought enormous spiritual benefits to the class, which, at least in part, became a community of faith and service as well as a setting for formal academic and ministerial training. In William Carroll's case, he found that the emotional bond between us, which was characterized by my active acceptance of the truth of his orientation, enabled him to experience self-love and a beginning sense of God's genuine care for him. It led him on a journey from loneliness to fellowship, from false-hood to truth, and from a sense of lovelessness to great dimensions of lov-ing communion. Christina found through a number of empathic connec-tions that her orientation did not stand under condemnation, but was valid in God's eyes. And although some of the contexts in which she learned this were ultimately inadequate, they were valuable "practice and rehearsal" for the mutuality that now exists with her permanent partner.

In discussing the nature of active welcoming and wholehearted valuing as a dimension of care for lesbian and gay persons, the Christian caregiver must find his or her touchstone in the gospel of Jesus Christ. In all the narratives of care, it was clear that the simple message of the gospel that there is no condemnation in Christ, but that God loves us as we are, conveyed enormous care and transformative potential. For Christians, any act of positive care that affirms and liberates persons is grounded in God's redemptive activity. It has the potential to evoke in all persons of faith the sense that we are cherished and precious and that we deserve to be treated accordingly by the church, if not the larger world.

In the case of lesbian and gay persons, it is especially important to rec-ognize the enduring core conflict between the message that God accepts and welcomes us as we are, and the social and ecclesiastical experience of rejection and vilification because of one's orientation. The expectation of affirmation, based often on early childhood religious education and spiritual experience, coupled with the later reality of rejection as a les-bian or gay person, eventuates for most in an acute spiritual and psycho-logical crisis. Faced with the double-bind choice between their love of God and the church and the positive affirmation of their sexuality, it is not uncommon for lesbians and gays to become angry, depressed, alien-ated, and conflicted. Sometimes they act on one side of their experience, against the other. To provide the type of care that can heal this split—or at least make it endurable—requires the church to embody the gospel of Christ's active welcome and wholehearted affirmation of the outsider and stranger as living members of the social body of believers in our congre-gations. It is only then that the Christian faith and sexual orientation may become mutually enriching and vital. Rather than alienation from God, self, neighbor, and the church, reconciliation, mission, and fellowship may emerge, with all the personal and communal spiritual vitality ac-companying these gifts. As we have seen, this movement from broken to full humanity points to what it means to realize the image of God in con-crete relational life.

The caregiver will recognize that it is not always possible for those who have been hurt or broken by the church to be meaningfully connected with it. The better course is to help gain a reconciled closure and move on to a setting that is authentic and spiritually vital for them. God's grace and presence are not confined to the social forms of Christianity in our culture. God is always doing a new thing, and God's image is reflected wherever authentic love and relational justice occur. Guiding persons to new forms and interpreting these in positive theological terms may assist those needing care authentically to find it outside of the church.

Communal Solidarity
and Liturgical Recognition

Communal solidarity, characterized by liturgical recognition, theological affirmation, and social inclusion in the formal and informal structures that govern the religious and larger environment, is the second pillar in the framework of care for lesbian and gay persons. Because the core difficulties in the lives of lesbian and gay persons derive primarily from deep-rooted social and cultural values and processes, it is essential that the ministry of care provide a countercultural dimension. In Christ, that which has been cut off has been included. Christian faith both affirms life and its fulfillment, and stands against forces of ignorance, evil, and injustice. Because heterosexism is social and collective, the ministry of care requires countervailing social and communal power. Thus Jack found it desirable to share his coming out of the closet with more than just the professors; having the whole class enter into his journey was necessary for overcoming his alienation and aloneness. Structuring a safe environment, within the context of the larger purposes of a seminary classroom, carried a spiritual and emotional weight that individuals in private and confidential counseling settings alone could not carry.

Temple Emanuel, described in chapter 2, engaged in an intentional process among its leaders to prepare for the possibility of having a lesbian or gay rabbi someday. They honestly confronted their differences, sought counsel from informed parties, and committed themselves to welcoming a lesbian or gay rabbi, if one applied who fulfilled the criteria of the job description. Such activity was more than passive acceptance; it involved intentional communal activity by which lesbian and gay persons would become an active and public part of the liturgical and organizational life of the congregation.

Communal solidarity and recognition are illustrated by Christina Troxell (chapter 1), who realized that if she were to value herself, she had to enter the larger religious and social environment with a clear message about her orientation. She found the Bay Area to be supportive of her orientation, and her church a source of spiritual growth as well as a setting for ministering to others.

The foregoing chapters provide many other examples of communal solidarity in which full inclusion and participation were encouraged and appreciated. A number of Christian congregations actively welcomed and intentionally utilized the "gifts and graces" of its lesbian and gay members. This normalized the presence and value of lesbian and gay persons for both the individuals themselves and, of equal importance, for the congregation as a whole. For example, Bill Weaver and Doug Johnson were asked to share in their Episcopal congregation what it meant to be celebrating their fortieth anniversary as a gay couple (chapter 4). They were members of a panel of resource people representing diverse family styles in the congregation. Being asked to share their experience was literally transforming for them. It was well received by the congregation and deepened understanding and affection in the church.

Another example of communal solidarity, mediated liturgically, took place in the same church at the time of the death of Andy, the partner of John, an openly gay member of the vestry. Andy's death was the result of complications from AIDS. E. Claiborne Jones (Andy and John's priest), their lesbian doctor, and immediate families were all in the hospital room when Andy died. During the funeral service, John reported that the priest "was at her best" in the sermon and that it was extremely moving to experience the outpouring of genuine love on the part of the congregation, even though at the time the congregation knew only that he had cancer. Andy's children and former wife were at the service. The children walked in with John, whom they had come to affectionately refer to as "their ugly stepmother." It was a time of communal solidarity in the extremities of dying, death, and bereavement. This solidarity was normalized in the liturgical life of the church and had an incalculable effect on John and others in the congregation, both gay and straight, who talked to me about it throughout the interview process.

In the interviews I conducted, two compelling examples of communal solidarity, theological affirmation, and liturgical recognition appeared. First, on repeated occasions it became clear to me how much the AIDS crisis has generated communal solidarity and sensitivity to ultimate values among the lesbian and gay community. One lesbian minister said, "After burying so many people who died from AIDS, we have come to realize that life is precious and we don't have time for bullshit!" In spite of enormous post-traumatic stress disorder and raw grief and ongoing terror, there is also an enormous sense of pride and political determination in the gay community regarding AIDS. This pride and determination have taken the form of mobilizing resources and increasing public political action to redirect research interests and medical resources toward the prevention, treatment, and cure of AIDS. The imminence of death for many has mobilized a courage to come out of the closet, to identify publicly as lesbian or gay, and to minister to one another as well as challenge the larger society. The communal solidarity and multiple collaborative partnerships that have emerged from this are quite significant and will likely become a stronger cultural dynamic. The various forms of AIDS support groups and healing services, pet care, and bereavement groups for those mourning the death of friends and family members through AIDS provide additional examples of the manner in which communal solidarity is essential for care.

The second notable expression of communal solidarity is the gay pride movement that emerged from the Stonewall Revolution in Greenwich Village in 1969. This has spawned a number of public activities to raise consciousness about the reality of lesbian and gay lives and to instill a sense of pride in the lesbian and gay community. Over and over in the interviews, people told me how much participation in these events instilled in them a sense of value and worth, and strengthened them to withstand the unrelenting hostility of church and society. For example, Michael and Paul attended the March on Washington in the spring of 1993 as a gay couple. Michael, a Mexican-American professor of ethics, said that it had incredible impact on him: "During the March on Washington, our numbers overwhelmed the others. You felt safer in sheer numbers. If you tried to beat me up, you couldn't get away. There were too many of us. It was the first time in our lives that we were a majority! On the Metro, everywhere. It was incredible!"

As Paul stated, "A little story in that regard, I'll never forget. We were taking a direct 747 from San Francisco to Dulles. It was obvious that there were lots of gays and lesbians on this flight. A group of gay and lesbian friends saw each other and started hugging and kissing; they were glad to see each other. They were having a great time saying hello and seeing each other. A straight man in his fifties or so was watching this and about to go through the ceiling. He was going ballistic. His wife was doing everything she could to divert his attention and keep him in his seat. Then it became clear to him that he was going to be stuck there for the whole flight with all of us around him! You could just read it on his face. It was significant to watch. It was so different to suddenly be in the majority."

Again, Michael reflects on this experience: "One of the most moving things for me was to go to the National Cathedral to a prayer service. We weren't going to go. There were so many other things to do besides going to church. We went because my cousin asked us to. The place was packed. It was the most moving spiritual experience in my life. The rector was a black man. I think of it as care. He welcomed us. He said, 'Everyone is welcome here.' We clapped, we cried. It almost makes me cry now. We sang with such devotion. I thought the roof would come down. People would be shocked. Here it is before one of the most significant political events in the recent past in our community's life, and we go to pray and to sing! The rector prayed for the march. It was justice and care all rolled together, in a real biblical sense of 'right relation' between people and God. I'll never forget it. We were blown away. It set a beautiful, beautiful way to start the march. There was a welcome—an honest welcome. There was community, solidarity, feeling close to God in a simple way. There was a sense of hope. It was just one of the most powerful things in my whole life. Hymns I sang a million times took on such power that I would get so choked up that I would not be able to sing.

"This experience reminds me of the movie *The Color Purple,* where at the end Sug, who has been estranged from her father, hears the singing in the church down the road from where she is singing in the nightclub. She walks into the church, and she and her father hug. Their estrangement is healed. There was a coming home. That image fits what I felt in the cathedral. There was the image of coming home, because we both come from strong religious backgrounds and we have struggled with that. This was not an alienating experience; it was coming home—in simple ways, such as honest welcome. There was celebrating diversity and the many styles of being gay. Paul once said, 'Why do we honor diversity of nature in God's creation, but not the diversity of people in God's creation?' It was very powerful to honor the diversity of all kinds of gay people at the cathedral! There were all kinds and styles of gay men and lesbians. It was just incredible! It was such a powerful, powerful experience! When we later reflected on this at our New Year's Eve dinner, everyone who had been there said that going to the march and to the National Cathedral in the spring had been the best part of the year for them."

From these examples, it is clear that communal solidarity involves welcome participation in the formal and informal life of the church and larger culture, expressed and embodied liturgically and in public events. It also involves theological validation and support for lesbian and gay life, affirming diversity and seeking creative forms of relational engagement. I have already pointed up how the gospel of "no condemnation" in Jesus Christ provides Christian grounding for this. It is also necessary to revise notions of sin and salvation, and what it means to be created in the image of God. Central to these considerations is the nature of the relationship of love to sexual orientation and the place of justice in the ecclesial and cultural environment. If sin consists of estrangement from the truth of one's created goodness, and salvation is restoration to a right relationship to one's self, to God, and to neighbor, then it seems plausible to suggest that lesbian and gay persons are capable of love and wholeness by virtue of their participation in loving and just relationships. Rather than their sexuality being a barrier to the possibility of being fully human in the image of God, it is one of the expressions of full humanity and one of the means of fulfilling the quality of life intended by God. Thus, to care for lesbians and gays is to affirm not only their acceptance in Christ, but to claim that when their relationships are loving and just, and eventuate in mission and ministry, they reflect what it means to be saved from sin and fully human in the image of God.[17]

It seemed clear to me that one of the sources of care was for the caregiver to affirm in word and action that loving relationships were in accordance with the will of God, who is love by nature. Caregivers recognized that the inability to love oneself, others, and God was an expression of sin and evil, and needed to be overcome by acceptance, reconciliation, and justice. It was essential to affirm that when issues of sin were connected to lesbian and gay experience, they not be connected to the orientation in itself. There is no sin in the orientation, but in the unjust response to persons with same-sex orientation and the multiple ways this injustice negated the capacity to love self, God, and neighbor. Empowering care necessitated theological thinking and revisioning core theological constructs.

Christina made explicit connections to gay love and the nature of God: "I think that sexual coming together is like the coming together of the Father, Son, and Holy Spirit. . . . We see in our holy, celebrative, directed, purposeful, and fulfilling love a type of the relation that we have in God. . . . I believe that homosexual relationships can reflect God's will for relationships just like others. I work on the quality and meaning of relationships, not their orientation." These words, along with countless other reports from those I interviewed, connected the transformative love they found in same-sex partnerships to the quality of life that they believed God calls us all to, whether gay or straight. To provide strategic care, then, is to help lesbians and gays—as well as straight persons—discern their sexual orientation in clear terms, validate it pastorally and communally, and help evaluate theologically and ethically the quality of life it makes possible in relation to self, God, and neighbor. When sexual orientation, including its erotic foundations and erotically mediated pleasures, promotes love, justice, communion, and service, it moves toward wholeness and salvation, and approaches what it means to be fully human in the image of God. When it fails in these dimensions, one's sexual orientation and activities are under the sway of sin and evil, and call for contrition and repentance.

Ecclesial Prophetic
and Pastoral Engagement

The third pillar in the framework of caregiving for lesbian and gay persons is concrete ecclesial prophetic and pastoral engagement in the struggle of lesbian and gay persons to overcome internalized oppression and to develop healthy relationships in a transformed social and ecclesial milieu. The dean of the National Cathedral's welcome and affirmation is an excellent example of ecclesial pastoral and prophetic engagement in affirming lesbian and gay experience, while opposing those structures of our society that denigrate it. Christina's description of her congregation's efforts to welcome the outcast as well as persons from all other segments of society fulfills this criterion. These examples reflect a conviction that to care for symptomatic persons, the caregiving community must also address the structures of life that impinge on the capacity to become fully human in the image of God. Caregivers must recognize the interplay of psychological, spiritual, and larger systemic factors, and address these conceptually and strategically.

One of the more impressive examples of how a person in his particular circumstances linked prophetic action to pastoral sensitivity to the care of lesbian and gay persons was recounted by Lamar, a man in his thirties who lives in Atlanta but was reared in rural Georgia. He said that there was a saying in rural Georgia that "we don't have any queers here." He commented that this was a correct saying, because "gay people left. There was no affirmation, so they went on to Atlanta or other places." Yet he himself had a positive experience that countered this dominant message. "My freshman history teacher was also the minister in my small town. He was also the debate coach. Because of my love of history and being on the debate team, I spent a lot of time with Jim. And I remember one day I came the closest I have come to having a nervous breakdown because there was no one to whom I could talk about my feelings. I was his student assistant that quarter, and he just looked at me and said, 'You're upset!' And I said, 'Yeah.' And he said, 'That's because you're gay.' I said, 'What?' He said, 'You are gay. You don't know it yet, but I have taught school for twenty years, and I had one of my kids commit suicide, and it turned out that he was gay, so I have made it a practice now that if I thought a gay student or lesbian was here, I would put them under my protection. I would counsel and try to help.' Jim said he had lost a student the first year he had taught. He introduced me to the idea of consenting adults and all these different books. And he explained to me about the Bible and how all these passages about homosexual acts were really dealing with male prostitution. He helped me work through the religious side. Since then we are still friends. He still stops by to see us, and we help him find antiques. Because of him, I was able to first deal with the church versus religion and so on. My big worry was to get out of town before someone else found out. I still have trouble trusting people. The ironic thing, however, is now that I am away and talk to other people, they say that they wanted to get away too for fear that some secret might come out! It wasn't about being gay always, but people said that they lived in fear that someone would find out that they were not the perfect son, or the perfect father, or perfect wife."

This vignette illustrates many dimensions of care, but for our purposes now, it most clearly points to the dimension of an agent of the church using his social location in a proactive manner to protect, guide, and befriend those most vulnerable in that context. Advocacy and education were combined with personal support to educate Lamar about his unjust situation and to provide a basis for interpreting his sexuality in more positive ways. Although it is not clear whether Jim took other steps toward public advocacy of lesbian and gay life, he did help Lamar find supportive social contexts and worked in a quietly pastoral way toward prophetic challenge of the dominant culture of righteous perfectionism that was destructive for Lamar as well as for others.

Conclusion

The narratives of care disclosed by those I interviewed and discussed in this book have helped us frame a profile of positive helpfulness toward lesbian and gay persons. I realize that generalizations from such a narrow base are always risky and that many other stories and resources need to be taken into account to provide an adequate portrait of care. However, certain common features are present in these situations that enable us to say with some confidence that positive care, when interpreted in the light of a relational view of what it means to become fully human in the image of God, is supported by the three pillars I have identified. First, active welcome and acceptance, characterized by a full affirmation of the validity and worthiness of lesbian and gay orientation, is essential. This is grounded in the gospel of God's acceptance in Christ, and in the validation by grace through faith apart from the works of the law. Second, care includes communal solidarity, characterized by liturgical recognition, social inclusion, and the theological affirmation that lesbian and gay experience, when characterized by loving communion and relational justice, may be a foundation for becoming fully human in the image of God. Third, care is expressed in pastoral and prophetic engagement with the destructive forces impinging on lesbian and gay persons. Prophetic care seeks to dislodge internalized oppression and limited self-definitions through the promotion of healthy relationships and transformed environments.

Notes

Notes to Introduction. Pastoral Theology and Lesbian and Gay Experience

1. This formulation of pastoral theology is based on the pioneering work of Seward Hiltner, in *Preface to Pastoral Theology* (Nashville: Abingdon Press, 1958). An elaboration of Hiltner's legacy can be found in Brian H. Childs and David W. Waanders, eds., *The Treasure of Earthen Vessels: Explorations in Theological Anthropology* (Louisville: Westminster John Knox Press, 1994).

2. After considerable thought, I have decided to use "lesbians and gay men" as the preferred nomenclature in this book. I originally was going to use "lesbian women and gay men," but this proved unwieldy and seemed redundant to some readers. To other readers, it was important to underscore that lesbians are "women" as a basis for political action against sexism in the larger culture and in the lesbian and gay subculture(s) as well. Though I have chosen to delete the redundancy, I believe that the book will amply demonstrate that pastoral care for lesbians includes opposition to sexist oppression, even when this occurs at the hands of their gay compadres.

3. As I indicated above, pastoral theology and care has always had a "social conscience," and from the beginning located its efforts with the marginalized, particularly the mentally ill. Current efforts in this direction are reflected in Pamela D. Couture and Rodney J. Hunter, eds., *Pastoral Care and Social Conflict* (Nashville: Abingdon Press, 1995), and Stephen Pattison, *Pastoral Care and Liberation Theology* (London: Cambridge University Press, 1994).

4. Many people who are quoted are named in the text; some are not. For those not named, I did not always seek specific permission to quote them. Each person named has reviewed both the material quoted and my interpretation of it. Some names are fictitious; some are real. I do not indicate in the text which is which. However, when a pseudonym was used, it was selected or approved by the person whose narrative was reported. It is unfortunate, yet telling, that these safeguards are necessary.

5. Dorothy Allison, "The Exile's Return: How a Lesbian Novelist Found Her Way into the Mainstream," *New York Times Book Review,* 26 June 1994, 15.
6. Ibid., 16.
7. The fuller theoretical background to this point is found in Larry Kent Graham, *Care of Persons, Care of Worlds: A Psychosystems Approach to Pastoral Care and Counseling* (Nashville: Abingdon Press, 1992). Chapters 6, 7, and 8 of this volume expand these points.
8. See John McNeill, *The Church and the Homosexual* (Kansas City, Kans.: Sheed Andrews & McMeel, 1976). McNeill also wrote *Taking a Chance on God: Liberating Theology for Gays, Lesbians, and Their Lovers, Families, and Friends* (Boston: Beacon Press, 1988), and *Freedom, Glorious Freedom: The Spiritual Journey to the Fullness of Life for Gays, Lesbians, and Everybody Else* (Boston: Beacon Press, 1994).
9. Narrative theory has become increasingly prominent in pastoral theology and care. Its most powerful statement is found in Charles V. Gerkin, *The Living Human Document: Re-visioning Pastoral Counseling in a Hermeneutical Mode* (Nashville: Abingdon Press, 1984). Other recent contributions are Andrew J. Lester, *Hope in Pastoral Care and Counseling* (Louisville: Westminster John Knox Press, 1995), and Edward P. Wimberly, *Using Scripture in Pastoral Counseling* (Nashville: Abingdon Press, 1994).
10. As I was finishing this volume, Leroy T. Howe's book, *The Image of God: A Theology for Pastoral Care and Counseling* (Nashville: Abingdon Press, 1995), appeared. Although his constructive view of the image of God and its centrality in defining the goal of pastoral care are nearly identical to the views developed in this book, we arrive at our conclusions from different starting points and sources. As far as I can see, he does not extend his views to include same-sex loving, or to draw on same-sex loving as a basis for his constructive ideas about what the concept *imago Dei* can mean for our time.
11. The concept of "relational justice" is a growing norm in pastoral theology and care. See Larry Kent Graham, "From Relational Humanness to Relational Justice: Reconceiving Pastoral Care and Counseling," in Couture and Hunter, eds., *Pastoral Care and Social Conflict.* I am also indebted to other writers for linking this concept to liberative concerns. See J. Michael Clark, *Beyond Our Ghettos: Gay Theology in Ecological Perspective* (Cleveland: Pilgrim Press, 1993), and Carter Heyward, *Touching Our Strength: The Erotic as Power and the Love of God* (San Francisco: Harper & Row, 1989).

Notes to Chapter 1. Affirmation and Solidarity: Establishing the Framework of Care

1. A briefer discussion of this pastoral situation can be found in chapter 7 of *Caught in the Crossfire: Helping Christians Debate Homosexuality,*

ed. Sally B. Geis and Donald E. Messer (Nashville: Abingdon Press, 1994). The case is used here with permission.

2. Beverly Barbo, *The Walking Wounded* (Lindsborg, Kans.: Carlson's Publishing, 1987).

3. See William Carroll, "God as Unloving Father," *The Christian Century,* 5 March 1991, 255.

4. Amendment 2 prohibited any municipality or legislative body in the State of Colorado from enacting or enforcing laws against discrimination based on sexual orientation. It was rejected by the United States Supreme Court in May 1996.

Notes to Chapter 2.
Breaking the Bubble: Care and Coming Out

1. For an illuminating discussion of coming out as a crisis experience, see Craig O'Neill and Kathleen Ritter, *Coming Out Within: Stages of Spiritual Awakening for Lesbians and Gay Men* (San Francisco: Harper & Row Publishers, 1992).

2. We have in this narrative a classic example of crisis understood as a "dangerous opportunity," in which a life or death choice must be made. The crisis cannot be averted, the individual (and often community) cannot avoid choice, the outcome of the choice is not known ahead of time, and the consequences of choosing or not choosing are fraught with ultimacy. The resolution may result in a spiritual gain or loss. In David's case, the gain was enormous.

3. James B. Nelson, *Embodiment* (Minneapolis: Augsburg Press, 1978).

4. Many Christian denominations have developed materials to help congregations become "open and affirming" to lesbian and gay persons. The process is usually more comprehensive than what is described about Temple Emanuel. Further information may be gained from The Reconciling Congregation Program, 3801 N. Keeler Ave., Chicago, IL 60641.

5. For fuller descriptions of the coming-out process, see Joretta L. Marshall, *Counseling Lesbian Partners.* Counseling and Pastoral Theology. (Louisville: Westminster John Knox Press, 1997).

Notes to Chapter 3. Partners and Lovers:
Bridging Eros and Agape Through Care

1. For a fuller interpretation of communication styles in African-American culture, see Thomas Kochman, *Black and White Styles in Conflict* (Chicago: University of Chicago Press, 1981), and Geneva Smitherman, "Black Language and Black Liberation," in *Black Psychology,* 2d ed., ed. Reginald Jones (San Francisco: Harper & Row, 1980).

2. The phrase "in the life," Don says, "is a term used by African-American gay and lesbian people to describe their sexual orientation. Many of us

do not prefer to use the terms 'lesbian' and 'gay' primarily because they are words of the dominant gay and lesbian culture, which does not always recognize the experiences of gays and lesbians of color."

3. For a fuller discussion of gay sexual ethics, see gay liberation theologian J. Michael Clark, "Gay Men, Masculinity, and an Ethic of Friendship," in *Redeeming Men: Essays on Men, Masculinities, and Religion,* ed. S. Boyd, M. Longwood, and M. Muesse (Louisville: Westminster John Knox Press, 1996).

4. A fuller description of Connie's "narrative of care" can be found in Larry Kent Graham, "From Relational Humanness to Relational Justice," in *Pastoral Care and Social Conflict,* ed. Pamela D. Couture and Rodney J. Hunter (Nashville: Abingdon Press, 1995), 220–34. The quotation used in this chapter is from pp. 225–26 and is used with permission.

5. See the Smalcald Articles, III, IV, "The Gospel," in *The Book of Concord: The Confessions of the Evangelical Lutheran Church,* trans. and ed. Theodore G. Tappert (Philadelphia: Fortress Press, 1959), 310.

Notes to Chapter 4. The Ark of Promise: Caring for Lesbian and Gay Families

1. Judy Dahl, *River of Promise: Two Women's Story of Love and Adoption* (San Diego: Lura Media, 1989).

2. For the concept of "mixed-status" relationships I am indebted to Archie Smith Jr., Foster Professor of Pastoral Psychology, Pacific School of Religion, Oakland, California. This concept emerged in private conversation and seems to be a promising way to identify the complexity of the social world currently facing pastoral theology and care.

3. For this section, I am informed by the articles in the Symposium on Pastoral Care and Spiritual Directing with Gay and Lesbian Persons in "A Symposium," *Journal of Pastoral Care* 50, no. 1 (Spring 1996): 57–104.

4. The text for this narrative is taken from the interview I conducted in their home and from written documents that they prepared for other purposes and made available to me.

5. This funeral is described more fully in chapter 8, p. 182.

Notes to Chapter 5. The Desolation of Our Habitations: Care in Loss and Crisis

1. For a fuller discussion of the theological and psychological dimensions of crisis, see Larry Kent Graham, *Care of Persons, Care of Worlds: A Psychosystems Approach to Pastoral Care and Counseling* (Nashville: Abingdon Press, 1992), chap. 4.

2. Bill Weaver's life and ministry to persons with AIDS is described in chapter 4 of this book.

3. For a fuller description of the Episcopal Church of the Epiphany and of Rev. E. Claiborne Jones, see Sally Purvis, *The Stained-Glass Ceiling:*

Churches and Their Women Pastors (Louisville: Westminster John Knox Press, 1995). References to "Cameron" and "Bethany Episcopal Church" correspond to Claiborne and Epiphany, and are disclosed here with permission. For a fuller description of the rector and congregation's ministry in the crisis of a gay couple, see chapter 8, p. 182.

Notes to Chapter 6. Affirmation, Advocacy, and Opposition: Dimensions of Comprehensive Communal Care

1. Michael has revisited the question of God's relationship to suffering in the light of the AIDS crisis. See J. Michael Clark, "AIDS, Death, and God: Gay Liberational Theology and the Problem of Suffering," *Journal of Pastoral Counseling* 21, no. 1 (Spring/Summer 1986): 40–54. See also "Abuse and Theodicy in Gay Theology and Ethics," *Journal of Men's Studies* 4, no. 2 (November 1995): 111–30.
2. J. Michael Clark, *Beyond Our Ghettos: Gay Theology in Ecological Perspective* (Cleveland: Pilgrim Press, 1993), 3f.
3. According to the *Denver Post,* 11 March 1996, the U.S. Census Bureau has identified 145,130 same-gender couples. The quotation about lack of benefits is from the same article.
4. Ibid.
5. The information and quotations that follow in this paragraph are taken from a news article in *Ecumenical News Bulletin,* no. 2 (January 30, 1996): 3–4.
6. KIDSOFGAYS can be contacted by e-mailing majordomo@vector.casti. com with the following in the message area: subscribe kidsofgays first-name lastname <name@e-mail. address>. For more information, contact COLAGE (Children of Lesbians and Gays Everywhere), a broad-based advocacy organization run by and for daughters and sons of lesbian, gay, bisexual, and transgendered persons. For more information, e-mail kidsofgays@aol.com, or write 2300 Market St. #165, San Francisco, CA 94114. COLAGE may be found on the Internet at http:// www.colage.org.
7. *New York Times,* 8 February 1996.
8. I have reconstructed this portion of the sermon from memory. It was very moving to hear it. Reverend Yvette Flunder, the ordained minister of City of Refuge UCC, is now co-chair of the National African-American Church Caucus on AIDS. See *United Church News,* April 1996.

Notes to Chapter 7. Constructing the *Imago Dei*

1. Traditionally, the tension surrounding the *imago Dei* symbolizing both the high status and unrealized potential of human beings is in the distinction between "image" and "likeness" of God. See Leroy T. Howe, *The*

Image of God: A Theology for Pastoral Care and Counseling (Nashville: Abingdon Press, 1995).

2. For a fuller discussion of the relationship between continuity and creativity in canon and tradition, see Delwin Brown, *Boundaries of Our Habitations: Tradition and Theological Construction* (Albany: State University of New York Press, 1994).

3. Paul A. Mickey, *Of Sacred Worth* (Nashville: Abingdon Press, 1993), 9, 45.

4. Ibid., 13, 14, 15, 16, 18.

5. Ibid., 18, 19.

6. Ibid., 19, 20.

7. Ibid., 23, 38, 39.

8. Ibid., 28.

9. Ibid., 23.

10. Ibid., 27.

11. Ibid., 32, 41.

12. Ibid., 42.

13. Ibid., 39.

14. Ibid., 27.

15. Ibid., 28.

16. Ibid., 28, 35.

17. Ibid., 27, 29, 35.

18. Ibid., 40.

19. Ibid., 47.

20. Ibid., 74.

21. Ibid., 77f, 96ff.

22. Ibid., 93.

23. This discussion is based on Dennis Ronald MacDonald, *There Is No Male and Female: The Fate of a Dominical Saying in Paul and Gnosticism,* No. 20, Harvard Dissertations in Religion, ed. Margaret R. Miles and Bernadette J. Brooten (Philadelphia: Fortress Press, 1987).

24. Ibid., 95.

25. Kari Elisabeth Borreson, "God's Image, Man's Image?" in *Image of God and Gender Models,* ed. Kari Elisabeth Borreson (Oslo: Solum Forlag, 1991).

26. Ibid., 188.

27. MacDonald, *No Male and Female,* 121.

28. Ibid., 126 (see also p. 130), 131.

29. Borreson, "God's Image," 188.

30. Ibid.

31. Ibid., 200.

32. Ibid., 202, 205.

33. Phyllis A. Bird, "Sexual Differentiation and Divine Image in the Genesis Creation Texts," in *Image of God and Gender Models,* ed. Kari Elisabeth Borreson (Oslo: Solum Forlag, 1991), 16, 17.

34. Ibid., 23.
35. Ibid., 25.
36. Ibid.

Notes to Chapter 8.
Disclosing the Image of God: Consequences for Care

1. Phyllis Bird, "Male and Female, He Created Them: Gen. 1:27b in the Context of the Priestly Account of Creation," *Harvard Theological Review* 74 (1981): 24.
2. Douglas John Hall, *Imaging God: Dominion as Stewardship* (Grand Rapids: Wm. B. Eerdmans, 1986).
3. Ibid., 98.
4. Ibid., 98, 115, 116.
5. Ibid., 122, 123.
6. Ibid., 127, 128.
7. Ibid., 131.
8. Ibid., 140ff.
9. Ibid., 149.
10. Ibid., 151.
11. Ibid., 156, 159, 158f.
12. Rosemary Radford Ruether, "Feminist Hermeneutics, Scriptural Authority, and Religious Experience: The Case of the *Imago Dei* and Gender Equality," in *Radical Pluralism and Truth: David Tracy and the Hermeneutics of Religion,* ed. Werner G. Jeanrond and Jennifer L. Rike (New York: Crossroad, 1991), 103f.
13. One of the most fully developed interpretations of love as the key to the image of God is found in Daniel Day Williams, *The Spirit and the Forms of Love* (New York: Harper & Row, 1968). Williams contends that "if love constitutes God's being, and if man [sic] is created in the image of God, then the key to man's being and to God's being is the capacity for free, self-giving mutuality and concern for the other" (160).
14. See Larry Kent Graham, "From Relational Humanness to Relational Justice," in *Pastoral Care and Social Conflict,* ed. Pamela D. Couture and Rodney J. Hunter (Nashville: Abingdon Press, 1995), 220–34.
15. J. Michael Clark, *Beyond Our Ghettos: Gay Theology in Ecological Perspective* (Cleveland: Pilgrim Press, 1993), 68.
16. Sallie McFague, *The Body of God: An Ecological Theology* (Minneapolis: Fortress Press, 1993), 54, 186, 200.
17. Reverend Melanie Morrison, one of the founders of Phoenix Community Church (UCC), a gay- and lesbian-affirming congregation in Kalamazoo, Michigan, is completing a Ph.D. dissertation at the University of Groningen in The Netherlands that addresses the subject of lesbian feminist models of sin and grace. She contends that "unless new models of sin and redemption can be developed and translated into ministry with les-

bian women, Christianity will not be liberating and life-giving for lesbians." She reconceives sin as "that which separates us from our deepest selves, from each other, and from God. Heterosexism is sin because it tries to accomplish all three separations. . . . Original sin is not 'trying to be like God' but rather denying the image of God in certain human beings" through "de-humanizing the other." The quotations are from personal communication and a paper that Morrison gave at a national gathering of CLOUT (Christian Lesbians OUT Together), Rochester, New York, on August 10, 1995: "Reflections on Sin and Redemption: A Lesbian Feminist Perspective." They are used with permission. See also her book of essays, *The Grace of Coming Home: Spirituality, Sexuality, and the Struggle for Justice* (Cleveland: Pilgrim Press, 1995).

For Further Reading

Alexander, Marilyn Bennett, and James Preston. *We Were Baptized Too: Claiming God's Grace for Lesbians and Gays.* Louisville: Westminster John Knox Press, 1996.

Appiah, K. Anthony. "The Marrying Kind." *The New York Review of Books,* 20 June 1996, 48–54.

Balka, Christie, and Andy Rose, ed. *Twice Blessed: On Being Lesbian or Gay and Jewish.* Boston: Beacon Press, 1989.

Berzon, Betty. *Permanent Partners: Building Gay and Lesbian Relationships That Last.* New York: E. P. Dutton, 1988.

Borreson, Kari Elisabeth, ed. *Image of God and Gender Models.* Oslo: Solum Forlag, 1991.

Boswell, John. *Christianity, Social Tolerance, and Homosexuality: Gay People in Western Europe from the Beginning of the Christian Era to the Fourteenth Century.* Chicago: University of Chicago Press, 1980.

———. *Same-Sex Unions in Premodern Europe.* New York: Villard Books, 1994.

Boyle, Sally M. *Embracing the Exile: A Lesbian Model for Pastoral Care.* Toronto: United Church Publishing House, 1995.

Brawley, Robert, ed. *Biblical Ethics and Homosexuality.* Louisville: Westminster John Knox Press, 1996.

Brooten, Bernadette. "Paul's Views on the Nature of Women and Female Homoeroticism." In *Homosexuality and Religion and Philosophy,* edited by Wayne R. Dynes and Stephen Donaldson, 57–83. New York: Garland, 1992.

Browning, Don. "Rethinking Homosexuality." Review of *The Construction of Homosexuality,* by David Greenberg. *The Christian Century,* 11 October 1989, 911–16.

Butler, Judith. *Bodies That Matter: On the Discursive Limits of "Sex."* New York: Routledge, 1993.

Buxton, Amity P. *Other Side of the Closet: The Coming-Out Crisis for Straight Spouses and Families.* Rev. ed. New York: John Wiley & Sons, 1994.

Carroll, William. "God as Unloving Father." *The Christian Century,* 5 March 1991, 255.

Clark, J. Michael. "AIDS, Death, and God: Gay Liberational Theology and the Problem of Suffering." *Journal of Pastoral Counseling* 21, no. 1 (Spring/Summer 1986): 40–54.

———. *Beyond Our Ghettos: Gay Theology in Ecological Perspective.* Cleveland: Pilgrim Press, 1993.

———. "Gay Men, Masculinity, and an Ethic of Friendship." In *Redeeming Men: Masculinities and Religion,* edited by S. Boyd, M. Longwood, and M. Muesse. Louisville: Westminister John Knox Press, 1996.

Clark, J. Michael, Joanne C. Brown, and Lorna M. Hochstein. "Institutional Religion and Gay/Lesbian Oppression." *Marriage and Family Review* 14, issue 3–4 (1989): 265–84.

Cleaver, Richard. *Know My Name: A Gay Liberation Theology.* Louisville: Westminster John Knox Press, 1995.

Dahl, Judy. *River of Promise: Two Women's Story of Love and Adoption.* San Diego: Lura Media, 1989.

DeCecco, John P., and John P. Elia, eds. *If You Seduce a Straight Person, Can You Make Them Gay? Issues in Biological Essentialism Versus Social Constructionism in Gay and Lesbian Identities.* New York: Haworth Press, 1993.

D'Emilio, John. *Making Trouble: Essays on Gay History, Politics, and the University.* New York: Routledge, 1992.

Dew, Robb Forman. *The Family Heart: A Memoir of When Our Son Came Out.* New York: Addison-Wesley, 1994.

Eskridge, William N., Jr. *The Case for Same-Sex Marriage: From Liberal Sexuality to Civilized Commitment.* New York: Free Press, 1996.

Ettelbrick, Paula. "Since When Is Marriage a Path to Liberation?" In *Lesbian and Gay Marriage: Private Commitments, Public Ceremonies,* edited by Suzanne Sherman, 20–26. Philadelphia: Temple University Press, 1992.

Falco, Kristine L. *Psychotherapy with Lesbian Clients: Theory in Practice.* New York: Brunner/Mazel, 1991.

Fortunato, John. *Embracing the Exile: Healing Journeys of Gay Christians.* Minneapolis: Winston-Seabury Press, 1983.

Furnish, Victor Paul. *The Moral Teaching of Paul.* Nashville: Abingdon Press, 1979.

Geis, Sally B., and Donald E. Messer. *Caught in the Crossfire: Helping Christians Debate Homosexuality.* Nashville: Abingdon Press, 1994.

Glaser, Chris. *Coming Out to God: Prayers for Lesbians and Gay Men, Their Families and Friends.* Louisville: Westminster/John Knox Press, 1991.

Goodman, Bernice. "Lesbian Mothers." In *Keys to Caring: Assisting Your Gay and Lesbian Clients,* edited by Robert J. Kus, 119–24. Boston: Alyson, 1990.

Gordis, Robert. "Homosexuality and Traditional Religion." *Judaism* 32, no. 4 (Fall 1983): 405–9.

Goss, Robert. *Jesus Acted Up: A Gay and Lesbian Manifesto.* San Francisco: Harper & Row, 1993.

Greenberg, David, and Marcia H. Bystryn. "Christian Intolerance of Homosexuality." *American Journal of Sociology* 88, no. 3 (1982): 515–48.

Greene, Beverly. "Lesbian Women of Color: Triple Jeopardy." In *Women of Color: Integrating Ethnic and Gender Identities in Psychotherapy,* edited by Lillian Comas-Diaz and Beverly Greene, 389–427. New York: Guilford Press, 1994.

Griffin, Horace L. "Giving New Birth: Lesbians, Gays, and 'The Family': A Pastoral Care Perspective." *Journal of Pastoral Theology* 3 (Summer 1993): 88–98.

Hall, Douglas John. *Imaging God: Dominion as Stewardship.* Grand Rapids: Wm. B. Eerdmans, 1986.

Heyward, Carter. *Touching Our Strength: The Erotic as Power and the Love of God.* San Francisco: Harper & Row, 1989.

Hunt, Mary E. *Fierce Tenderness: A Feminist Theology of Friendship.* New York: Crossroad, 1991.

Isay, Richard. *Being Homosexual: Gay Men and Their Development.* New York: Farrar, Straus, & Giroux, 1989.

"A Symposium." *Journal of Pastoral Care,* 50, no. 1 (Spring 1996): 57–104.

Kassoff, Elizabeth. "Nonmonogamy in the Lesbian Community." *Women and Therapy: A Feminist Quarterly* 8, no. 1/2 (1988): 67–182.

Lebacqz, Karen, and Ronald G. Barton. *Sex in the Parish.* Louisville: Westminster/John Knox Press, 1991.

LeVay, Simon, and Dean H. Hamar. "Evidence for a Biological Influence in Male Homosexuality." *Scientific American* 270, no. 5 (May 1994): 44–49.

Lewes, Kenneth. *Psychoanalysis and Male Homosexuality.* New York: Aronson, 1995.

Lorde, Audre. *Sister Outsider.* Freedom, Calif.: Crossing Press, 1984.

MacDonald, Dennis Ronald. *There Is No Male and Female: The Fate of a Dominical Saying in Paul and Gnosticism.* Number 20, Harvard Dissertations in Religion, edited by Margaret R. Miles and Bernadette J. Brooten. Philadelphia: Fortress Press, 1987.

Markowitz, Laura M. "When Same-Sex Couples Divorce." *Family Therapy Networker* 18, no. 3 (May/June 1994): 31–33.

Marshall, Joretta L. *Counseling Lesbian Partners* (Counseling and Pastoral Theology). Louisville: Westminster John Knox Press, 1997.

———. "Pedagogy and Pastoral Theology in Dialogue with Lesbian/Gay/Bisexual Concerns." *Journal of Pastoral Theology* 6 (Summer 1996): 55–69.

McFague, Sallie. *The Body of God: An Ecological Theology.* Minneapolis: Fortress Press, 1993.

McNeill, John. *Freedom, Glorious Freedom: The Spiritual Journey to the Fullness of Life for Gays, Lesbians, and Everybody Else.* Boston: Beacon Press, 1994.

McWhirter, David P., and Andrew P. Mattison. *The Male Couple: How Relationships Develop.* Englewood Cliffs, N.J.: Prentice Hall, 1984.

McWhirter, David P., Stephanie A. Sanders, and June Reinisch Machover. *Homosexuality/Heterosexuality: Concepts of Sexual Orientation.* New York: Oxford University Press, 1990.

Mollenkott, Virginia Ramey. *Sensuous Spirituality: Out from Fundamentalism.* New York: Crossroad, 1993.

Morrison, Melanie. *The Grace of Coming Home: Spirituality, Sexuality, and the Struggle for Justice.* Cleveland: Pilgrim Press, 1995.

Murray, Elwood J. "A Search for God in Story and Time." *America* 169, no. 11 (October 16, 1993): 10–13.

Nelson, James B. *Body Theology.* Louisville: Westminster/John Knox Press, 1992.

———. *Embodiment: An Approach to Sexuality and Christian Theology.* Minneapolis: Augsburg Publishing House, 1978. See especially chapter 8.

Nelson, James B., and Sandra P. Longfellow, eds. *Sexuality and the*

Sacred: Sources for Theological Reflection. Louisville: Westminster John Knox Press, 1994.

O'Neill, Craig, and Kathleen Ritter. *Coming Out Within: Stages of Spiritual Awakening for Lesbians and Gay Men.* San Francisco: Harper & Row, 1992.

Rafkin, Louise. *Different Mothers: Sons and Daughters of Lesbians Talk About Their Lives.* Pittsburgh: Cleis Press, 1990.

Rich, Adrienne. "Compulsory Heterosexuality and Lesbian Existence." *Signs* (Summer 1980): 139–68.

Ruether, Rosemary Radford. "Feminist Hermeneutics, Scriptural Authority, and Religious Experience: The Case of the *Imago Dei* and Gender Equality." In *Radical Pluralism and Truth: David Tracy and the Hermeneutics of Religion,* edited by Werner G. Jeanrond and Jennifer L. Rike, 95–106. New York: Crossroad, 1991.

———. *Sexism and God-Talk: Toward a Feminist Theology.* Boston: Beacon Press, 1983.

Scanzoni, Letha, and Virginia Ramey Mollenkott. *Is the Homosexual My Neighbor? Another Christian View.* New York: Harper & Row, 1980.

Scroggs, Robin. *The New Testament and Homosexuality.* Philadelphia: Fortress Press, 1983.

Sedgewick, Eve Kosofsky. *Epistemology of the Closet.* London: Penguin, 1994.

Seow, Choon-Leong, ed. *Homosexuality and Christian Community.* Louisville: Westminster John Knox Press, 1996.

Siker, Jeffrey S., ed. *Homosexuality in the Church: Both Sides of the Debate.* Louisville: Westminster John Knox Press, 1994.

Slaskerud, Jacquelyn Haak, and Peter J. Unguarski. *HIV-AIDS: A Guide to Nursing Care.* 2d ed. Philadelphia: W. B. Saunders, 1992.

Slater, Suzanne. *Lesbian Family Life Cycle.* New York: Free Press, 1995.

Soloff, Rav A. "Is There a Reform Response to Homosexuality?" *Judaism* 32, no. 4 (Fall 1983): 417–24.

Switzer, David. *Coming Out as Parents: You and Your Homosexual Child.* Louisville: Westminster John Knox Press, 1996.

Tasker, Fiona, and Susan Golombok. "Adults Raised as Children in Lesbian Families." *American Journal of Orthopsychiatry* 65 (April 1995): 202–15.

Trible, Phyllis. *Texts of Terror.* Philadelphia: Fortress Press, 1984.

Ussher, Jane M. "Family and Couples Therapy with Gay and Lesbian

Clients: Acknowledging the Forgotten Minority." *Journal of Family Therapy* 13, no. 2 (1991): 131–48.

Verghese, Abraham. *My Own Country: A Doctor's Story of a Town and Its People in the Age of AIDS*. New York: Simon & Schuster, 1994.

Weston, Kath. *Families We Choose: Lesbians, Gays, Kinship.* New York: Columbia University Press, 1991.

Wezeman, Phyllis Vos. *Creative Compassion: Activities for Understanding HIV/AIDS.* Cleveland: Pilgrim Press, 1994.

Williams, Daniel Day. *The Spirit and the Forms of Love.* New York: Harper & Row, 1968.

Wiltshire, Susan Ford. *Seasons of Grief and Grace: A Sister's Story of AIDS.* Nashville: Vanderbilt University Press, 1994.

Index

Index

Lamar, 186f.
Lawton, Doug, 110–14, 128, 139, 142
Liberation, 20, 38, 61, 75f., 129, 132f., 164, 177
liturgy, 126f.
love
  and change, 117
  relation to justice and care, 119f.
  of self, God, and neighbor, 25
Luther, Martin, 77, 131

MacDonald, Dennis, 156f.
March on Washington, 109, 130
Marcy, 84–85
marriage
  mixed status, 81
  same-sex, 57f., 98, 133f.
Martínez, Donaciano, 116–20, 121, 130, 138, 176
McFague, Sallie, 177f.
McNair, Barbra, 106–8, 127, 139
Meadows, Dan. See Douglas, Giff
Messer, John, 122, 143, 182
Michael and Paul, 130, 183f.
Mickey, Paul A., 150–55, 159ff., 178
Miller, Terryl, 78

narratives/stories, 10f., 123
Neal, Teresa, 82–85, 129f., 142
network, 134–42
normalizing ethos, 125

Parkin, Robert, 61
pastoral leadership, 122, 142f.
pastoral theology, 1–4, 124, 146, 162, 164
Paul (apostle), 157ff., 161, 170, 184
Paul and Cliff, 122f., 126, 140
pet care, 90, 131f.
Project Angel Heart, 105
Project Open Hands, 90
prophetic action, 130, 185f.

Racism, 28, 48f., 66, 70, 104, 123, 129, 132
Ralph, 62
Raymond, 135f.
relational justice, 11, 50, 144
  and the family, 100
  and heteropatriarchy, 132f.
  and the image of God, 171, 175f.
Ruether, Rosemary Radford, 171

Sandoval, Diana, 47–50
St. Bartholomew's Episcopal Church, 62
sexism, 28, 48f., 66, 70f., 106, 123, 129, 132
sexuality
  centrality of, 57
  and Christian faith, 25

and sprituality, 57
and the Trinity, 26
and truth, 57
  See also spritualilty
sin, 10, 20, 66f., 87, 109f., 153, 154f., 178, 184f.
  and heterosexism, 75
  and promiscuity, 75
Smith, Archie, Jr., 191 n.2
solidarity, 52, 171, 182
spirituality
  advanced by care, 88f., 136f., 145
  African-American, and eros, 68
  ambiguity of, 51
  assisted by prayer, 96
  to avoid sexual orientation, 65
  and coming out, 60
  and healing, 36f.
  in grief, 122
  linked to God's providence, 103, 112
  links to creation, 151
  links to ecology, 131
  links to sexuality, 26, 27, 71f., 151, 163, 184
  in same-sex unions, 99
  and self-acceptance, 34f.
  at the time of death, 116
  See also sexuality
Stonewall Revolution, 117, 130, 183
subculture, gay and lesbian, 140f.
support resources, 139

Temple Emanuel, 43–46, 128, 181
Teresa, 82–85, 129f., 142
theology, theological task, 148f., 155f.
  experience influencing norms, 164
  primary question, 163
  sexuality as source of knowledge, 163, 184
  See also pastoral theology
therapy and therapists, 138–40
  changing orientation, 62
  contribution, 56f., 70
  criteria, 58f., 62, 80, 111, 118, 138
  goals, 80
  methods, 106f.
  moral attitude, 74
Troxell, Christina, 22–29, 61, 99, 142, 165, 170, 175, 179, 181, 185, 186
Tutu, Desmond, 134

Ulrich, Kenneth, 108–10

Weaver, Bill and Johnson, Doug, 86–91, 126, 127, 182
welcome, active, 128, 179f.
Wilkonson, David, 34–40, 73, 127, 171
Windham, Allen, 73–75

205